PROJECT BASED LEARNING

25 PROJECTS FOR 21ST CENTURY LEARNING

RALPH MALTESE

This edition published by
Dog Ear Publishing
4010 W. 86th Street, Ste H
Indianapolis, IN 46268

www.dogearpublishing.net

ISBN: 978-145751-059-5
This book is printed on acid-free paper.

Printed in the United States of America

For my parents, Jim and Lee Maltese.
I thank them every day for making me one of their projects.

Table of Contents

Project Based Learning

"Something Old, Something New…"

A few years ago I attended a conference on public education, and an administrator from a university was a keynote speaker. In his speech, he stated that he rarely awarded a research grant to an educator. He would award research money to researchers studying diabetes or researchers examining volcanoes in the ocean or researchers probing the air quality around the Arctic Circle. Those who wanted to study how students learn…not as much. As an educator I felt slighted, and, with a colossal chip on my shoulder, I confronted him afterward to ask him why he rarely funded educational research. He replied, "Because the findings of the research rarely reach the classroom." I had no retort. He was right. By the time any significant information about how people learn or how groups interact reaches the classroom teacher, *if* it reaches the classroom teacher, the results are often distilled through a filtration system that ultimately dismisses the research as an educational "fad" that will soon evaporate.

Politics plays an enormous role in the failure of educational reform to move forward. Despite the many claims by politicians that we are "data driven," they are actually driven by "data discrimination," choosing only that research that supports their political platform. A governor may commission a fact finding team to research best practices. The team, depending on its quality and honesty, may actually deliver useful results and findings relevant to the classroom. In rare cases the governor might actually act on these results and attempt a true educational reform. Across the state, necessary reform might be initiated. And then the governor loses the next election or finishes out his term. The incoming governor, especially if he is from the opposing party, then literally throws out the research gathered by the previous administration. Political wisdom dictates that one never give a predecessor credit, nor does a new governor build on previous experience. This explains why veteran teachers and administrators, weary of the recycling of information, tell novice teachers, "I've seen that before. Don't pay attention to that research. It will come and go." In the course of 38 years of teaching high school students, I have written the "new and improved" district standards at least three times. Seemingly every new state administration comes to the bully pulpit with a demand for tougher academic standards, as if simply demanding them will result in their achievement.

Even when policy makers and administrators are enamored of a particular educational program, their commitment is often lukewarm. For example, I was sent to a number of writing workshops built around a peer editing approach to improving student work. Most of us liked the approach and presented the program at our schools as part of a professional development workshop. The writing program, extensive as it was, demanded a good deal of time (skills always take longer to develop than content), and its implementation demanded we remove some content from the curriculum. For example, to make room for the writing program, the English department decided to give up Samuel Johnson and his essays on dictionary writing.

Not much of a sacrifice as far as I was concerned. The administration nixed the deletion of Samuel Johnson from the curriculum, and suggested that we use only a "part" of the writing program (the chosen "part" was the least important section and the easiest to implement). The most important element, the peer editing aspect, was, of course, omitted because it required "too much class time." At the next school board meeting, the administration proudly announced that it had implemented a new writing program. I shared these events with the creator of the writing program who replied, "That is why programs aren't successful. Districts do not implement the program."

There is one major reason why this discarding of educational research and the bowdlerizing of successful programs occur. To act on the research and to fully implement programs of reform would mean change. **Educational communities would have to face the fact that the current structural model of most public schools is embarrassingly outdated**. We would have to think anew about our educational goals and the best methods and structures to achieve those goals. If honest in our reflection, we would have to rethink predicating student advancement based on the number of times the student's body has orbited the sun. We would have to move, especially in our high schools, from a content based system to a skills based system. This is a daunting task, because developing skills takes time and requires another type of assessment than the usual bubble-sheet-multiple-choice type of assessment currently in vogue.

For educational reform to begin, we must consider metaphors, particularly those metaphors that describe the schools as factories churning out "students" on an assembly line. The teachers are the factory workers alongside the assembly line pounding the heads of their students with tonnage of math, social studies, science and language arts. The factory model of schools is all about information, once a relatively rare commodity now made cheap and easily accessible through a number of media. The factories, for the most part, are gone and the United States, to participate in the geopolitical arena, must structure schools along the lines of a new metaphor---one which stresses the development of higher level thinking skills as opposed to rote memorization. Policy makers will state that, in a standards based system, most of the standards are skills. And, as Hamlet would say, "There's the rub." The factory model treats skills in the same way it treats content---in terms of poundage. . One fourth grade teacher, frustrated by edicts imposed by a "revolutionary program," was asked to "cover" 39 skills in 30 days with her fourth graders. Students do not learn the sixty million skills outlined in a state's standardized system in one year. People learn a few skills, and they learn them over a period of time. Project based learning focuses on students developing important skills over a period of time. Conventional classrooms expect skills to be mastered in one shot deals (think about asking students to develop research skills while writing a term paper). Imagine a basketball coach teaching dribbling on Monday and forgetting about teaching it the rest of the season. But our factory model says we do not have the time to teach thinking skills because of the amount of content we have to cram into the student's head….information which the best students, studies tell us, promptly forget.

We also have an obsession with digitizing everything. If we cannot measure it, or if it takes too much time to evaluate it, we tend to dismiss whatever it is. If it can be measured, we make the assumption it must have some value. Even if it doesn't. If we want to know if a person can play the piano, we drag her up on the stage and ask her to perform. But our modern educational culture wants the piano player to be tested on a series of micro-skills through a computerized test. These micro-skills are measured and evaluated and written about, interventions implemented to make sure each micro-skill is maximized, and little attention is paid to the music coming out of the piano. If you doubt this, examine many reading programs in elementary schools.

I was asked by a very motivated and energetic math teach to visit his class of calculus honor students. The teacher was energetic, the class attentive (although it was obvious they just wanted to learn what they needed to learn to get an "A" on the weekly test), and the instructor did everything expected of the conventional math teacher. After class, he asked for my opinion. I have learned not to give my opinion directly, but instead I asked him what he thought. He shared his disappointment that though "the kids were good students and nice," he did not see any enthusiasm in their eyes for the content. I asked him, "John, what do you like about calculus?" His eyes lit up. John explained how he appreciated most the artistry of math, the beautiful symmetry and interlacing dynamics. I then suggested that perhaps his primary goal would be to share that passion with his students. Wouldn't school be a much more efficient institution if teachers began their lessons with a focus on having students develop the same enthusiasm for their subject area as their instructors? But then, again, it is difficult to measure intellectual curiosity, let alone passion, so conventional wisdom cautions against allowing any of that "stuff" (as one principal explained to me) in the curriculum-- especially when there is so much other "stuff" to cram into our students' crania, and we cannot waste resources on learning elements that cannot be put on a bar graph, or so I have been told. Funding resources are limited and have to be carefully allocated.

This is not to say that education is not big business. Quite the contrary. There are hundreds of companies advertising programs and approaches "guaranteed" to improve reading/writing/math scores on standardized tests. Of course, improved test scores do not translate into improved learning which is very hard to assess quantitatively (a fact many policy makers fail to acknowledge), and this "guaranteed success" implies that all students are equivalent to identical little widgets coming off the assembly line. Ironically we have available to us more programs that guarantee success through a differentiated approach to teaching….as if good teachers have not been differentiating for decades, if not centuries.

The nomenclature in education is also a contributing factor to the dismissal of any educational reform by instructors, especially veteran instructors. The educational lexicon has exploded with new names for old processes. Project based learning is an example. When I engaged my students in project based learning back in the seventies and eighties, I did not call it "project based learning." It was simply an assignment. Sometimes I called it a group project to differentiate it from an individualized assignment or a lecture by me. The more sophisticated a culture becomes, the more its vocabulary has to expand to satisfy that culture's communication and understanding. So it is with the educational culture. Education includes many other cultures, including the disciplines in cognitive sciences as well as sociology and even anthropology. I knew that project based learning worked, and I knew eventually how to structure it so that it was effective, but I needed a vocabulary that I could share with others. Still, the new vocabulary involving any educational methodology remains descriptive rather than prescriptive because learning is a messy activity. Learning is not linear nor is human intellectual growth. The best that an educational jargon could do is the same as any grammar can do—describe how a language operates rather than claim to be totally definitive. But some project based learning enthusiasts insist on being prescriptive in a fashion that I describe as "Fascist Formulae for Project Based Learniing(PBL)." Some proponents of PBL will insist that, in order for it to be a true and pure PBL, the following must be observed stringently: "In order to have pure Project Based Learning, you must have a project that solves a real world problem and the audience must be members of the community, hopefully U.S. Congressmen or ideally the President of the United States, etc." One teacher who wanted to initiate a project for her students confessed, "But the audience is just my class….is that okay?" Of course it is okay. One of my projects included in this book involved students converting a novel to a musical, and they were required to sing in front of the class. This was certainly a high threat activity, and my focus was on building class trust. We did not need to have the state senator in the audience to make it a legitimate project based learning experience. Teachers know their students and the classroom climate, and have to develop their own rubrics both for the process and the final evaluation.

I want to emphasize that project based learning is not new. A number of us have been using that methodology/best practice or whatever else you would like as a descriptor for many years. **What is new is that we have research to back up what many of us already knew---that project based learning works because, if structured properly, it is a more successful strategy than lecturing or class discussions, or individual assignments *most of the time*.** In the late seventies and eighties I immersed myself in studying collaborative learning (a fundamental element of project based learning). I also experimented with my classes for most of that school year, so much so that my students complained about always doing "group work." They were right, of course. There is the necessary time for individual work and reflection, class discussions, and even lectures. I did know that, if I wanted to teach something really important or have my students reflect on something truly significant, and I wanted to reach most of my students, I employed pbl. But even then I knew one size does not fit all. For example, while teaching *Animal Farm*, I wanted my classes to consider the fact that there is also propaganda formulated by the government of the United States. I constructed some projects involving the creation of posters, radio and television broadcasting, etc. Almost all my students were heavily engaged, although I realized that some would have internalized the initial concepts I wanted them to learn if they had an individualized approach. While that was true, I also had to recognize that besides the initial concept involving propaganda, I wanted my students to develop certain skills such as collaboration. So even though a few of them might have learned the content better on their own, they would never have worked on essential 21st skills such as collaboration if they had worked on their own.

I was part of a program, Classrooms for the Future, a Pennsylvania state-wide initiative for genuine classroom reform, which asked teachers to rethink the goals, structures and methodologies of the classroom. In order to reward districts for successfully applying for a grant to enter the program, the state gave districts varying amounts of technology—activboards, classroom sets of laptop computers, projectors, video cameras, etc. The program also included professional development, the main focus of which was to help teachers rethink the challenge of teaching. While the program, in my view, was a success, some districts only saw the "gift" of free technology without considering the requirement that teachers NOT use their activboards to display their twenty year old overhead transparencies. Using technology without a sound methodology is a waste of economic and human resources. The projects included in this text were successfully implemented without computers, activboards or web 2.0 tools. There are teachers who do not have access to these technology tools, and I did not want them to feel unable to conduct these projects because they did not have those tools. I included technology as options for those who are fortunate to have access to those aids, but the most important aspect of these projects are their structures and processes. Teachers can readily adapt those structures and processes to fit any discipline.

Project based learning is built on the concept that higher level thinking skills are developed by engaging students in higher level thinking. Conservative educators sometimes argue that this means content is not valued. This is not true. Students retain concepts and information better through a project based approach than through cramming for a test. But teachers who employ PBL understand that their educational goals go beyond Bloom's lowest level of intellectual behavior, and these teachers challenge students to think creatively and constructively. **When I taught literature in high school, I knew that the literary work we studied was a gateway, an excuse to study great issues and to challenge students to problem solve.** Had I taught calculus or social studies or biology or visual arts, the goals would have been the same.

Just as the conclusion of an essay should lead to further explorations and ideas, so the conclusion of a project should lead students into new and exciting realms, to "Beyond Infinity," to provide a variation on Buzz Lightyear's catchphrase from my granddaughter's favorite movie, *Toy Story 3*. These follow up activities/ideas at the end of each project include a generic section (identical questions designed to help students become metacognitive about their studies), and a project-specific set of ideas that we hope students would ponder before moving on to the next lesson. I once asked my honors students if they ever reflected on what they learned in class. The overwhelming majority answered in the negative. "We just move on from assignment to assignment," one highly intelligent and personable student told me. We cannot assume students incorporate this very important reflective piece in their studies no more than we should assume that students make transfers from one discipline to the other.

The next chapter is devoted to collaborative learning. We assume that students know how to work together at our own peril. If students do not develop effective collaborative skills, the project based learning falls apart.

Structuring Collaborative Learning

One day a colleague approached me with a huge frown on her face. "You talk about group work and how good it is, but I just gave my class this really cool assignment, and while I was marking papers, they just sat in their groups and gossiped and laughed and played around. This collaborative learning thing stinks. I'll never try it again."

I was sorry that my colleague had such a sour experience with the methodology. The first concept I try to explain to colleagues who are considering employing collaborative learning is that successful strategies have essential precepts that must be followed. All methods of medicine are not equal in effectiveness. I can claim that one way to fix an earache is to snake a probe up from the big toe through the main arteries and finally to the inner ear canal...the same is true of all teaching. There may be many many ways to teach something, but not all those methods will necessarily be effective. Lecturing 186 days a year falls into this category. The same is true of collaborative learning.

Assuming that students know automatically how to work well together is one of the first major mistakes teachers make. Cooperating effectively with others is not a gene, no more than catching a fly ball is an inborn skill. Collaboratively working well with others might be a skill enhanced by family background, initial brain matter, and the temperature of the room, but it is a skill nevertheless and needs to be learned. A corollary to this maxim is that it is often a false assumption that traditionally excellent students likewise automatically know how to work well with others.

I believe that leadership is definitely contextualized. In a discussion with colleagues who taught physics, I do not imagine I would be a leader in the conversation. And even if I were a leader in a discussion about teaching Shakespeare, it is quite another thing to encourage successfully those same colleagues to teach Shakespeare "my way."

One honors student approached me in the middle of a project and asked, "Mr. Maltese, why don't my group members follow my ideas? I have the best ideas in the group."

I have often pondered the irony that, in so many facets of school life like sports and band and orchestra and drama, we emphasize the need to submerge individuality for the betterment of the team or the group. But in the classroom we traditionally champion individual goals, even encouraging academic competition rather than cooperation. As we become adults we realize that, as one scholar claimed, we move from dependency as a child, to an emphasis on independency as a young adult, to the understanding of the importance of interdependency as a wise adult.

But we do little in school to share this awareness.

I asked my frowning colleague, "Did you spend some time aforehand helping students develop collaborative skills?" The blank look on her face gave me that answer.

I then asked her if she chose the groups.

"No, I let them choose."

This is always the easy way out for the teacher, but, as I relate below, not a good instructional strategy.

The third mistake my colleague made was to not monitor students while they worked. This I discuss in the Power of the Clipboard below.

One of the mistakes that I believe inexperienced teachers make is that they assume students already have the skills necessary for collaborative work. *Cooperative* skills, like other skills, must be *learned*.

Groups that function efficiently demonstrate mastery of the following skills:

1) Communication   Members communicate well and have the ability to both **articulate** their ideas and to **listen** to the ideas of others.

2) Trust. Members send and receive two trust messages: "I trust that when I express my opinion, you will listen and critique appropriately, not confusing the person with the idea." Likewise, "I hope you understand that when you make a contribution, I will consider and critique the idea and not you."

3) Shared leadership. No one student dominates the group, and everyone participates in brainstorming and developing ideas.

4) Creative problem solving. Students bring their own talents to a project and resolve collaborative issues.

Particularly in the beginning of the school year, when I randomly assign groups to address individual lessons, I grade students in large part on how well they attempt to master the skills above. Everything has to count. If they know I will grade them on their mastery of these skills, they are more likely to work on them.

Groups are chosen by the teacher.

Too often teachers allow students to choose groups. Students frequently choose their friends, and consequently much useful time is lost on maintaining those friendships instead of remaining on task. Also, friends develop internal cliques within groups that often undermine successful group functioning. When students complain about not choosing their own groups, offer the following:

1) In real life people do not often have the opportunity to work with their friends. An employer expects the newly hired employee to get along with co-workers. This learned skill (to get along with others in problem solving enterprises) is extremely important in the adult world, and this is why schools must teach this skill.

2) Often it is not easy to tell a friend to stop gossiping or playing and get back on task.

Choose groups usually by your appraisal of their abilities and work ethics. I usually assign the top students in a class, say the top six students, to six different groups. Then I assign the six most inexperienced students to those same groups. I continue this process until the entire class is assigned.

Alternatively you can assign students based on their talents/interests (visual, verbal, etc.), but be careful not to make the same student the illustrator all the time. The visual student will also have to write and act and perform. Our task as educators is not primarily to indulge student interests , but to expand them. This is one belief that seems to differentiate experienced teachers from the theorists who never actually taught. After all, if we ask many blooming adolescents what their primary interests are, would we really want to make projects out of them? And will indulging those interests help them learn how to build bridges, explore space, or find a cure for cancer?

Time is an Issue

I learned collaborative time management from my father who was a supervisor overseeing a crew of workers. If he gave them three days to complete a project, most of them would not start really working until halfway through the second day. He did not mind because the time allotted was decided by his boss, and, as long as his crew was done on time and job was satisfactory completed, my father was content. Students are less experienced about time management.

If you give students three days to complete a project, they might not start working until the third day in the last fifteen minutes and then complain they need more time.

If I know a project, completed satisfactorily, necessitates three days, I give the class two days to complete the assignment. There should be enough work so that at the beginning they seem overwhelmed. If they have been working steadily and everyone in the group is on task, I can always extend the collaborative time a day or even more. "Well, I have my own schedule to maintain, but you all seem to be working hard and on task, so, okay, I will extend it another day." Not only do you keep them on task, but you become the kindly authority figure!

The Power of the Clipboard

Early in my teaching career, one of my colleagues, whose preferred method of "teaching" was to sit behind her desk and pontificate to her class, told me that "Collaborative learning is a lot of bunk. I know a teacher who broke the kids into groups and then went outside to have a cigarette." I do not know of any instance where this has occurred, and I certainly have never lit up while my students were working in groups, but there is a point here. When the students are working, especially in the early stages of a document, be *visible*. Walk around the room. Stop at each group and ask about the progress. For me, these times were some of the most satisfying teaching experiences. I got to sit with small groups of students and work with them.

When I felt that some students were off task I made a point of walking the room with a clipboard under my arm. I would stop at an offender's desk and make some notes on a chart. Sometimes there was actually a chart! Especially if students know that they are in a sink and swim situation, that any student's off task behavior diminishes them all, making myself proximate to the groups often makes them return to the task at hand. For certain projects and for certain reasons at certain times of the year (particularly at the beginning of the school year in order to establish climate), I do grade individual contributions to group work.

Some teachers try to employ collaborative learning and project based learning because they think it is easier. Done correctly, PBL is more work than traditional approaches. I have taught Shakespeare so many times that if you ask me to stop writing this book and give a twenty minute lecture on Shakespeare and the Great Chain of Being, I can do it with no difficulty. But to develop a viable project to engage students in a project on The Great Chain of Being, its pre-project activities, the project itself, assessments and classroom monitoring and management, would tax my energy and skills.

Some old timers, critics of any methodology practiced after 1950, will argue that "In group work there is always the kid that piggy backs on the work of others." My response is two fold. One, a teacher can structure collaborative projects with individual accountability. Two, this implies that in the conventional classroom, teacher lecture/student listen or large group discussion, the recalcitrant student is highly involved. In truth, that same student *hides better* than he or she can in a small group. Those same students would often complain to me my keeping them on task because their off task behavior was much more visible in small groups. In large groups they simply feigned interest or went unnoticed as the teacher focused on the students who did respond. Even good students know that, if they answer one or two discussion questions in the beginning of the period, they can get credit for participation and then mentally drop out for the rest of the class.

One final note about structuring collaborative learning. In the early eighties, I threw myself into studying collaborative learning both by reading extensively about it and employing it in my classroom.....so much so that one day one of my students asked me, "Mr. Maltese, couldn't we not do a group work thing and just you lecture to us?" Learning does not lend itself to one supreme overarching effective strategy. But during those two years I learned that, while some fundamental sociological concepts might apply to choosing groups, the selection of members for groups was NOT solidified in a formula. I grouped students by gender, by apparent intelligences, interests, skills, and combinations of these. Near the end of one school year, in an exceptionally talented and trustworthy class, I allowed them to choose their own groups. This I did rarely. One racial minority, all of its members good friends, were assigned a project on Macbeth. The result was the best project any of the groups in any of my five classes completed that year. So, the question raised for me is, do we emphasize the skills necessary to successfully cooperate across lines of race and gender and age and interests, or are we interested in the final product? The caveat to this example is that all four members of the group were not only best friends and of the same race, but they were all highly academically motivated. Still, the question persists.

Collaborative learning is the both the strategy and the goal of project based learning. It is the essential means of student engagement in creative problem solving, and it is also an achievement as students learn to work together.

If you would like to discuss collaborative skills and their assessment, please feel free to contact me.

The Ten Commandments of Group Work

1) THOU SHALL STAY ON TASK.

2) THOU SHALL NOT DO MR. BEAGLE'S OR ANY OTHER TEACHER'S HOMEWORK.

3) THOU SHALL NOT DISCUSS THE NEWEST HUNKS ON *AMERICAN IDOL*.

4) THOU SHALL NOT DISCUSS THE COOLEST DUNK WITNESSED IN LAST NIGHT'S NBA GAME.

5) THOU SHALL NOT DISCUSS THE GENDER OF BIG BIRD.

6) THOU SHALL NOT LEAVE FACE IMPRINTS ON THY DESK.

7) THOU SHALL CRITICIZE IDEAS, NOT OTHER MEMBERS OF THE GROUP FOR THEIR IDEAS.

8) THOU SHALL ATTEMPT TO BE CLEVER AND NOT CUTE.

9) THOU SHALL NOT ATTEMPT TO DRAW ATTENTION TO ONESELF BY BEHAVING LIKE A HYPER HAMSTER WITH A CAFFEINE ADDICTION.

10) THOU SHALL NOT INSULT THE TEACHER'S INTELLIGENCE BY PRETENDING TO BE ON TASK WHEN HE DRAWS NEAR, ESPECIALLY WHEN YOU ARE REALLY DISCUSSING THE WARDROBE OF RYAN SEACREST.

Rules of Engagement

We live in a culture that places a high value on things that can be measured. This is fine when we operate within certain fields like medicine and surgery. I do not want my surgeon to use a metaphor to determine how long to make an incision. I do not want my family physician to approximate my correct dosage of antibiotic. But "measurement" has its shortcomings when it is applied to an activity such as "learning." Many policy makers in the educational community possess this burning desire to "measure" how much a student learns, as if learning can be packaged and measured like discrete quanta of energy or grams of matter. Not everything that can be measured is of value, and there are things that cannot be measured that are extremely important….like love, or hate, or commitment, or passion or curiosity.

The same limitation applies to student engagement. We tend to imagine the human brain to be this highly organized and single-minded entity. In truth, the brain is composed of warring factions---that part of the brain that prioritizes survival above all else often conflicts with that element of the brain that champions an ethical approach to decision making. My theory about how engaged a class is during an activity follows the Heisenberg Principle of Uncertainty, which posits that "measuring the present *position* while determining future *momentum* of a particle is impossible. Both cannot be simultaneously done to arbitrarily high precision. In other words, the more precisely one property is measured, the less precisely the other can be controlled, determined, or known." (Wikipedia, http://en.wikipedia.org/wiki/Uncertainty_ principle) How deeply a student is engaged and with what he is engaged are difficult to ascertain, let alone measure. What happened to the student at home during breakfast, how he relates to the other group members of the project, what slings and arrows of outrageous fortune he suffered in the halls, the cafeteria or gym class all impact on the quality of the engagement. If a teacher creates a highly engaging problem, some of those conditions that impact on the student's learning slide into the subconscious. We know what engagement looks like, but the thermometer has not been invented that could measure this. My point is that we can watch a class and "tell" whether students are engaged, but individual scientific determination of engagement will only be possible when every student's brain is connected to a super computer and software has been developed to measure content specific electrical impulses.

This is the point where a teacher's professional evaluation is extremely important. The current trend in the standards based community is to view students moving along an assembly line, like so many widgets, all of the same ability and quality, and the expectation is that, after being worked on by the teachers on the assembly line, all the students exit school with the same tonnage of mathematics, science, language arts, and history. Teachers know that not all students enter the conveyor belt with the same personal history, perspective, and talents, and the very best teachers can only bring all students as far along that continuum as they can, knowing full well that not all students will wind up at the same educational terminus.

Spectators measure a college coach's success by wins and losses. True educators know that the strength of a coach is how far along he brings his players, despite the wins and losses.

Having stated that caveat, there are still some "rules" that will maximize student engagement. **Project based learning is predicated, in most cases, on problem based learning, and the challenge a teacher has in creating a good project involves creating a good problem.**

What is a good problem for project based learning? First, the problem must satisfy what I call "Ralph's Goldilocks Theory of Essential Questions." The question we ask students to explore must not be so difficult and amorphous that they do not know where to begin. "What are some major themes and concepts in Hemingway's work?" At the other end of the spectrum of "problem development," the question must not be so easy that it is not intellectually challenging. "In *The Old Man and the Sea*, who is the hero?" A good question might be "Did Hemingway, himself, in his lifestyle and by his actions, exemplify the Hemingway code hero?" Or "Does the Hemingway code hero exist in modern film?" The last two questions are doable and require some neural pathways to be activated.

The second criterion for a good project is an attempt to engage multiple intelligences. This takes some careful thinking. We can assign the project of restaging a Shakespearean drama and require that music be provided for each act. Without a more academically valuable qualification, the student assigned this task will simply choose the most popular trendy song. Instead, I would be more inclined to demand that whatever music is chosen should be in line with the theme of the play or should give a different perspective on the theme. Almost every one of my assignments requires that the music be non-lyrical. This really upsets some students because they want to play the latest music by their favorite group, but that is not the purpose of the assignment. Besides, one of my major goals is to expand their interests, so, if they have to go outside their preference zone to listen to classical music or jazz, I do not think that is a bad thing. My point is that whatever the intelligence addressed, it must be academically engaging on a high level of thinking. If we stay within the concept that our goal is to expand student interests, then we must also be careful that the same student with a primary dependency on visual intelligence not always be responsible for the art work. He has to learn to develop his writing skills as well.

One of my best examples of a successful addressing of an intelligence involves a young man who played the clarinet in the school orchestra. As part of a larger project on the novel *The Great Gatsby*, Dean wrote small musical pieces to identify the major characters in the novel. When it came time for his performance, he handed me a list of the characters in the order of the pieces he was going to play on his clarinet. His classmates had no such list. Dean would play the first selection, and he would ask the class which character that music represented. Students would shout out the correct answer every time. To me, that represents understanding on a deep and different level. Dean understood those characters in such a way as to interpret them musically.

The third rule of engagement focuses on the element of fantasy in developing an assignment. Term paper assignments often fail because they are framed as topics. "Write a paper on Abraham Lincoln's assassination." "Write a paper on Edgar Allan Poe." "Write a paper on Black Holes." All of these topics cry out, from a student's perspective, for plagiarism or, at most, a great deal of cutting and pasting rather than interaction with the content. We sometimes, as teachers, forget that the academic world is motivated by questions rather than answers. Scholars are exploring problems which are interesting. "Write a paper on what would have happened to Reconstruction if Abraham Lincoln had NOT been assassinated." "Write a paper on how Edgar Allan Poe's super sleuth Monsieur Dupin is similar to and different from Sherlock Holmes." "Write a paper on what happens to time at the edge of a black hole."

A teacher can eliminate the propensity for plagiarism (not to mention reading 120 boring papers on Edgar Allan Poe) by constructing a fantasy analogy for which there is no research. "If Abraham Lincoln were running for president of the United States today, what would be his stand on the following issues: illegal immigration, public school reform, spending money on space exploration." "If Edgar Allan Poe wrote the following three chapters of *Alice in Wonderland*, what would they look like. Explain your choices in the course of your paper." "Basing your opinion on what you have learned about the physics of black holes, write a paper arguing either that the universe is expanding or contracting."

Using fantasy analogies such as the ones above may seem odd at first because we are so content driven, especially in high schools, but if we remember that our primary focus should be on the student's development of high level thinking skills, I think we will agree that the focused questions above will invoke more head scratching than the topics above that require little more regurgitation via cutting and pasting. As a wise educator once told me, elementary school teachers are more focused on the student, and high school teachers are more focused on the content. English/Language Arts lends itself to be more expansive. The projects in this book have a decidedly English bent, but, with a little imagination the science/math/social studies teacher can alter the project to fit his discipline. The necessity here is for the teacher to abandon the notion that his responsibility is to cover the material (the teacher may be on Chapter 10 of the math textbook, but the students might still be on Chapter 1!), in favor of fulfilling his responsibility to develop high level skills. In my experience, this is a tough concept for many teachers to embrace.

A fourth consideration in developing a project for your classes involves the affective domain. When to choose to assign which project is a subjective choice that I often made predicated on what I sensed my students were experiencing. I would not assign a sophisticated project at the beginning of the year, before students had developed some collaborative skills and a sense of trust. Other projects which would focus on developing those skills and trust I would assign in the beginning of the year. Some projects are more fun for the students, and these I might place at that time of the year when I perceived students would most benefit from them---after a boring bout of standardized testing for example.

Before I administered any projects, I focused on developing collaborative skills by mini-lessons on the subject matter. For example, I would randomly assign groups, and ask each group to choose a cartoon character to represent each of the characters in a short story. I told the class I would grade the groups on how well they exercised the collaborative skills outlined in the previous chapter. Or I would give every student a set of questions to ask on a literary work, and, after they completed the questions they would turn them in. I would then assign groups, and issue each group the same set of questions which they are to answer as a group. (This method assures individual accountability. Student engagement is minimized if the "slackers" know that they can piggy back on the group's answers.)

One of the current trendy foci in education is differentiated education. Differentiating learning for students who are individuals rather than widgets on an assembly line is an important consideration. What I find troubling is the notion that somehow this is new. Even though we had tracking for most of my teaching career (a structure I found appalling even as a novice teacher), I learned early on that there really is no such thing as a class of students who are all "lower track." Any experienced teacher can tell you that honors classes are collections of disparate personalities, talents, and aspirations, with, perhaps, the only possible commonality being a similar socioeconomic background. Now we have numerous books on how to formulaically instill differentiated education in the classroom. One text postulates that we indulge individual student interests and assign books accordingly. This may be possible in elementary school, but in high school it is a virtual impossibility. And, if we are truly honest, we might ask ourselves if we really want to find a book that would illuminate the interests of many high school students. Or we may differentiate by reading levels within the same class which ultimately becomes homogeneous tracking within a class....everyone knows who the Red Robins, Blue Jays, and Yellow Finches are. By the time the texts give us the scientific measurements for initiating differentiated education, we are back to the students as assembly line widgets.

The second aspect I find disturbing about this educational reform is the unwillingness to recognize that American public schools were designed to mass manufacture students in the same way as we mass produced tanks and rifles and airplanes and pencils. If, as a culture, we truly want educational reform we must revisit this structure and recognize its limitations for individualized education. Only then can we rethink the school schedule, and have dialogues about how to engage all students in higher level thinking. If you want a private room in a hospital, rather than to be one patient amongst fifty in a large room, then you have to be willing to pay the price.

Without knowing I was differentiating education, I tended to differentiate on the "back end" of a unit. Rather than indulge their interests, I tried to give options for students to demonstrate their understanding of the content or to showcase their improvement of skills through another means than paper and pencil. (See Dean and his clarinet above). The more options students have to participate in the project using their own talents, the richer the project usually is. However, the student who draws well should also be given the opportunity to improve his writing skills, or his skills in articulation and collaboration. As I stressed earlier, allowing the same student to always be the illustrator is not a sound idea. In this facet, "differentiating" to allow for the student's ability is limiting his ability to grow in other areas.

My point is that this is the art part of teaching rather than the science part. Knowing what projects to assign when depends on a teacher's subjective evaluation.

An associative element of the Classrooms For the Future program was the integration of technology into the classroom. This text and my other works holds sacred the premise that methodology and teacher skills precede the use of technology. A teacher who has an activboard in his classroom and uses it to display his twenty year old overhead transparencies is not necessarily more successful than a teacher who does not even have an overhead projector. As a coach mentor for Classrooms for the Future, I visited schools attempting to implement the program. I remember visiting an English teacher (who was pointed out to me by my school escort) who was proud that her entire class was using laptop computers. The assignment, as she joyfully explained, involved each student using the laptop to research one poem assigned by the teacher. "Research" in this example meant identifying the poet, the poet's country of origin, and some information about the poem. I asked the teacher what the students were going to do with the information after they gathered it digitally. She gave me the blankest glare, as if to say, "I used the laptops. What else do you want from me?"

A poorly designed project will not be enhanced by web 2.0 tools, just as a school board chosen textbook or reading program will not make a poor teacher a model teacher. And an exceptionally good teacher will make something positive out of a bad textbook or flawed program. The emphasis on school reform should always be on the strengths of the teacher.

I debated on the structure of these projects, using built in technological enhancements. But I am aware of two facts. I did not want a teacher who intended to use these projects to be frustrated because he did not have available any emerging technologies. Besides, All of these projects were implemented long before any of those technologies were available to me, so while some digital tools are included, they are not required.

Please also remember that these projects are templates. Use them to help you initiate your own ideas on how to teach your own subject matter and to your individual goals for your individual classes. My goal was to share the structures and the processes that I think are the skeleton of successful project based learning. Flesh these out according to your teaching talents and skills. Good luck.

Project Assessments—How to Use the Spreadsheets

I used spreadsheets and databases for many many administrative and assessment duties in my teaching career. I have included (in Word Document form) several spreadsheets I used to assess the projects. I wanted individual as well as group accountability in my projects, and this meant that if I used the first sheet of an Excel spreadsheet, things would get pretty messy. Then I realized that the various sheets in an Excel workbook could be interrelated. I could have a sheet just for individual accountability (say on task behavior), and the results of this sheet could automatically be entered in another spreadsheet. For example, I could track individual student contributions to group work on Sheet #2 and those tallies would be calculated into a total group performance on Sheet #1. In other words, students who were off task would not only suffer from an individual viewpoint, but would also detract from their group's grade.

Let's start with the simple.

The Pediment File Evaluation Sheet is a simple way to tally performances on the Greek Pediment Project. Just enter the numbers in the categories.

Tracking Students for a Project is also simple. Type in the class roster in the left column. Print out this spreadsheet and latch it onto a clipboard. As students work, walk around the room, and periodically award points to individual students for being actively engaged. Of course, there are students who will be off task, and, as you approach, will jump into gear as if they have been engaged the whole time. I would point out to them that I was not as dumb as I looked. Rather than direct my warning to the miscreant, I addressed the group. "Do you understand that Harry being off task negatively affects all your grades?" Often that was enough. Let them police themselves.

Evaluation Sheet for The Canterbury Tales Olympics is a little more complex. The scores for the individual events are entered on Sheet #1, and the ultimate tallies automatically show up for the groups on Sheet #2.

Group Project Evaluation Sheet 2006 is also relatively simple. Sheet #1 is used to set up the groups. In the beginning of the school year, I set up a database of all my students. I can then simply choose a class and cut and paste their names into Column J. From Column J I cut and paste the names into the various groups. I try to choose groups based on a combination of talents and strengths and inexperienced and experienced students mixed in. Notice that when a student's name is placed in Sheet #1, it automatically appears in Sheets #2 and #3. I hate doing things over and over again that the computer likes to do. Enter the scores on Sheet #3 and the final totals come out on Sheet #2 which you can print out and then enter into your gradebook (hopefully you can copy and paste into an online gradebook).

Group 2001 Evaluation Sheet with Individual Test Scores and **Hard Times Evaluation Sheet** have the same template. I just wanted to demonstrate how you can tailor your spreadsheet easily by changing the column headings. Sheet 1, Column A has the groups and the individual members of the groups. Sheet 4 is the location for entering individual test scores on an reading assessment of the novel **Hard Times**. Notice that a student is not only held accountable individually for his test score, but contributes to the group's score. Sheet # 3 is the one you print out and latch to a clipboard. Walk around the room and enter points for each student for being on task. Not only will the student receive an individual grade, but will contribute (or detract from) his group's grade. On Sheet #2 enter the categories you want to assess for the project (in Rows 5 and 6). Then, using base 10, evaluate the project for each group. All the totals automatically appear on Sheet #1 which you can print out and use to record the final grades in your gradebook. You can also use Sheet #1 to point out to your students where their strengths and weaknesses were.

You will notice that there is a column titled "Project Points." That is because I wanted to work on the 100 point scheme even though, if it was a complicated project involving much time and effort, I wanted the project to be worth, say, 150 points. I simply entered "150" in Column B, Row 6 on Sheet #1, and the computer made all the adjustments. For those teachers who want an easy conversion scale (changing scores based on 100 points to, say, 300 points, or a project based on 100 points converted to one based on 50 points, there is a conversion scale I created on my website, ralphmaltese.com under Teacher Tools. It's free.

I spent a great deal of time developing these spreadsheets. I would gladly send you the spreadsheets in their Excel form on a disk, but I would have to charge, and I truly have not thought that part through. If enough people email me and want the spreadsheet ready-made, I will have to work out something. Any ideas?

Pediment File Page 1 of 1

Pediment File

JUDGE _____

DATE _____

PERIOD

GROUP	GROUP 1	GROUP 2	GROUP 3	GROUP 4	GROUP 5	GROUP 6	GROUP 7	GROUP 8
ROUND ONE 10 @								
SPEED								
ORGANIZATION								
CREATIVITY								
TOTALS	0	0	0	0	0	0	0	0
ROUND TWO A 10 @								
SPEED								
ORGANIZATION								
CREATIVITY								
TOTALS	0	0	0	0	0	0	0	0
ROUND THREE 10@								
BEAUTY								
CREATIVITY								
TOTALS	0	0	0	0	0	0	0	0

Tracking Students Page 1 of 1

tracking students for a project				Day 1	Day 2	Day 3	Day 4	Day 5	Day 6	Day 7	Day 8	Day 9	Day 10
Mr. MalteseActivity is worth =	100	Adjust	Total	Here	Here	Here	Here	Here	Here	Here	Here	Here	Here
				Ready	Ready	Ready	Ready	Ready	Ready	Ready	Ready	Ready	Ready
Student Name	%	Points	Points	Active	Active	Active	Active	Active	Active	Active	Active	Active	Active
		0	0	0									
		0	0										
		0	0										
		0	0										
		0	0										
		0	0										
		0	0										
		0	0										
		0	0										
		0	0										
		0	0										
		0	0										
		0	0										
		0	0										
		0	0										
		0	0										
		0	0										
		0	0										
		0	0										
		0	0										
		0	0										
		0	0										
		0	0										
		0	0										
		0	0										
		0	0										
		0	0										
		0	0										
		0	0										
		0	0										
		0	0										
		0	0										
		0	0										
		0	0										
		0	0										
		0	0										
Possible PTs =	30												

Evaluation Sheet for Canterbury Tales Olympics Page 1 of 3

Evaluation Sheet for Canterbury Tales Project

Sheet 1

SEE SHEET 2 FOR TOTALS

Period =

Project Pts. = 100

Page 1 of 3

			Categories	Prologue	Phone	Pilgrim	Panto			1					2					
	%	Project Pts.	Total Pts.	Group	Message	Plea	Mime	Party	Questions	Alpha	Whose	Party	Questions	Alpha	Whose	Cook	Closure
GROUP 1				40	10	10	10	10	10	10	10	10	10	10	10	50	50
	4%	4	250	40	10	10	10	10	10	10	10	10	10	10	10	50	50
	0%	0	10	10													
	0%	0	0														
	0%	0	0														
	0%	0	0														
	0%	0	0														
Group Points =	10	4	10	10	0	0	0	0	0	0	0	0	0	0	0	0	0
GROUP 2				40	10	10	10	10	10	10	10	10	10	10	10	50	50
	4%	4	250	40	10	10	10	10	10	10	10	10	10	10	10	50	50
	0%	0	10	10													
	0%	0	0														
	0%	0	0														
	0%	0	0														
	0%	0	0														
Group Points =	10	4	10	10	0	0	0	0	0	0	0	0	0	0	0	0	0
GROUP 3				40	10	10	10	10	10	10	10	10	10	10	10	50	50
	4%	4	250	40	10	10	10	10	10	10	10	10	10	10	10	50	50
	0%	0	10	10													
	0%	0	0														
	0%	0	0														
	0%	0	0														
	0%	0	0														
Group Points =	10	4	10	10	0	0	0	0	0	0	0	0	0	0	0	0	0
GROUP 4				40	10	10	10	10	10	10	10	10	10	10	10	50	50
	4%	4	250	40	10	10	10	10	10	10	10	10	10	10	10	50	50
	0%	0	10	10													
	0%	0	0														
	0%	0	0														
	0%	0	0														
	0%	0	0														
Group Points =	10	4	10	10	0	0	0	0	0	0	0	0	0	0	0	0	0

Evaluation Sheet for Canterbury Tales Project Page 2 of 3

Sheet 1

2	2	2		
Questions	Alpha	Whose	Cook	Closure
10	10	10	50	50
10	10	10	50	50
0	0	0	0	0
>>>>>	>>>>>	>>>>>	>>>>>	>>>>>
Questions	Alpha	Whose	Cook	Closure
10	10	10	50	50
10	10	10	50	50
0	0	0	0	0
>>>>>	>>>>>	>>>>>	>>>>>	>>>>>
Questions	Alpha	Whose	Cook	Closure
10	10	10	50	50
10	10	10	50	50
0	0	0	0	0
>>>>>	>>>>>	>>>>>	>>>>>	>>>>>
Questions	Alpha	Whose	Cook	Closure
10	10	10	50	50
10	10	10	50	50
0	0	0	0	0
>>>>>	>>>>>	>>>>>	>>>>>	>>>>>

Evaluation Sheet for Canterbury Tales Project Page 3 of 3

Sheet 2

PERIOD =

TOTALS FOR OLYMPIC EVENTS

GROUPS	TOTALS		Prologue	Phone	Plea	Mime	Party	Questions	Alpha	Whose	Party	Questions	Alpha	Whose	Cook	Closure
GROUP #1	10		10	0	0	0	0	0	0	0	0	0	0	0	0	0
>>>	>>	>>>>>>>>>>>>>>>>>>>>>>>>>>>>														
GROUP #2	10		10	0	0	0	0	0	0	0	0	0	0	0	0	0
>>>>>>	>>	>>>>>>>>>>>>>>>>>>>>>>>>>>>>														
GROUP #3	10		10	0	0	0	0	0	0	0	0	0	0	0	0	0
>>>>>>	>>	>>>>>>>>>>>>>>>>>>>>>>>>>>>>														
GROUP #4	10		10	0	0	0	0	0	0	0	0	0	0	0	0	0
>>>>>>	>>	>>>>>>>>>>>>>>>>>>>>>>>>>>>>														
GROUP #5	10		10	0	0	0	0	0	0	0	0	0	0	0	0	0
>>>>>>	>>	>>>>>>>>>>>>>>>>>>>>>>>>>>>>														
GROUP #6	10		10	0	0	0	0	0	0	0	0	0	0	0	0	0
>>>>>>	>>	>>>>>>>>>>>>>>>>>>>>>>>>>>>>														
GROUP #7	10		10	0	0	0	0	0	0	0	0	0	0	0	0	0
>>>>>>	>>	>>>>>>>>>>>>>>>>>>>>>>>>>>>>														
GROUP #8	0															
>>>>>>	>>	>>>>>>>>>>>>>>>>>>>>>>>>>>>>														
GROUP #9	0															
>>>>>>	>>	>>>>>>>>>>>>>>>>>>>>>>>>>>>>														
GROUP #10	0															
>>>>>>		>>>>>>>>>>>>>>>>>>>>>>>>>>>>>>>>														
>>>>>>	>>>	>>>>>>>>>>>>>>>>>>>>>>>>>>>>>>>>>														
>>>	>>>	>>>>>>>>														

Group Project Evaluation Sheet 2006 Page 1 of 4

Sheet 1

Project =

| PERIOD = | | MALES = | |
| TOTAL = | **0** | FEMALES = | |

	GROUP #1			GROUP #2	
1			1		
Grade	2	Grade	2	Grade
3			3		
4			4		
5			5		
6			6		
Topic			Topic		

	GROUP #4			GROUP #5	
1			1		
Grade	2	Grade	2	Grade
3			3		
4			4		
5			5		
6			6		
Topic			Topic		

	GROUP 7			GROUP #8	
1			1		
Grade	2	Grade	2	Grade
3			3		
4			4		
5			5		
6			6		
Topic			Topic		

	GROUP #10			GROUP #11	
1			1		
Grade	2	Grade	2	Grade
3			3		
4			4		
5			5		
6			6		
Topic			Topic		

			STUDENTS WORKING ALONE	
Grade		Grade		Grade
1			7	
2			8	
3			9	

Group Project Evaluation Sheet 2006 Page 2 of 4

Sheet 1 Continued

		STUDENTS COPIED FROM DATABASE
	GROUP #3	
1		
2		
3		
4		
5		
6		
Topic		
	GROUP #6	
1		
2		
3		
4		
5		
6		
Topic		
	GROUP #9	
1		
2		
3		
4		
5		
6		
Topic		
	GROUP #12	
1		
2		
3		
4		
5		
6		
Topic		
13		
14		
15		

PASSWORD IS MOUNTAIN

ENTER SCORES ON SHEET #2   Project =

SHEET #3   0

Sheet 2

| Period = | 0 |
| PROJECT IS WORTH = | 100 |

	Total Possible Pts. =				Weight Value	Weight Value	Weight Value	Weight Value	Weight Value	Weight Value
		Adjusted Points	70 Total Points		20 Collabor 10	10 Organiz 10	20 Thought 10	10 Punctual 10	10 Creativity 10	0
	Percent									
GROUP 1	0.0%	0	0		0	0	0	0	0	0
	0.0%	0	0		0	0	0	0	0	0
0	0.0%	0	0		0	0	0	0	0	0
0	0.0%	0	0		0	0	0	0	0	0
0	0.0%	0	0		0	0	0	0	0	0
0	0.0%	0	0		0	0	0	0	0	0
GROUP 2										
#REF!	0.0%	0	0		0	0	0	0	0	0
0	0.0%	0	0		0	0	0	0	0	0
0	0.0%	0	0		0	0	0	0	0	0
0	0.0%	0	0		0	0	0	0	0	0
0	0.0%	0	0		0	0	0	0	0	0
0	0.0%	0	0		0	0	0	0	0	0
GROUP 3										
0	0.0%	0	0		0	0	0	0	0	0
0	0.0%	0	0		0	0	0	0	0	0
0	0.0%	0	0		0	0	0	0	0	0
0	0.0%	0	0		0	0	0	0	0	0
0	0.0%	0	0		0	0	0	0	0	0
0	0.0%	0	0		0	0	0	0	0	0
GROUP 4										
0	0.0%	0	0		0	0	0	0	0	0
0	0.0%	0	0		0	0	0	0	0	0
0	0.0%	0	0		0	0	0	0	0	0
0	0.0%	0	0		0	0	0	0	0	0
0	0.0%	0	0		0	0	0	0	0	0
0	0.0%	0	0		0	0	0	0	0	0
GROUP 5										
0	0.0%	0	0		0	0	0	0	0	0
0	0.0%	0	0		0	0	0	0	0	0

Group Project Evaluation Sheet 2006 Page 4 of 4

Sheet 3		Enter Student Project Scores Here			Total Points	Collabor	Organiz	Thought	Punctual	Creativity	
Project 0						Weight Value 20	Weight Value 10	Weight Value 20	Weight Value 10	Weight Value 10	Weight Value 0
Period =				Based on a Value of 10	0	10	10	10	10	10	0
											0
GROUP 1	>>>>>>	>>>>>>	>>>>>>	>>>>>>	>>>>>>	>>>>>>	>>>>>>	>>>>>>	>>>>>>	>>>>>>	>>>>>>
					0						
					0						
					0						
					0						
GROUP 2	>>>>>>	>>>>>>	>>>>>>	>>>>>>	>>>>>>	>>>>>>	>>>>>>	>>>>>>	>>>>>>	>>>>>>	>>>>>>
#REF!					0						
					0						
					0						
					0						
					0						
GROUP 3	>>>>>>	>>>>>>	>>>>>>	>>>>>>	>>>>>>	>>>>>>	>>>>>>	>>>>>>	>>>>>>	>>>>>>	>>>>>>
					0						
					0						
					0						
					0						
					0						
GROUP 4	>>>>>>	>>>>>>	>>>>>>	>>>>>>	>>>>>>	>>>>>>	>>>>>>	>>>>>>	>>>>>>	>>>>>>	>>>>>>
					0						
					0						
					0						
					0						

Group 2001 Evaluation Sheet with Individual Test Scores Page 1 of 4

Group Evaluation Sheet 2001

SHEET 1

USE WITH SHEET 2, SHEET 3   SHEET 4

PERIOD =	8		CRITERIA VALUES						
PROJECT POINTS =		100	40	20	30			10	
GROUP	PROJECT	PERCENT	TOTAL	GROUP	ORG	THEME			TEST
# 1	POINTS	AGE	POINTS	WORK	QUALITY	QUALITY			POINTS
	#####	#####	#####	#####	13.333	0	######	#####	#DIV/0!
>>>>>>>>>>>>>>	>>>>>	>>>>>	>>>>>	>>>>>	>>>>>	>>>>>	>>>>>>	>>>>>	>>>>>
GROUP	PROJECT	PERCENT	TOTAL	GROUP	ORG	THEME			TEST
# 2	POINTS	AGE	POINTS	WORK	QUALITY	QUALITY			POINTS
	#####	#####	#####	#####	0	0	#######	#####	#DIV/0!
>>>>>>>>>>>>>>	>>>>>	>>>>>	>>>>>	>>>>>	>>>>>	>>>>>	>>>>>>	>>>>>	>>>>>
GROUP	PROJECT	PERCENT	TOTAL	GROUP	ORG	THEME			TEST
# 3	POINTS	AGE	POINTS	WORK	QUALITY	QUALITY			POINTS
	#####	#####	#####	#####	0	0	#######	#####	#DIV/0!
>>>>>>>>>>>>>>	>>>>>	>>>>>	>>>>>	>>>>>	>>>>>	>>>>>	>>>>>>	>>>>>	>>>>>
GROUP	PROJECT	PERCENT	TOTAL	GROUP	ORG	THEME			TEST
# 4	POINTS	AGE	POINTS	WORK	QUALITY	QUALITY			POINTS
	#####	#####	#####	#####	0	0	#######	#####	#DIV/0!
>>>>>>>>>>>>>>	>>>>>	>>>>>	>>>>>	>>>>>	>>>>>	>>>>>	>>>>>>	>>>>>	>>>>>
GROUP	PROJECT	PERCENT	TOTAL	GROUP	ORG	THEME			TEST
# 5	POINTS	AGE	POINTS	WORK	QUALITY	QUALITY			POINTS
	#####	#####	#####	#####	0	0	#######	#####	#DIV/0!

Group 2001 Evaluation Sheet with Individual Test Scores Page 2 of 4

EVALUATION SHEET FOR
GRAMMAR CRITERIA

SLAVERY UNIT
CRITERIA

PERIOD
= 8

SHEET 2

GROUP #	TOT PTS	ORGANIZATI CIT	PARA	#	TOT PTS	THEME ORG	CREA	ALL	TOT PTS	EFF		TOT PTS			TOT PTS
1	30	10	10	10	30	10	10	10	0			0			0
	20	10	10		0				0			0			0
	TOT	ORGANIZATI			TOT	THEME			TOT		0	TOT		0	0	TOT
GROUP #	PTS	CIT	PARA	#	PTS	ORG	CREA	ALL	PTS	EFF	0	PTS			0	PTS
2	30	10	10	10	30	10	10	10	0		0	0			0	0
	0				0				0			0			0
	TOT	ORGANIZATI			TOT	THEME			TOT		0	TOT		0	0	TOT
GROUP #	PTS	CIT	PARA	#	PTS	ORG	CREA	ALL	PTS	EFF	0	PTS			0	PTS
3	30	10	10	10	30	10	10	10	0		0	0			0	0
	0				0				0			0			0
	TOT	ORGANIZATI			TOT	THEME			TOT		0	TOT		0	0	TOT
GROUP #	PTS	CIT	PARA	#	PTS	ORG	CREA	ALL	PTS	EFF	0	PTS			0	PTS
4	30	10	10	10	30	10	10	10	0		0	0			0	0
	0				0				0			0			0
	TOT	ORGANIZATI			TOT	THEME			TOT		0	TOT		0	0	TOT
GROUP #	PTS	CIT	PARA	#	PTS	ORG	CREA	ALL	PTS	EFF	0	PTS			0	PTS
5	30	10	10	10	30	10	10	10	0		0	0			0	0
	0				0				0			0			0
	TOT	ORGANIZATI			TOT	THEME			TOT		0	TOT		0	0	TOT
GROUP #	PTS	CIT	PARA	#	PTS	ORG	CREA	ALL	PTS	EFF	0	PTS			0	PTS
6	30	10	10	10	30	10	10	10	0		0	0			0	0
0	0				0				0			0			0
	TOT	ORGANIZATI			TOT	THEME			TOT		0	TOT		0	0	TOT
GROUP #	PTS	CIT	PARA	#	PTS	ORG	CREA	ALL	PTS	EFF	0	PTS			0	PTS
7	30	10	10	10	30	10	10	10	0		0	0			0	0
Hiram Walker	0				0				0			0			0
	TOT	ORGANIZATI			TOT	THEME			TOT		0	TOT		0	0	TOT

Group 2001 Evaluation Sheet with Individual Test Scores Page 3 of 4

Slavery Unit
PERIOD = 8
INDIVIDUAL PTS. = 200
Sheet 3

GROUP	PROJ PTS.	PER CENT	TOTAL PTS.	#IN GROUP	SESS #1	#IN GROUP	SESS #2	#IN GROUP	SESS #3	#IN GROUP	SESS #4	#IN GROUP	SESS #5	#IN GROUP	SESS #6	#IN GROUP	SESS #7
#1	####	####	####		10		10										
	####	####	0														
	####	####	0														
	####	####	0														
	####	####	0														
	####	####	0														
	####	####	0	0													
	0	0	0	####	0	####	0	####	0	0	0	0	0	0	0	0	0
#2	####	####	####		10		10										
	####	####	0														
	####	####	0														
	####	####	0														
	####	####	0														
	####	####	0														
	####	####	0														
	0	0	0	####	0	####	0	####	0	0	0	0	0	0	0	0	0
#3	####	####	####		10												
	####	####	0														
	####	####	0														
	####	####	0														
	####	####	0														
	####	####	0														
	####	####	0														
	0	0	0	####	0	####	0	####	0	0	0	0	0	0	0	0	0
#4	####	####	####														
	####	####	0														
	####	####	0														
	####	####	0														
	####	####	0														
	####	####	0														

Group 2001 Evaluation Sheet with Individual Test Scores Page 4 of 4

Period =	8
Individual Test Pts.	200
Group Project Points	10

Sheet 4

Use this sheet for entering test data

Highest Possible Individual Test Grade = 100

GROUP	Percent %	Adjusted Points	Test Score	# Test Takers	Total Pts. Possible	Total Pts. All Takers	Adjusted Grp. Pts.	Average Group
#1	90%	180	90	2	200	340	17	85
	80%	160	80					
	#VALUE!	#VALUE!						
	#VALUE!	#VALUE!						
	#VALUE!	#VALUE!						
0	#VALUE!	#VALUE!						

GROUP	Percent %	Adjusted Points	Test Score	# Test Takers	Total Pts. Possible	Total Pts. All Takers	Adjusted Grp. Pts.	Average Group
#2	90%	180	90	2	200	340	17	85
	80%	160	80					
	#VALUE!	#VALUE!						
	#VALUE!	#VALUE!						
	#VALUE!	#VALUE!						
	#VALUE!	#VALUE!						

GROUP	Percent %	Adjusted Points	Test Score	# Test Takers	Total Pts. Possible	Total Pts. All Takers	Adjusted Grp. Pts.	Average Group
#3	90%	180	90	2	200	340	17	85
	80%	160	80					
	#VALUE!	#VALUE!						
	#VALUE!	#VALUE!						
	#VALUE!	#VALUE!						
	#VAL!	#VALU!						

Hard Times Evaluation Sheet Page 1 of 4

Hard Times Eval Sheet

Hard Times Eval Sheet

Sheet 1

USE WITH SHEET 2, SHEET 3   SHEET 4

PERIOD =	1		CRITERIA VALUES							
PROJECT POINTS =			100	30	20	30	20			
GROUP	PROJECT	PERCENT	TOTAL	GROUP	ORG	THEME	Creative		TEST
#1	POINTS	AGE	POINTS	WORK	QUALITY	QUALITY	Presentation		POINTS
	######	######	######	######	13.333	0	#DIV/0!	######	######
>>>>>>>>>>>>>>	>>>>>	>>>>>	>>>>>	>>>>>	>>>>>	>>>>>	>>>>>>	>>>>>	>>>>>
GROUP	PROJECT	PERCENT	TOTAL	GROUP	ORG	THEME	Creative		TEST
#2	POINTS	AGE	POINTS	WORK	QUALITY	QUALITY	Presentation		POINTS
	######	######	######	######	0	0	#DIV/0!	######	######
>>>>>>>>>>>>>>	>>>>>	>>>>>	>>>>>	>>>>>	>>>>>	>>>>>	>>>>>>	>>>>>	>>>>>
GROUP	PROJECT	PERCENT	TOTAL	GROUP	ORG	THEME	Creative		TEST
#3	POINTS	AGE	POINTS	WORK	QUALITY	QUALITY	Presentation		POINTS
	######	######	######	######	0	0	#DIV/0!	######	######
>>>>>>>>>>>>>>	>>>>>	>>>>>	>>>>>	>>>>>	>>>>>	>>>>>	>>>>>>	>>>>>	>>>>>
GROUP	PROJECT	PERCENT	TOTAL	GROUP	ORG	THEME	Creative		TEST
#4	POINTS	AGE	POINTS	WORK	QUALITY	QUALITY	Presentation		POINTS

Hard Times Evaluation Sheet Page 2 of 4

**EVALUATION SHEET FOR
GRAMMAR CRITERIA**

PERIOD
= 1   **Sheet 2**

GROUP #	TOT PTS	ORGANIZATI CIT	PARA	#	TOT PTS	THEME ORG	CREA	ALL	TOT PTS		EFF		TOT PTS			TOT PTS
1	30	10	10	10	30	10	10	10	0				0			0
	20	10	10		0				0				0			0
2	30	10	10	10	30	10	10	10	0			0	0		0	0
	0				0				0				0			0
3	30	10	10	10	30	10	10	10	0			0	0		0	0
	0				0				0				0			0
4	30	10	10	10	30	10	10	10	0			0	0		0	0
	0				0				0				0			0
5	30	10	10	10	30	10	10	10	0			0	0		0	0
	0				0				0				0			0
6	30	10	10	10	30	10	10	10	0			0	0		0	0
0	0				0				0				0			0
7	30	10	10	10	30	10	10	10	0			0	0		0	0
	0				0				0				0			0

Hard Times Evaluation Sheet Page 3 of 4

Slavery Unit

PERIOD = 1
INDIVIDUAL PTS. = 200
Sheet 3

GROUP	PROJ PTS.	PER CENT	TOTAL PTS.	#IN GROUP	SESS #1	#IN GROUP	SESS #2	#IN GROUP	SESS #3	#IN GROUP	SESS #4	#IN GROUP	SESS #5	#IN GROUP	SESS #6	#IN GROUP	SESS #7
GROUP #1	####	####	####		10		10										
	####	####	0														
	####	####	0														
	####	####	0														
	####	####	0														
	####	####	0														
	####	####	0														
	0	0	####	####	0	####	0		0		0		0		0		0
GROUP #2	####	####	####		10		10										
	####	####	0														
	####	####	0														
	####	####	0														
	####	####	0														
	####	####	0														
	####	####	0														
	0	0	####	####	0	####	0		0		0		0		0		0
GROUP #3	####	####	####		10												
	####	####	0														
	####	####	0														
	####	####	0														
	####	####	0														
	####	####	0														
	####	####	0														
	0	0	####	####	0	####	0		0		0		0		0		0
GROUP #4	####	####	####														
	####	####	0														
	####	####	0														
	####	####	0														
	####	####	0														
	####	####	0														

Hard Times Evaluation Sheet Page 4 of 4

Period =	1
	Use this sheet for entering test data
Individual Test Pts.	200
Highest Possible Individual Test Grade =	100
Group Project Points	

Sheet 4

GROUP #1

Percent	Adjusted	Test	# Test	Total Pts.	Total Pts.	Adjusted	Average
%	Points	Score	Takers	Possible	All Takers	Grp. Pts.	Group
90%	180	90	2	200	340	######	85
80%	160	80					
#VALUE!	#VALUE!						
#VALUE!	#VALUE!						
#VALUE!	#VALUE!						
0 #VALUE!	#VALUE!						

GROUP #2

Percent	Adjusted	Test	# Test	Total Pts.	Total Pts.	Adjusted	Average
%	Points	Score	Takers	Possible	All Takers	Grp. Pts.	Group
90%	180	90	2	200	340	######	85
80%	160	80					
#VALUE!	#VALUE!						
#VALUE!	#VALUE!						
#VALUE!	#VALUE!						
#VALUE!	#VALUE!						

GROUP #3

Percent	Adjusted	Test	# Test	Total Pts.	Total Pts.	Adjusted	Average
%	Points	Score	Takers	Possible	All Takers	Grp. Pts.	Group
90%	180	90	2	200	340	######	85
80%	160	80					
#VALUE!	#VALUE!						
#VALUE!	#VALUE!						
#VALUE!	#VALUE!						

Architecture-Walk Right In, Sit Right Down

Teacher Notes—Walk Right In, Sit Right Down, Baby Let Your Mind Roll On

This project focuses on architecture, but the creative teacher can use it as a preliminary project before studying math (geometry, e.g.), science or social studies. Architecture, as one artist defined it, is the use of space. This project is comprised of two lessons and a final project. You can develop your own list of structures depending on where you live or on national/world monuments. We actually used a field trip to local structures for this assignment. All I can say is that it worked well.

As a follow up to this project, I asked students, in the same groups as for the project above, to examine the architecture of their school. Groups reported back their findings, and then agreed as a class on some basic principles underlying the physical structure of their school and the culture that designed it. (I related to the class my visit to Okinawa, Japan, where I was surprised to learn that almost all the schools and universities used a more or less concrete pillbox structure.....not so aesthetically pleasing but functional in a land where typhoons are common). I then asked each group to prepare the blueprints of a modern school. There are a number of software tools like geosketch and online software to accomplish this, but paper and pencil is fine if those tech tools are not available. Of course, first results included vending machines in every room, automated walkways, music in the halls, lounge seats in every oom, etc. Expecting this, and allowing them to get it out of their systems, I then ordered them back to the drawing boards with the caveat that the design of the school must improve learning. I asked each group to also choose one member who would estimate the cost to the taxpayer for whatever design they came up with. This resulted in conversations that went beyond architecture.

This project worked out so well that I wanted to bring more teachers and their classes on board in one large collaborative project involving the art teacher, physics and math teachers. Alas, the prime directive from administration was on improving standardize test scores, and, so, I could not enlist more participants. This project was a success, however, and the students seemed to really enjoy it...and to learn something.

Walk Right In, Sit Right Down,

Baby Let Your Mind Roll On

Lesson 1

Consider the following questions as you examine your assigned structure:

1) Name of the Structure _____

2) Is there a particular purpose that the structure is intended to serve? If so, what is it?

_____

_____

3) How well does it accomplish its purpose?

_____

_____

4) How does space seem to be used? Does the area seem cluttered or spacious?

_____

_____

5) What ornamentation, if any, seems to exist in this structure?

_____

_____

6) What conclusions can you make about what values the designer possessed? What conclusions can you make about the people the structure is supposed to serve?

_____

_____

7) Explore your feelings when you are in this structure. How do you feel when first entering?

_____

_____

Lesson 2

Home is Where I Am

Let's explore where we live. Answer the following questions about the establishment where you eat and sleep most often.

1) Pretend you are a stranger and enter your home. What are your first impressions?

_____

_____

2) What conclusions could you draw about the culture which built and lives in this establishment if you were a person seeing it for the first time?

_____

_____

3) What are some things about the establishment that make it feel more comfortable?

_____

_____

4) What are some things about the establishment that make it seem uncomfortable?

_____

_____

5) Examine your room or the room you may share with someone. What does its arrangement and construction say about you as a person?

_____

_____

Project

Lincoln Logs and Legos

As a world reknown architect you have been commissioned to do all of the following:

Choose *one* and make a design. You may construct a model using whatever materials you wish. Online tools and computer software are certainly welcome. Be prepared to defend your use of space and its purpose according to sound architectural principles and your understanding of human nature.

1) A spiritual center. It may be a church/synagogue/mosque/temple for your faith or a center for meditation.
2) An office building for a huge and powerful corporation
3) A high school for a suburban population
4) A sports center that would house baseball, basketball and football among other sports
5) A retirement community
6) An art museum
7) A science museum
8) A township administration building
9) A building that is the seat of government for a state
10) A structure that will enclose a war memorial
11) A monument to a president or other historical figure
12) A monument to the 21st century common man/woman

Beyond Infinity: Walk Right In, Sit Right Down

1) Ask the students either through class discussion or in groups to consider how their group functioned. What were the challenges and how did they overcome those challenges?
2) What could the group have done better?
3) What did the group excel at doing?
4) What did students learn about the subject matter (literary work, middle ages, time, interpersonal relations, etc.)?
5) What, if anything, did students learn about themselves, other people, life in general?
6) What questions do they have about themselves, other people, life in general?

Specific to the unit studied:

1) Since architecture, ultimately, is about the use of space, what does our society's use of space say about our values and beliefs?
2) Physicists discuss space as if it is an entity, a thing as in the phrase "space-time." (The space/time continuum). Is space something or is it nothing? To reflect more deeply on this question, research "dark energy."
3) Now that you have thought about architecture, do you see the buildings around you in a different way? If so, how?
4) Do you think the architecture of the school you attend makes the best use of space, especially considering the school's function?

The Black Cat and Dark Emotions

Teacher Notes—The Black Cat and Dark Emotions

During my last few years at my high school, I served as the "embedded coach," working with teachers to integrate emerging educational technologies into the classroom and to develop learning units that engaged the students in high level thinking. One of my younger colleagues, Mr. Dan Rendine, approached me somewhere in the middle of the school year and asked me to observe his class. Dan was not happy with the way his classes were going. I observed once or twice, and saw that Dan was teaching the way so many people teach in the conventional classroom. He gave a reading assignment for homework, a short story, and on the following day expected students to show up ready to discuss the work. The next day he had, what research tells us, are the normal number of students who engage in class discussions---six. The rest of the class politely listened (or daydreamed), unless Dan called on them, and then they gave a typical superficial response.

I told Dan that, if he wanted to work with me to develop a project, he would have to spend some time with the class developing collaborative skills. So he planned several quick lessons involving small groups and told students they would be held accountable for exercising good collaborative skills. I also advised Dan that everything must count, so, if he gave a reading assignment, he must quiz students on the reading the next day. Even in classes with highly motivated students (perhaps especially in classes with highly motivated students!), if the students know they will not be held accountable for a homework assignment, they will prioritize their responsibilities and abandon those that the teacher will not hold them accountable for. If I am a very good student taking a challenging course load, one in which I have homework in every subject, and I know Mr. Einstein will quiz me on my physics homework and Mr. Shakespeare will not on my reading assignment, if time and energy are limited, I know where I am going to trim effort. So Dan created some quizzes and worked on collaborative learning, and I furnished him with the following project.

After he executed the project, I asked for a follow-up conference. He told me that initially the students were engaged and working well, but soon there was a rebellion in class. When Dan and I processed the dynamic, we realized that it was difficult for the slackers in class to hide in groups of four. In effect, the rebellion was predicated on the students having to actually work for the first time. They wanted a return to class-as-usual, teacher talking and six or eight students carrying the load.

Do not be surprised if you experience this same protest. To help eliminate the clamor for mediocrity, begin the school year with small group enterprises, holding the students accountable for working well together. You will still get the outcry from some students who will request that you be more like last year's English teacher who followed the conventional classroom mode of teacher discuss and students get credit for seat time. Project based learning is not easy. Developing those neural pathways, thinking and problem solving consume energy…..both yours and your students'.

Notes on the project I gave to the teacher:

Before starting, please review my notes on collaborative learning. Before attempting any collaborative project, students must learn the skills inherent in successful cooperation.

I Goals:

1) Students are going to learn to read for meaning, and they are going to demonstrate higher level thinking skills such as analysis and synthesis.

2) Students will improve their vocabularies.

3) Students will learn the elements of suspense.

II Context

Provide students with a context of what they are going to learn.

So, begin a five to ten minute discussion of horror films. Ask them to write down (bullet style) three qualities of a really good horror film and three qualities of a really bad horror film. After about two minutes of silent writing, ask the class to share their opinions (You may ask one volunteer to go to the board and write the findings down or do it yourself). In the process of the listing, try to steer them to what creates suspense in movies or in books.

III Necessary background

There are some essential terms that you need to explain to the class. Ask them what they know about Edgar Allan Poe. Guaranteed a few will say he was a dope fiend, alcoholic, pervert...all the adolescent obsessions. After they have gotten that out of their systems, give as much or as little biographical background on Poe as you choose, but focus on the following:

1) Poe's narrators give reasons for their strange behaviors (in the "Cask of Amontillado" the narrator claims it was an offense by Fortunato that prompts him to wall up his victim; in "The Black Cat" the narrator blames excessive drinking), but those are the ostensible reasons. The real reasons Poe wants the reader to discover are more subtle and profound—the "desire of the soul to vex itself....to do wrong for the sake of doing wrong." Ask the students as they read the short story to look for the reasons given and the real reasons for the behavior of the characters (character motivations).

2) In Poe's essay on the art of writing, "Philosophy of Composition," he theorizes that one of the key elements of good short stories is that "every word contributes to the emotional effect." (the other criteria is that they can be read in one sitting in order to maintain that emotional effect, hence, a "short" story rather than a novel.) To demonstrate this concept, ask the students how many times, while watching a drama on television, the feeling is lost by interruptions of commercials.

3) Explain "foreshadowing." Ask for examples of foreshadowing in other stories or movies.

IV Assign the Reading of the Short Story (in this case, "The Black Cat" which I have provided in word document form for reasons that will be explained later).

1) Require that students read the story silently and take notes on the following three areas:

a) the reasons the author gives for his actions and the real reasons why he behaves the way he does.

b) vocabulary words that needed to be looked up

c) vocabulary words that contribute to the emotional effect of the story

V Quiz the students on a close reading of the story. *Do not be afraid to be picky here. A major way of discouraging Spark Notes, etc. is to be choosy. My suggestion is a ten question, fill in the blank (no multiple guess), quiz that can be graded fairly quickly. We are asking them to read for meaning and to study, not just cursorily read the material.*

VI Discuss the story.   **Choose your method of discussion:**

1) make lists—(ask students to share their notes, or check their notes) of vocabulary words that need to be defined, words that contribute to the emotional effect, reasons for behavior, foreshadowings, etc.

2) discuss elements of plot, characterization and theme.

3) ask students to make two lists—

   a) Reasons why I think the narrator is simply mad

   b) Reasons why the supernatural is really responsible (the cat is truly getting revenge, the similarities of the second cat to the first)

4) make a class list of all the vocabulary words that need to be defined. Ask a student to copy down this list. Make copies to redistribute later. See Vocabulary List #1.

VII Divide the class into collaborative groups. *Please see my thoughts on collaborative structures and concepts accompanying this project. Do Not announce the groups at this point.*

VIII Individual Assignment *(see "Individual Assignment 1" attached)*

*Assign this to be done **in class**. This is to provide individual accountability as well as to make certain everyone is involved. The story is divided into several sections. Assign one or two sections (depending on how many people are in each group—my suggestion is that, for this project, you try to keep the maximum number of students in each group to four). So in Group 1, member 1 is responsible for section 1, member 2 is responsible for section 2, etc. **DO NOT** announce the groups now. Save that for later. After you collect the individual translations, announce the groups and assign Group Assignment #1.*

You can assign weights to the criteria or add your own as you wish. You can give a cursory look at their translations and just award points if they made an honest effort. I would not count this assignment too heavily. I want students to be individually accountable and on the same page as their future group members. This individual assignment is three pages long, most of which is space for them to write, but if you choose to use composition paper, feel free to do so.

IX Announce the Groups and Assign Group Assignment #1

Time allotted—two periods maximum.

Distribute one (1) Vocabulary List #1 to the groups. It is up to them to define the words using a dictionary, thesaurus, etc. This may take another class period (a visit to an online dictionary/thesaurus) or for homework.

After the assignment is completed, discuss with the class the challenges in this particular project, including problems in working with other people. Emphasize the importance of collaboration and shared responsibilities.

Consider a group peer editing of the projects with groups reading other groups' work and commenting. Grade these assignments according to the criteria shared with the class.

X Assign Group Assignment #2

Time allotted—two to three periods maximum, depending on how well they are working. Shorter if they are off task, longer if they are working hard.

When the students have created the presentations, collect the recorded files. Either have them listen to one presentation and then comment and critique or play the file on the classroom computer and have them comment and critique.

Grade this assignment according to the criteria you shared with the class.

XI Assessment

*Using one of the assessment spreadsheets included earlier, you can use the columns or cells to grade the individual and group projects. Each individual student should receive individual grades for the rewritten section he/she was responsible for as well as a subjective individual grade for remaining on task and contributing to the group. Each individual student should also receive two group grades, Group Assignment #1, and Group Assignment #2. This grade must be the same for everyone in a group. It **must** be emphasized that they are in a sink or swim environment for collaborative projects to succeed.*

XII Follow-up

There are several options that may be taken:

1) class discussion concerning

    a) differences between reading a story and hearing a story

    b) importance of vocabulary to storytelling

    c) challenges in working together

    d) use of a narrator in telling a story

    e) how suspense is created and maintained

2) assign another Poe short story. After the reading make comparisons and contrasts. What elements of Poe's work seem to be consistent from story to story.

The story "The Black Cat"

THE BLACK CAT

by Edgar Allan Poe
(1843)

Section #1

FOR the most wild, yet most homely narrative which I am about to pen, I neither expect nor solicit belief. Mad indeed would I be to expect it, in a case where my very senses reject their own evidence. Yet, mad am I not --and very surely do I not dream. But to-morrow I die, and to-day I would unburden my soul. My immediate purpose is to place before the world, plainly, succinctly, and without comment, a series of mere household events. In their consequences, these events have terrified --have tortured --have destroyed me. Yet I will not attempt to expound them. To me, they have presented little but Horror --to many they will seem less terrible than baroques. Hereafter, perhaps, some intellect may be found which will reduce my phantasm to the common-place --some intellect more calm, more logical, and far less excitable than my own, which will perceive, in the circumstances I detail with awe, nothing more than an ordinary succession of very natural causes and effects.

From my infancy I was noted for the docility and humanity of my disposition. My tenderness of heart was even so conspicuous as to make me the jest of my companions. I was especially fond of animals, and was indulged by my parents with a great variety of pets. With these I spent most of my time, and never was so happy as when feeding and caressing them. This peculiar of character grew with my growth, and in my manhood, I derived from it one of my principal sources of pleasure. To those who have cherished an affection for a faithful and sagacious dog, I need hardly be at the trouble of explaining the nature or the intensity of the gratification thus derivable. There is something in the unselfish and self-sacrificing love of a brute, which goes directly to the heart of him who has had frequent occasion to test the paltry friendship and gossamer fidelity of mere Man.

I married early, and was happy to find in my wife a disposition not uncongenial with my own. Observing my partiality for domestic pets, she lost no opportunity of procuring those of the most agreeable kind. We had birds, gold fish, a fine dog, rabbits, a small monkey, and a cat.

This latter was a remarkably large and beautiful animal, entirely black, and sagacious to an astonishing degree. In speaking of his intelligence, my wife, who at heart was not a little tinctured with superstition, made frequent allusion to the ancient popular notion, which regarded all black cats as witches in disguise. Not that she was ever serious upon this point -- and I mention the matter at all for no better reason than that it happens, just now, to be remembered.

Pluto --this was the cat's name --was my favorite pet and playmate. I alone fed him, and he attended me wherever I went about the house. It was even with difficulty that I could prevent him from following me through the streets.

Our friendship lasted, in this manner, for several years, during which my general temperament and character --through the instrumentality of the Fiend Intemperance --had (I blush to confess it) experienced a radical alteration for the worse. I grew, day by day, more moody, more irritable, more regardless of the feelings of others. I suffered myself to use intemperate language to my At length, I even offered her personal violence. My pets, of course, were made to feel the change in my disposition. I not only neglected, but ill-used them. For Pluto, however, I still retained sufficient regard to restrain me from maltreating him, as I made no scruple of maltreating the rabbits, the monkey, or even the dog, when by accident, or through affection, they came in my way. But my disease grew upon me --for what disease is like Alcohol! --and at length even Pluto, who was now becoming old, and consequently somewhat peevish --even Pluto began to experience the effects of my ill temper.

One night, returning home, much intoxicated, from one of my haunts about town, I fancied that the cat avoided my presence. I seized him; when, in his fright at my violence, he inflicted a slight wound upon my hand with his teeth. The fury of a demon instantly possessed me. I knew myself no longer. My original soul seemed, at once, to take its flight from my body; and a more than fiendish malevolence, gin-nurtured, thrilled every fibre of my frame. I took from my waistcoat-pocket a pen-knife, opened it, grasped the poor beast by the throat, and deliberately cut one of its eyes from the socket! I blush, I burn, I shudder, while I pen the damnable atrocity.

Section 2

When reason returned with the morning --when I had slept off the fumes of the night's debauch --I experienced a sentiment half of horror, half of remorse, for the crime of which I had been guilty; but it was, at best, a feeble and equivocal feeling, and the soul remained untouched. I again plunged into excess, and soon drowned in wine all memory of the deed.

In the meantime the cat slowly recovered. The socket of the lost eye presented, it is true, a frightful appearance, but he no longer appeared to suffer any pain. He went about the house as usual, but, as might be expected, fled in extreme terror at my approach. I had so much of my old heart left, as to be at first grieved by this evident dislike on the part of a creature which had once so loved me. But this feeling soon gave place to irritation. And then came, as if to my final and irrevocable overthrow, the spirit of PERVERSENESS. Of this spirit philosophy takes no account. Yet I am not more sure that my soul lives, than I am that perverseness is one of the primitive impulses of the human heart --one of the indivisible primary faculties, or sentiments, which give direction to the character of Man. Who has not, a hundred times, found himself committing a vile or a silly action, for no other reason than because he knows he should not? Have we not a perpetual inclination, in the teeth of our best judgment, to violate that which is Law, merely because we understand it to be such? This spirit of perverseness, I say, came to my final overthrow. It was this unfathomable longing of the soul to vex itself --to offer violence to its own nature --to do wrong for the wrong's sake only --that urged me to continue and finally to consummate the injury I had inflicted upon the unoffending brute. One morning, in cool blood, I slipped a noose about its neck and hung it to the limb of a tree; --hung it with the tears streaming from my eyes, and with the bitterest remorse at my heart; --hung it because I knew that it had loved me, and because I felt it had given me no reason of offence; --hung it because I knew that in so doing I was committing a sin --a deadly sin that would so jeopardize my immortal soul as to place it --if such a thing were possible --even beyond the reach of the infinite mercy of the Most Merciful and Most Terrible God.

On the night of the day on which this cruel deed was done, I was aroused from sleep by the cry of fire. The curtains of my bed were in flames. The whole house was blazing. It was with great difficulty that my wife, a servant, and myself, made our escape from the conflagration. The destruction was complete. My entire worldly wealth was swallowed up, and I resigned myself thenceforward to despair.

I am above the weakness of seeking to establish a sequence of cause and effect, between the disaster and the atrocity. But I am detailing a chain of facts --and wish not to leave even a possible link imperfect. On the day succeeding the fire, I visited the ruins. The walls, with one exception, had fallen in. This exception was found in a compartment wall, not very thick, which stood about the middle of the house, and against which had rested the head of my bed. The plastering had here, in great measure, resisted the action of the fire --a fact which I attributed to its having been recently spread. About this wall a dense crowd were collected, and many persons seemed to be examining a particular portion of it with every minute and eager attention. The words "strange!" "singular!" and other similar expressions, excited my curiosity. I approached and saw, as if graven in bas relief upon the white surface, the figure of a gigantic cat. The impression was given with an accuracy truly marvellous. There was a rope about the animal's neck.

When I first beheld this apparition --for I could scarcely regard it as less --my wonder and my terror were extreme. But at length reflection came to my aid. The cat, I remembered, had been hung in a garden adjacent to the house. Upon the alarm of fire, this garden had been immediately filled by the crowd --by some one of whom the animal must have been cut from the tree and thrown, through an open window, into my chamber. This had probably been done with the view of arousing me from sleep. The falling of other walls had compressed the victim of my cruelty into the substance of the freshly-spread plaster; the lime of which, had then with the flames, and the ammonia from the carcass, accomplished the portraiture as I saw it.

Section #3

Although I thus readily accounted to my reason, if not altogether to my conscience, for the startling fact 'just detailed, it did not the less fall to make a deep impression upon my fancy. For months I could not rid myself of the phantasm of the cat; and, during this period, there came back into my spirit a half-sentiment that seemed, but was not, remorse. I went so far as to regret the loss of the animal, and to look about me, among the vile haunts which I now habitually frequented, for another pet of the same species, and of somewhat similar appearance, with which to supply its place.

One night as I sat, half stupefied, in a den of more than infamy, my attention was suddenly drawn to some black object, reposing upon the head of one of the immense hogsheads of Gin, or of Rum, which constituted the chief furniture of the apartment. I had been looking steadily at the top of this hogshead for some minutes, and what now caused me surprise was the fact that I had not sooner perceived the object thereupon. I approached it, and touched it with my hand. It was a black cat --a very large one --fully as large as Pluto, and closely resembling him in every respect but one. Pluto had not a white hair upon any portion of his body; but this cat had a large, although indefinite splotch of white, covering nearly the whole region of the breast.

Upon my touching him, he immediately arose, purred loudly, rubbed against my hand, and appeared delighted with my notice. This, then, was the very creature of which I was in search. I at once offered to purchase it of the landlord; but this person made no claim to it --knew nothing of it --had never seen it before.

I continued my caresses, and, when I prepared to go home, the animal evinced a disposition to accompany me. I permitted it to do so; occasionally stooping and patting it as I proceeded. When it reached the house it domesticated itself at once, and became immediately a great favorite with my wife.

For my own part, I soon found a dislike to it arising within me. This was just the reverse of what I had anticipated; but I know not how or why it was --its evident fondness for myself rather disgusted and annoyed. By slow degrees, these feelings of disgust and annoyance rose into the bitterness of hatred. I avoided the creature; a certain sense of shame, and the remembrance of my former deed of cruelty, preventing me from physically abusing it. I did not, for some weeks, strike, or otherwise violently ill use it; but gradually --very gradually --I came to look upon it with unutterable loathing, and to flee silently from its odious presence, as from the breath of a pestilence.

What added, no doubt, to my hatred of the beast, was the discovery, on the morning after I brought it home, that, like Pluto, it also had been deprived of one of its eyes. This circumstance, however, only endeared it to my wife, who, as I have already said, possessed, in a high degree, that humanity of feeling which had once been my distinguishing trait, and the source of many of my simplest and purest pleasures.

With my aversion to this cat, however, its partiality for myself seemed to increase. It followed my footsteps with a pertinacity which it would be difficult to make the reader comprehend. Whenever I sat, it would crouch beneath my chair, or spring upon my knees, covering me with its loathsome caresses. If I arose to walk it would get between my feet and thus nearly throw me down, or, fastening its long and sharp claws in my dress, clamber, in this manner, to my breast. At such times, although I longed to destroy it with a blow, I was yet withheld from so doing, partly it at by a memory of my former crime, but chiefly --let me confess it at once --by absolute dread of the beast.

Section #4

This dread was not exactly a dread of physical evil-and yet I should be at a loss how otherwise to define it. I am almost ashamed to own --yes, even in this felon's cell, I am almost ashamed to own --that the terror and horror with which the animal inspired me, had been heightened by one of the merest chimaeras it would be possible to conceive. My wife had called my attention, more than once, to the character of the mark of white hair, of which I have spoken, and which constituted the sole visible difference between the strange beast and the one I had y si destroyed. The reader will remember that this mark, although large, had been originally very indefinite; but, by slow degrees --degrees nearly imperceptible, and which for a long time my Reason struggled to reject as fanciful --it had, at length, assumed a rigorous distinctness of outline. It was now the representation of an object that I shudder to name --and for this, above all, I loathed, and dreaded, and would have rid myself of the monster had I dared --it was now, I say, the image of a hideous --of a ghastly thing --of the GALLOWS! --oh, mournful and terrible engine of Horror and of Crime --of Agony and of Death!

And now was I indeed wretched beyond the wretchedness of mere Humanity. And a brute beast --whose fellow I had contemptuously destroyed --a brute beast to work out for me --for me a man, fashioned in the image of the High God --so much of insufferable wo! Alas! neither by day nor by night knew I the blessing of Rest any more! During the former the creature left me no moment alone; and, in the latter, I started, hourly, from dreams of unutterable fear, to find the hot breath of the thing upon my face, and its vast weight --an incarnate Night-Mare that I had no power to shake off --incumbent eternally upon my heart!

Beneath the pressure of torments such as these, the feeble remnant of the good within me succumbed. Evil thoughts became my sole intimates --the darkest and most evil of thoughts. The moodiness of my usual temper increased to hatred of all things and of all mankind; while, from the sudden, frequent, and ungovernable outbursts of a fury to which I now blindly abandoned myself, my uncomplaining wife, alas! was the most usual and the most patient of sufferers.

One day she accompanied me, upon some household errand, into the cellar of the old building which our poverty compelled us to inhabit. The cat followed me down the steep stairs, and, nearly throwing me headlong, exasperated me to madness. Uplifting an axe, and forgetting, in my wrath, the childish dread which had hitherto stayed my hand, I aimed a blow at the animal which, of course, would have proved instantly fatal had it descended as I wished. But this blow was arrested by the hand of my wife. Goaded, by the interference, into a rage more than demoniacal, I withdrew my arm from her grasp and buried the axe in her brain. She fell dead upon the spot, without a groan.

This hideous murder accomplished, I set myself forthwith, and with entire deliberation, to the task of concealing the body. I knew that I could not remove it from the house, either by day or by night, without the risk of being observed by the neighbors. Many projects entered my mind. At one period I thought of cutting the corpse into minute fragments, and destroying them by fire. At another, I resolved to dig a grave for it in the floor of the cellar. Again, I deliberated about casting it in the well in the yard --about packing it in a box, as if merchandize, with the usual arrangements, and so getting a porter to take it from the house. Finally I hit upon what I considered a far better expedient than either of these. I determined to wall it up in the cellar -- as the monks of the middle ages are recorded to have walled up their victims.

For a purpose such as this the cellar was well adapted. Its walls were loosely constructed, and had lately been plastered throughout with a rough plaster, which the dampness of the atmosphere had prevented from hardening. Moreover, in one of the walls was a projection, caused by a false chimney, or fireplace, that had been filled up, and made to resemble the rest of the cellar. I made no doubt that I could readily displace the at this point, insert the corpse, and wall the whole up as before, so that no eye could detect anything suspicious.

Section #5

And in this calculation I was not deceived. By means of a crow-bar I easily dislodged the bricks, and, having carefully deposited the body against the inner wall, I propped it in that position, while, with little trouble, I re-laid the whole structure as it originally stood. Having procured mortar, sand, and hair, with every possible precaution, I prepared a plaster could not ever possibly be distinguished from the old, and with this I very carefully went over the new brick-work. When I had finished, I felt satisfied that all was right. The wall did not present the slightest appearance of having been disturbed. The rubbish on the floor was picked up with the minutest care. I looked around triumphantly, and said to myself --"Here at least, then, my labor has not been in vain."

My next step was to look for the beast which had been the cause of so much wretchedness; for I had, at length, firmly resolved to put it to death. Had I been able to meet with it, at the moment, there could have been no doubt of its fate; but it appeared that the crafty animal had been alarmed at the violence of my previous anger, and forebore to present itself in my present mood. It is impossible to describe, or to imagine, the deep, the blissful sense of relief which the absence of the detested creature occasioned in my bosom. It did not make its appearance during the night --and thus for one night at least, since its introduction into the house, I soundly and tranquilly slept; aye, slept even with the burden of murder upon my soul!

The second and the third day passed, and still my tormentor came not. Once again I breathed as a free-man. The monster, in terror, had fled the premises forever! I should behold it no more! My happiness was supreme! The guilt of my dark deed disturbed me but little. Some few inquiries had been made, but these had been readily answered. Even a search had been instituted --but of course nothing was to be discovered. I looked upon my future felicity as secured.

Upon the fourth day of the assassination, a party of the police came, very unexpectedly, into the house, and proceeded again to make rigorous investigation of the premises. Secure, however, in the inscrutability of my place of concealment, I felt no embarrassment whatever. The officers bade me accompany them in their search. They left no nook or corner unexplored. At length, for the third or fourth time, they descended into the cellar. I quivered not in a muscle. My heart beat calmly as that of one who slumbers in innocence. I walked the cellar from end to end. I folded my arms upon my bosom, and roamed easily to and fro. The police were thoroughly satisfied and prepared to depart. The glee at my heart was too strong to be restrained. I burned to say if but one word, by way of triumph, and to render doubly sure their assurance of my guiltlessness.

"Gentlemen," I said at last, as the party ascended the steps, "I delight to have allayed your suspicions. I wish you all health, and a little more courtesy. By the bye, gentlemen, this --this is a very well constructed house." (In the rabid desire to say something easily, I scarcely knew what I uttered at all.) --"I may say an excellently well constructed house. These walls --are you going, gentlemen? --these walls are solidly put together"; and here, through the mere phrenzy of bravado, I rapped heavily, with a cane which I held in my hand, upon that very portion of the brick-work behind which stood the corpse of the wife of my bosom.

But may God shield and deliver me from the fangs of the Arch-Fiend! No sooner had the reverberation of my blows sunk into silence than I was answered by a voice from within the tomb! --by a cry, at first muffled and broken, like the sobbing of a child, and then quickly swelling into one long, loud, and continuous scream, utterly anomalous and inhuman --a howl --a wailing shriek, half of horror and half of triumph, such as might have arisen only out of hell, conjointly from the throats of the damned in their agony and of the demons that exult in the damnation.

Of my own thoughts it is folly to speak. Swooning, I staggered to the opposite wall. For one instant the party upon the stairs remained motionless, through extremity of terror and of awe. In the next, a dozen stout arms were tolling at the wall. It fell bodily. The corpse, already greatly decayed and clotted with gore, stood erect before the eyes of the spectators. Upon its head, with red extended mouth and solitary eye of fire, sat the hideous beast whose craft had seduced me into murder, and whose informing voice had consigned me to the hangman. I had walled the monster up within the tomb!

-- THE END --

Vocabulary List #1   Name_____

                              Period_____ Group #_____

CLASS VOCABULARY LIST

#	POE'S WORD	OUR WORDS

Poe Group Assignment #1   Name_____

                                 Period_____   Date_____

 Chiller Novels Presents

Chiller Novels, the leading producer of graphic novels, is looking for a graphic writing translation of Poe's short story, "The Black Cat." Your group's task is to produce a graphic short story for modern day audiences. The audience is a young audience but sophisticated, and a third grade vocabulary is not acceptable. The story must be at least as long as Poe's original, must contain the same emotional effect Poe tried to maintain, and must be accompanied by appropriate graphics. Your group may draw the graphics or use clip art.

You may combine the individual sections of the story that each member translated, but *as a group* you must come to a decision as to the quality of the storytelling, the sophisticated vocabulary employed in telling the story, the words chosen to maintain an emotional effect, the graphics employed, the distinguishing features of your storytelling.

Your group will receive 1 grade for this project. Each student will receive the same grade. The project will be graded according to the following criteria:

1) In-class on-task time. Everyone must be working in the time allotted for this project. **Any** student off task will subtract points from the entire group.

2) Quality of the storytelling. Is the story an accurate and exciting recreation?

3) Appropriate vocabulary. Are the words substituted for Poe's words valid?

4) Emotional effect. Has your retelling maintained the emotional effect that Poe strove for?

5) Quality of the graphics. Are the graphics appropriate to the mood and theme of the story?

6) Distinguishing features. How will your retelling be superior to the retelling by the other groups? What elements of your recreation will raise the eyebrows of the producers of Chiller Novels and cause them to choose *your* story?

You will have a limited time to complete this project. Work cooperatively and efficiently.

Poe Group Assignment #2   Name_____

                            Period_____   Date_____

Chiller Theater Presents

Congratulations!   Your collaboration on a graphic story for *Chiller Novels* was so impressive that the sister company of *Chiller Novels*, *Chiller Theater*, is hiring you to recreate the same story only this time instead of being read, the story is to be heard.

Your group's task is to retell Poe's story as a dramatic podcast. You may add dialogue, character voices, background music and special effects. When you have rewritten the story to be heard, **rehearse** the dramatic presentation. When your group is ready, record your presentation and give the file to your instructor.

Your group will receive one (1) grade for this project based on the following criteria:

1) In-class on-task time. *Any* student in the group off task will significantly decrease the grade for the entire group. It is in everyone's interest to see that all members are responsible and engaged in the task. Is your presentation organized and *smoothly* presented?

2) Quality of the rewriting. Have you changed the writing of the story to be more appropriate as a script to be heard? Did you maintain suspense, for example?

3) Quality of the enhancements. Have you added background music when appropriate? Sound effects?

4) Creativity. Have you distinguished your presentation among the other presentations that are presented?

You will have a limited time to create this presentation. Work cooperatively and efficiently. I stand ready to assist you in any way possible.

Poe Individual Assignment #1   Name_____

                                      Period_____ Date_____

TRANSLATING POE

You will be assigned a section of Poe's short story to "translate."

Rewrite your section using a modern vocabulary (substituting contemporary words for some of Poe's more esoteric words.) Make certain that when you substitute a Poe word from the vocabulary list generated by your class. Next to the word you choose to replace Poe's word, place in parentheses the vocabulary word that Poe used.

As you translate, look for key words that contribute to the emotional effect Poe was trying to create. Either retain these words or substitute them with your own. Remember, you are rewriting your section for a modern day audience.

You will have one class period to do this, so work efficiently.

You will be graded on the following criteria:

1) How well you followed instructions

2) Time on task

3) Appropriate Substituted Vocabulary

4) Accurate retelling of your section of the story

Use the next sheet to retell your section.

Poe retelling

Section of the Story You are Retelling

_____

_____

_____

_____

_____

_____

_____

_____

_____

_____

_____

Beyond Infinity: The Black Cat and Dark Emotions

1) Ask the students either through class discussion or in groups to consider how their group functioned. What were the challenges and how did they overcome those challenges?
2) What could the group have done better?
3) What did the group excel at doing?
4) What did students learn about the subject matter (literary work, middle ages, time, interpersonal relations, etc.)?
5) What, if anything, did students learn about themselves, other people, life in general?
6) What questions do they have about themselves, other people, life in general?

The teacher can use the questions below as either closures for the projects or as the inceptions of new projects.

Specific to the unit studied:

1) Have you ever made a self-destructive choice, knowing at the time that it was the wrong choice? If so, why do you think you made that choice?
2) Do all human beings have a capacity to do the wrong thing, knowing that it is wrong (may lead to bad consequences)?
3) The narrator in "The Black Cat" blames alcoholism as the reason for his actions, but the author leads us to believe other factors are responsible for the narrator's behavior. Can we ever really be objective about our motives and our behavior?
4) Studies have demonstrated that crime victims invariably describe their attackers as taller and larger than they actually are. In other words, fear distorts our perceptions. What other emotions shape our views of reality?
5) Can you recall a situation in which your fear was almost paralyzing, preventing you from acting? What can we do to overcome our irrational fears?
6) Like the narrator, are most human beings inclined to make the wrong decision, wrong in the sense that in the long run, the decision they make does not lead to their benefit?

Canterbury Tales Olympics

Teacher Notes—Canterbury Tales Olympics

This was one of my favorite projects because we got a great deal of learning mileage out of it while, at the same time, students had a great deal of fun. As one student said to me, "I'm doing all this stuff in your class, and I wonder where it is going, learning wise, and later I look back and see how much I really have learned."

I had two major goals for this project. First, since I usually teach The Canterbury Tales in the beginning of the year, I wanted students to develop collaborative skills. Secondly, I hoped students would study the elements of characterization for which Chaucer is so well known. Many of my colleagues, with this latter goal in mind, created exceptional projects asking students to create a modern day pilgrimage to a selected "shrine" using stereotypes from the contemporary culture. So after quizzing students on the prologue and the selected tales (see assignment for part I in this section) I chose to focus on, we discussed the theme of modern stereotyping as well. I asked students to describe the groups in school---"the goths, the jocks, the cheerleaders, the nerds, etc." They easily fell into my trap. Of course, none of them professed to belong to a group, since they were all unique individuals. That was an "Aha" moment for many of them. With that caveat about typecasting medieval people as well, we looked at what I think are the two major Chaucerian themes of the Canterbury Tales:

1) the male/female dynamic. A number of Chaucer's tales examine the relationship between male and female, from the viewpoint of marriage, love, and sex. The Wife of Bath's tale lectures on marriage on one extreme and The Miller's Tale exploits the realities of cuckoldry and lust. Chaucer's own marriage apparently was not always smooth sailing, so, as a class we discuss the tales in this context.

2) hypocrisy of religious figures The only admirable pilgrim with any religious affiliation is the parson whose prime directive is the welfare of his flock. All the others, from the pardoner who is greedy to the monk and friar who overindulge in worldly delights are subtly (and sometimes not so subtly satirized) for their hypocrisy. We also discuss these themes in light of contemporary life, asking groups to discuss how much has changed since Chaucer's day in terms of these two themes.

I also asked students in the same groups as part I above to develop five conclusions about medieval life. Then I issue assignment part II which begins the fun part of the Canterbury Tales Olympics. Students really got into it. I had suggested that they name their group using medieval motifs---The Knights of South Street. Not suggested to me but delightful was the costuming. On the days of the Olympics some students showed up dressed as the Knight (tin foil---looked more like the Tin Man from The Wizard of Oz), Yeoman (cardboard bow and arrow), Wife of Bath (outrageous outfit), monk, etc.

For the *Whose Line is it Anyway?* I show students clips from the show demonstrating the following activities:

- **All Questions** (in which students are given a situation and are required to speak only in questions)
- **Alphabet** (two students are given a scenario and asked to begin each sentence with the next letter of the alphabet—student 1—Wife of Bath-- says, "Are you all right?" student 2—Yeoman--says, "Boy, I am tired of fighting.")
- **Whose Line Is It** (two students are given two slips of paper on which are written two phrases they have never seen and are told not to look at. They place these strips of paper in their pockets and are given a scenario and asked to begin the conversation as the pilgrims they are assigned. Then, in the conversation, one at a time brings out one of the strips and reads it as part of the conversation. The sillier the better.)
- **Party Quirks** (all four members of the group participate. One member is the party host. Every other pilgrim enters one at a time and each has been given an index card with a quirk on it. For example, the student who is the Wife of Bath might receive the following quirk—"Wife of Bath has just had dental work and has been shot with an overdose of Novocain." The host pilgrim, after all the guests have arrived, tries to guess the pilgrim his classmates are impersonating and their party quirk.

My preparation for the Canterbury Tale Olympics include the following:

1) Hamming it up. I started the whole Olympics by lighting a candle (the Olympic torch) and placing it on my desk. One year I convinced a student in another class to enter my room in his gym outfit carrying the lit candle above his head.
   I also played music to introduce the Olympics. Aaron Copeland's Fanfare for the Common Man is a good choice.
2) Decide on the tales, and prepare quizzes for them and the prologue
3) Prepare the Prologue Pentathalon (which you have in this book)
4) Prepare the scenarios/situations for All Questions activity (around ten per class) See my scenarios for this.
5) Prepare the scenarios/situations for Alphabet activity (around ten per class) See my scenarios for this.
6) Prepare the scenarios/situations for Whose Line Is It activity (around ten per class) as well as the phrases on strips of paper. See my scenarios for this as well as the phrases
7) Prepare the party quirks. This was time consuming. I put the quirks on index cards, four quirks per group. Then I had to figure out a way to show the class (while the group's collective backs were turned) the quirks. These I put on a transparency and used the overhead projector. During my last few years of teaching, I put these on a word document and simply displayed them on my Smartboard. I included my quirks in this book.

8) Realizing that students could use some practice in improvisation, I made up additional scenarios for all the activities above and on one day we had a practice run. That proved useful. A number of the hot shot boys who thought "I am gonna be great at this" soon realized how difficult it truly was. Not only were they thinking on the spot, but, to be effective, they had to react and respond in the character of the assigned pilgrim! They found this very very challenging, and the hot shots went back to study more.

9) Create a table for pilgrim assignment. I wanted to make certain that each student was responsible for at least three pilgrims. I included this table at the end of Assignment 2.

10) Create a spreadsheet not only to award points but to keep track of participation in the activities. Use one of the spreadsheets provided earlier.

11) Creating a closure (see the group closure sheet for ct Olympics)

12) Provide a closure for the entire class to reflect on the entire unit. What did they learn about the medieval time period, about stereotyping, the battle of the sexes, hypocrisy, and non-verbal communication as well as body language? So many students attempted to reveal their pilgrimess through their body language.

This project demanded a great deal of preparation for me and my students, but years later they still talked about this unit. And I doubt that any of them will ever forget the Wife of Bath. Enjoy.

Assignment CT Olympics Part II

Name_____

Period_____ Group ID#_____

The Prologue Pentathalon

Or

The Pardoner's Shalom

The Canterbury Tales by Geoffrey Chaucer provides us not only with some entertaining and enlightening tales, but also with insight into medieval culture and the people that inhabit that culture. Chaucer's unique vantage point at court allowed him to observe humanity, and the descriptions of the pilgrims are the results of those observations. This work is noted for its characterization of medieval stereotypes, and this project is designed to help you understand and appreciate Chaucer's depictions of those caricatures.

The frame for this project is the Olympics. Let's face it. You always wanted to be an Olympian. Now is your chance. Your group will enter into competition with other groups for the Olympic medals made of gold (well, silver, maybe bronze, what's that tinsely stuff that surrounds peanut butter cups?) through "events" that challenge your knowledge and understanding of Chaucer's pilgrims.

Each member of your group should choose several pilgrims. You will become experts on these pilgrims by studying them in depth. Read the text to discover their motivations, their tastes, their desires, and their aspirations. Almost all of this information is contained in the Prologue, but additional information can be obtained by reading the tales associated with them (providing they have tales associated with them). After becoming experts on your respective pilgrims, the Olympics will commence amidst much pomp and circumstance. The Marine Corps Band will perform at the opening ceremonies (actually, a recording of the Marine Corps Band, actually some oldies sung by guys who almost made it into the Marines, actually, if truth be told, a third grader playing the kazoo, well, really, a recording of a third grader playing the kazoo), and your mettle as a Canterbury Tales Scholar will be sorely tested.

THE EVENTS

Your group will participate in the following events:

1) Phone Tag Moguls

"Hello, you have reached the Pardoner's residence. Leave your name and address and I will send you a catalogue of jawbones that Samson used to slay the Philistines."

Your group must write and present a phone message from a pilgrim assigned by your instructor.

2) Down on Your Knees Pleading Biathlon

Prepare a pilgrim's plea for its life.

3) Downhill Pantomiming

Prepare a pantomime for one of the following situations:

a) a pilgrim on his/her deathbed

b) a pilgrim hailing a taxi

4) Culinary Canterbury Curling

Your group must prepare a five-minute cooking show with one of the assigned pilgrims as host. You may use index cards when you present, but memory is even better.

We must be able to guess who the pilgrim is from your pantomime.'

5) Prologue Pentathlon

Each group will be given a list of questions to answer. These questions will relate to information contained in the *Prologue* to *The Canterbury Tales.* Each group will attempt to answer the questions *in the shortest time possible.* For each *correct question* the group will receive 5 points. The first team to turn in their questions will receive a bonus of 5 points, the second team to turn in their questions will receive a bonus of 4 points, etc. The team which racks up the most points will win this event.

The next series of events will be predicated on the *Whose Line Is It, Anyway?* Improvisation show. Members of your group will be called upon to engage in several activities. Points will be awarded on the cleverness, *smoothness,* and **most of all,** the quality of "pilgrim characterization" that is revealed in those activities.

This is a point to reemphasize: Since this assignment has, among other goals, your greater understanding of literary characters, the more depth of understanding is displayed through your participation in these events, the more points will be awarded. Each student should become an expert on three of the pilgrims. (see pilgrim list for ct Olympics).

Procedure

1) Study your respective pilgrims

2) Prepare events 1,2,3, and 4.

3) Prepare and Practice, Prepare and Practice, Prepare and Practice for other events.

4) Go for the Gold!!

Suggested Pilgrim Assignments. Each student is responsible for at least 3 pilgrims.

Student 1	Student 2	Student 3	Student 4
Wife of Bath	Prioress	Friar	Pardoner
Knight	Squire	Clerk	Monk
Physician	Reeve	Yeoman	Miller

Fifth Student

Skipper

Manciple

Merchant

CTIO

Prologue Pentathalon

Group Name_____

Period_____ Group ID_____

Time_____

Prologue Questions

All Questions

_____1) Including the narrator and the host, how many pilgrims are there?

_____2) In what part of England is the city of Bath?   A) northeastern   b) northwestern c)southeastern d) southwestern e) it is not in England

_____3) How many pilgrims are clerics or religious people who represent the Church? (do NOT count the Summoner)

_____4) A yeoman is a a) soldier b) bow hunter c) naval officer d) ship's steward e) none of the above

_____5) Which of the pilgrims is most similar to the role of students of this school?

_____6) Which of the pilgrims has a red beard and tells "dirty" stories?

_____7) Which of the pilgrims seems most like a farmer?

_____8) Which of the pilgrims liked garlic and onions and drinking strong wine?

_____9) Which of the pilgrims is a steward or minor official on the estate?

_____10) Which of the pilgrims liked to serve the people in his county the finest food and drink?

_____11) Which of the pilgrims was fat and had a bald head?

_____12) Which of the pilgrims had excellent table manners?

_____13) What is the name of the inn where the pilgrims began their pilgrimage?

_____14) In what month do the pilgrims begin their trip?

_____15) Which pilgrim knew all the taverns, liked to drink and sing and did not like to associate with the lower class?

_____16) Which of the pilgrims was an expert navigator?

_____17) Which of the religious members seems to be the most honest and generous?

_____18) Which of the pilgrims was a first rate carpenter?

_____19) How many tales was EACH pilgrim supposed to tell?

_____20) Which pilgrim had a special love of gold?

_____21) Which pilgrim wore a Flemish beaver hat?

_____22) Which pilgrim had an ulcer on his knee?

_____23) Which of the pilgrims had been in fifteen battles?

_____24) Which of the pilgrims is wearing an article of clothing inscribed with the saying "Love overcometh all?"

_____25) Which of the pilgrims will be the judge of the stories?

WARM UPS FOR CANTERBURY TALES

WHOSE LINE IS IT

ACTIVITIES

ALL QUESTIONS—WIFE OF BATH AND PARDONER AT HER BIRTHDAY PARTY

ALPHABET—THE KNIGHT AND THE NUN SHOOTING THE RAPIDS

ALL QUESTIONS—SKIPPER AND SQUIRE ON A ROLLER COASTER

ALPHABET—FRIAR AND MILLER BUILDING A PYRAMID

ALL QUESTIONS—MILLER AND REEVE FISHING FROM AN ICE FLOE

ALPHABET—PARDONER AND COOK TAKING A CHEMISTRY FINAL EXAM

Use these scenarios for the Canterbury Tales Olympics activities All Questions, and Alphabet.

Lines for dialogue between two pilgrims, all questions

1) pilgrims are on a lifeboat on the ocean   (wife of bath and parson)
2) pilgrims are standing at the spot where Becket was killed (friar and prioress)
3) pilgrims are walking around the cathedral   (monk and knight)
4) pilgrims are riding along talking about the other pilgrims (squire and oxford cleric)
5) pilgrims meet for the first time   (parson and wife of bath)

Lines for dialogue between two pilgrims, alphabetical order

1) pilgrims are attending the hanging of another pilgrim   (merchant and yeoman)
2) pilgrims are on a runaway carriage   (skipper and cook)
3) pilgrims are hiding in a ditch from bandits   (squire and manciple)
4) pilgrims are suspended by their thumbs in a dungeon   (miller and reeve)
5) pilgrims are sneaking into the kitchen of the inn for a late night snack (wife of bath and friar)

These are lines for "Whose Line Is it Anyway?" for Canterbury Tales Olympics.

Print out this sheet and cut out each sentence. Choose two pilgrims, give them a scenario, and have them engage in conversation. Before they start, give them each two slips **FOLDED UP***. They place one slip in each pocket, start the conversation, and, at random points, take out a slip and read it aloud.*

"My dog has fleas."

"These pretzels are making me thirsty."

"The milk on my oatmeal has curdled."

"There are not enough marshmallows in my jello!"

"Look, the sewers are backing up!"

"Always wash your feet in warm water."

"I wasn't expecting the Spanish Inquisition!!"

"My pen has run out of ink!"

"Never extinguish your cigarette in a full mug of hot chocolate."

"Dance until your feet have blisters."

"It's been a long time since I have danced to the Funky Chicken."

"Wash your delicate clothes in cold water."

"Hold the pickles, hold the lettuce; special orders don't upset us."

""Spit and spiderwebs are great things to stop a wound from bleeding."

"The person I love sips soup through his nose."

"Always buy your seaweed salad fresh."

"Put your hands up. This is a holdup."

"The fish in my tank are floating upside down."

"You have to work hard to clean your ears well."

"Never mix Captain Crunch with Count Chocula!!"

"Hold him down while I extract his tooth!"

"Gather around and watch the elephant's stomach explode."

"Death to the Energizer Bunny!"

"Richard Simmons is a fun date."

PARTY QUIRKS   GROUP 1

1) PILGRIM IS THE **PARDONER** WHO

HAS RECENTLY EATEN SOME VERY BAD OYSTERS.

2) PILGRIM IS THE **OXFORD CLERIC** WHO

LOVES TO ICE SKATE ALL THE TIME.

3) PILGRIM IS THE **MERCHANT** WHO

WANTS TO BE A DETECTIVE.

The Canterbury Tales

PARTY QUIRKS   GROUP 2

4) PILGRIM IS THE **KNIGHT** WHO

   HAS RECENTLY HAD TOO MUCH CAFFEINE.

5) PILGRIM IS THE **PARSON** WHO

   CANNOT GET WATER OUT OF HIS EAR (FROM

   SWIMMING AT BEACH).

6) PILGRIM IS THE **PRIORESS** WHO

   HAS A BAD CASE OF POISON IVY.

The Canterbury Tales

PARTY QUIRKS   GROUP 3

7) PILGRIM IS THE **WIFE OF BATH** WHO

HAS AN OVERDOSE OF NOVOCAIN IN MOUTH.

8) PILGRIM IS THE **FRIAR** WHO

HAS RECENTLY INHALED HELIUM.

9) PILGRIM IS THE **OXFORD CLERIC** WHO

THINKS HE HAS MAD COW DISEASE

The Canterbury Tales

PARTY QUIRKS GROUP 4

10)PILGRIM IS THE **WIFE OF BATH** WHO

WANTS TO BE A FIREMAN (FIREWOMAN?)

11)PILGRIM IS THE **MONK** WHO

LOVES TO DANCE ALL THE TIME.

12)PILGRIM IS THE **KNIGHT** WHO

FEARS THAT ALIENS ARE AMONG US.

The Canterbury Tales

PARTY QUIRKS   GROUP 5

13)PILGRIM IS THE **YEOMAN** WHO

ALWAYS SPEAKS IN RHYMING COUPLETS.

14)PILGRIM IS THE **COOK** WHO

IS CURRENTLY STARVING FOR FOOD.

15)PILGRIM IS THE **SKIPPER** WHO

FEARS HE WILL TURN INTO A WEREWOLF AT ANY TIME.

The Canterbury Tales

PARTY QUIRKS   GROUP 6

16)PILGRIM IS THE **PRIORESS** WHO

   HAS A PHOBIA ABOUT CONTRACTING DISEASES FROM OTHER PEOPLE

17)PILGRIM IS THE **SQUIRE** WHO

   SUFFERS FROM SCHIZOPHRENIA.

18)PILGRIM IS THE **PARDONER** WHO

   WANTS TO BECOME PROM QUEEN

The Canterbury Tales

PARTY QUIRKS   GROUP 7

19)PILGRIM IS THE **WIFE OF BATH** WHO

BELIEVES HER DEAD HUSBANDS SPEAK TO HER

20)PILGRIM IS THE **KNIGHT** WHO

BELIEVES OTHERS ARE TRYING TO KILL HIM.

21)PILGRIM IS THE **FRIAR** WHO

IS TRYING TO LOSE WEIGHT

The Canterbury Tales

Name_____

Period_____ Group Id_____

CLOSURE FOR CT Olympics 1

The Canterbury Tales

The response to the following questions should reflect the depth of the group's creativity and intelligence. A *collaborative* effort is essential to attaining a good score on this assignment.

1) Which pilgrim seems to represent the best of the medieval period and why?
Pilgrim_____

Why?_____

_____

_____

_____

2) Which pilgrim seems to represent the worst of the medieval period and why?
Pilgrim_____

Why?_____

_____

3) What pilgrim would have the cleverest epitaph and what would it be?

Pilgrim_____

_____

_____

4) What two (2) pilgrims would be the most fun to watch in a sumo wrestling match and why?

Pilgrim _____ and

Pilgrim_____

Why?_____

_____

5) What three (3) pilgrims would you choose for the basis of a modern television situation comedy and what would be the show's name and premise?

Pilgrims 1)_____ 2)_____ 3)_____

Name of Show_____

Premise of Show_____

_____

6) If the prologue to *The Canterbury Tales* was the only document surviving from Chaucer's time, what conclusions would we draw about life in the Middle Ages? Remember, the conclusions must come solely from information contained in this literary work.

_____

_____

_____

_____

7) What seems to be Chaucer's attitude toward religious professions?

_____

_____

_____

8) What seems to be Chaucer's attitude toward women?

_____

_____

_____

9) What observations by Chaucer about medieval life and medieval people seem to be also true about life and people in the modern age?

_____

_____

_____

10) Themes, about life or about human nature, can be drawn from the prologue to *The Canterbury Tales*?

_____

_____

_____

Beyond Infinity: The Canterbury Tales Olympics

1) Ask the students either through class discussion or in groups to consider how their group functioned. What were the challenges and how did they overcome those challenges?
2) What could the group have done better?
3) What did the group excel at doing?
4) What did students learn about the subject matter (literary work, middle ages, time, interpersonal relations, etc.)?
5) What, if anything, did students learn about themselves, other people, life in general?
6) What questions do they have about themselves, other people, life in general?

Specific to the unit studied:

1) What stereotypes appear to exist in your school? Are you stereotyped or are you one of those you listed?
2) There are four ways that characterization is revealed by an author:
    a. By what a character says
    b. By what a character does
    c. By what another character says about that first character
    d. By what the author describes about that character
        Of the four above, which do you think is the most effective? Least effective? Why?
3) What problems may evolve from stereotyping?
4) Why do human beings seem to have a tendency to stereotype?
5) What have you learned about improvisation?
6) How similar are Chaucer's characters to people in our contemporary culture?

Clowning Around

Teacher Notes—Clowning Around

We had recently finished a unit in our Interdisciplinary Studies course on the culture of the Ancient Greeks and another unit on Native American mythology. Our next unit involved a study of Asian culture, the Silk Road, Siddhartha, Sound of Waves, etc. One of the themes we wanted our students to explore was the concept that some societies mistrust words because words often contain lies. Meaning and truth are often conveyed more through context (for example, in a funeral home, everyone behaves according to implicit norms about voice volume and behavior without anyone spelling these rules out) and body language/facial expressions than through endless chatter (understanding this might change the course of American politics!). We also wanted our students to explore nonverbal communication, especially since future assignments included play acting.

As a prelude to the projects, we required students to read the articles on False Faces and Zuni Clowns, respond to the questions on these articles both individually and in groups, and then issued the Clown Mask assignment. Simultaneously, we issued the Clowning Around assignment. Both projects, in my opinion, were successes. In follow up discussions, students determined that nonverbal communication, particularly body language, is more precise than voice verbalization. They also developed a greater understanding of rituals like Japanese Tea Ceremonies in which context and body language convey more meaning than speech, and students also understood that, in other cultures, pauses in conversations did not need to be filled up with meaningless chatter. In fact, silences convey information as well.

To execute this project, students need to have developed strong collaborative skills, especially the skill of building and maintaining trust. Give it a show. I think you will be happily satisfied with the results.

Name_____

Period___ Group_____

This is excerpted from Peter Farb's *Man's Rise to Civilization*

FALSE FACES

"Despite the sophistication of much of Iroquois society, its religious ritual were still shamanistic-with the difference that they were not carried on by a religious free-lancer but by an organized shamanistic group. The individual shaman's songs, dances, and other hocus-pocus were restricted to the False Face society, whose members cured with the aid of large woode masks. These distorted facial nightmares consisted of twelve basic types-- crooked mouth, straight-lipped, spoon-lipped, hanging mouth, tongue protruding, smiling, whistling, divided red and black, long nosed, horned, pig, and blind. There were also some additional local types, such as the diseased face, as well as color variations. A catalog of all combinations probably would number several dozen kinds. The society members always functioned as a group, and they put on a frightening performance at the house of the sick person. They lurched, humped, 'crawled, and trotted to the house, grunting and issuing weird cries from behind their masks. They danced around the sick person, sprinkled him with ashes, shook their large rattles made from the carapaces of turtles, and sang out their incantations.

In 1751 the pioneer American naturalist and a friend of the Indian, John Bartram, described what it was like to encounter one of the members of the False Face society:

He had on a clumsy vizard of wood colour'd black, with a nose 4 or 5 inches long, a grinning mouth set awry, furnished with long teeth, round the cycs circles of bright brass, surrounded by a larger circle of white paint, from his forehead hung long tresses of buffaloes hair, and from the catch part of his head ropes made of the plated husks of *Indian* corn; I cannot recollect the whole of his dress, but that it was equally uncouth: he carried in one hand a long staff, in the other a calabash with small stones in it, for a rattle . . . he would sometimes hold up his head and make a hideous noise like the braying of an ass.

The false faces really should not be regarded as masks, since they were not intended to hide anything. There has been considerable discussion and dispute about them, and a common explanation is that they represent merely a form of idolatry. It is true that in addition to the large masks intended to be worn, there were much smaller "maskettes," often only two or three inches long. They were kept partly as charms, much as some people keep a lucky stone, but they were primarily compact substitutes for, and reminders of, the larger masks, similar to the Saint Christopher statuettes some drivers place on their automobile dashboards. If the word "idolatry" is pronounced with a condemnatory tone, as many good White Protestants often do, then the Iroquois must be defended. The Iroquois worshiped-and they, the few that are left, still worship today despite the inroads of Christianity-their supernatural beings and not idols. They regarded their masks as portraits into which the supernatural has made itself manifest. The wearer behaved as if he were the supernatural being whom he impersonated. He had obtained the mask by carving in the trunk of a living tree the vision he had of a False Face, and then cutting the mask free. During this ceremony, the spirit revealed itself to the maker, who then finished carving the features and painted the mask. The Iroquois did not worship the images themselves, only what they signified. Iconism is undoubtedly a better description than idolatry." Peter Farb *Man's Rise to Civilization.* Pages 108-110

FACE IT!

1) In the excerpt from Peter's Farb's *Man's Rise to Civilization*, what function in society did the False Faces seem to serve?

_____

_____

2) Farb says that the masks the False Faces used should not really be regarded as masks. Why does he say this?

_____

_____

3) Think of examples of masks that we have in our society. (For example, an automobile is a mask.) Make a list of masks that exist in our culture.

_____

_____

_____

4) Chose one of the masks listed above and describe what purpose it seems to serve, from both a sociological and psychological view.

_____

_____

_____

5) "A mask provides us with the opportunity to hide a private identity while simultaneously displaying a communal face." RM How valid is this observation compared to your own experience?

_____

_____

_____

Name_____

Period ____ Group_____

This is excerpted from Peter Farb's *Man's Rise to Civilization*

RITES OF REBELLION

"Even though Ruth Benedict drew the wrong conclusions, some of her observations about Zuni are true: Its society is structured, overtly unemotional in behavior, controlled in its obedience. But can people continue to survive in a society from whose psychological strictures they cannot escape? Or are there hidden mechanisms in Zuni society that allow repressed aggressions to be worked off?

There assuredly are. Before the enforced peacefulness brought by Whites, the Pueblo Indians had enthusiastic war cults that channeled aggression into socially acceptable paths. Before the coming of the Spaniards, and even for some time thereafter, considerable internecine warfare took place between various Pueblo tribes, a common excuse being a suspicion of witchcraft. The war cult, which nowadays functions solely as an internal police force, in pre-White times must have safely evaporated a tremendous amount of aggression. To become a member of the Bow Priests, for example, a warrior had to bring back an enemy's scalp. The war ceremonies in recent times have of necessity become more symbolic than real. The ceremonies make do with one of the old scalps still kept in the Zuni kivas, instead of one from a fresh victim. The scalp is kicked into the village by four aunts of the "warrior" while the onlookers whoop it up and shoot off guns. If a mere symbolic dramatization produces such a frenzy today, imagine what must have been the commotion when a warrior returned with the actual scalp of a Navaho or a Ute. In those days, dances continued for twelve nights around a scalp pole erected in the plaza.

Rebellion against conventional behavior nowadays shows up in certain rites that mock the gods, ridicule the ceremonials, revile conventional behavior, and merge obscenity with religion. During these rites of rebellion, hostility that Zuni society represses during most of the year comes to the surface in a socially approved fashion. The prime agents of these rites are members of the cult of Kachina Priests known as Koyemshi, or Mudheads. They are sacred clowns, grotesque in appearance, wearing mud-daubed masks in which the nose and eyes are bulging knobs, the mouth a gaping hole, the face covered with large warts.

The Mudheads are believed to have been born of an incestuous union; they are therefore excused from conventional behavior while they utter obscenities or mock things held in reverence. They cavort around the serious dancers, speaking whatever their unconscious throws out about the ceremony or the audience. Their antics are funny in the same way a circus clown is funny and partly for the same reason, both being excused from conventional behavior. A Mudhead may satirize the dancers by a toometiculous attention to ceremony; he, may keep dancing long after the conventional dancers have finished, focusing attention on himself until he finally realizes his "mistake." One routine, reminiscent of vaudeville or television, is the Zuni clown who uses an imitation telephone to carry on an imaginary conversation with the gods.

Some observers have thought that these routines originated only in recent decades, perhaps inspired by movies or by television-but one account of clowning at Zuni in 1881 reveals there is nothing new about them. The account states that twelve members of a religious society dressed themselves in odd bits of clothing that allowed them to caricature a Mexican priest, an American soldier, an old woman, and several other types. The principal performance of the evening was a devastating parody of Roman Catholic ritual. The dancers rolled on the ground, and with extravagant beating of the breast mocked a Catholic service. One bawled out the paternoster; another portrayed a passionate padre; a third mimicked old people reciting the rosary. The dancers then started to eat such things as corn husks and filthy rags. One called out, in the same way that a diner might summon a waiter in a restaurant, for a portion of dog excrement. Instead of sacramental wine, several of the dancers drank long draughts of human urine, smacked their lips, and pronounced it very tasty indeed. The account reports that the audience of men, women, and children howled with un-controlled merriment.

What do these rites of rebellion indicate? Are they as infantile as they seem, or is some more complex social mechanism at work? Obviously, they release the audience emotionally by permitting to tread, a socially acceptable manner, in forbidden areas. Comic relief, though, is probably only part of the answer, for these rites assuredly are not solely negative. They are of positive value in supporting the Zuni social order and in resolving conflicts. On one level, burlesque is negative because it undermines convention. Contrariwise, though, it emphasizes through contrast and the very enormity of the obscenity exactly what everyone in the audience knows all along-the proper social behavior.

An examination of those American Indian societies that had ritual clowns reveals an interesting fact: Clowns were prevalent only in societies that possessed an unchallenged and established social order, those societies that were sure of themselves. Modern American society has little place for institutionalized rites of rebellion, because it is a democratic society;

it is characteristic of a democratic society always to question and to challenge, never to be certain of itself. Modern Americans cannot conceive of a television comic parodying sacred ritual or eating excrement; such conduct would be adjudged the symptoms of a nervous breakdown rather than an expression of rebellion. Modern American society is so unsure of itself that it has not been able to endure even the rebellious humor of the "sick comedians," and as outcasts of Modern America they were hounded until they retired, escaped into the fantasy world of narcotics, or committed suicide. Most Americans seem unable to endure anything stronger than the mild television barbs of a Bob Hope or the buffoonery of the circus clown." Peter Farb's *Man's Rise to Civilization*, pages 92-94   Answer the questions on the next page.

CLOWING AROUND

1) List all the terms that you can think of that use the word "clown."

_____   _____

_____   _____

_____   _____

2) In the excerpt from Peter Farb's *Man's Rise to Civilization*, what fundamental purposes do the Zuni clowns serve?

_____

_____

3) Why does Farb claim that Americans could not accept clowns in the same way as the Zuni do?

_____

_____

4) In question #3 above, do you think that Farb is correct? Give reasons for your answers.

_____

_____

_____

_____

5) Is it good for a society to be so sure of itself (see Farb's excerpt) that it can accept clowns, at least clowns in the Zuni style of clowns? Why or why not?

_____

_____

_____

_____

6) Name some clowns in American culture—

_____

_____

7) Do you find any commonalties in the list you devised in #6? What purpose, if any, do clowns serve in our culture?

_____

_____

_____

_____

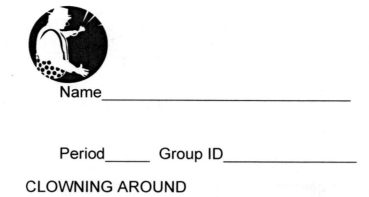

Name_____

Period_____ Group ID_____

CLOWNING AROUND

"Ladies and Gentlemen, and Children of All Ages..."

I was at a social gathering when I met a gentleman, and we started sharing old college stories. Immediately upon graduation from our respective universities, we applied and were accepted into graduate schools, but his was a little different from mine. He enrolled in Clown College somewhere in Florida, and, so, his graduate school experience was far more interesting than mine was. According to my acquaintance, Clown College was extremely challenging. There was the sheer physicality of it all, requiring fitness and stamina, and he needed to learn the fine art of Clowning. Facial expressions, gestures, nuances of body language, all had to be mastered in a sort of *ballet of burlesque* if he was to make it to the big ring.

Let's see if you are up to the challenge. Your group is to develop a three-minute clown act. Each member will construct a mask for himself/herself. The mask can be as simple or as elaborate as he or she wishes. The group does not have to have masks that all reflect one theme. This allows for individual diversity. What the group must do is create and develop a short pantomime to perform for the class. This clown act should attempt to spoof (like the Zuni clowns) some aspect of school life. The major difference between the Zuni performances and the performances of your group is that your group must operate within the boundaries of acceptable taste. The key here is to be clever rather than cute.

These are the criteria for success:

1) Group Involvement—all members are actively engaged both in preparation and performance.
2) Quality of the Masks—masks do not have to be elaborate, but they must fit the demeanor of the wearer's "performance identity."
3) Quality of the Performance—the act must be organized and display thought and creativity.

This is actually a challenging assignment. I know it might be difficult to find anything to spoof in our perfect school, but try anyway. The real difficulty is to think about the body language and movements that convey your message, and to operate in concert with one another. At the very least, I hope you realize how serious clowning around is. Oh, yes, my acquaintance flunked out of Clown College. Good luck.

Name_____

Period_____   Group ID_____

"Who Was That Masked Man?"
various characters from *The Lone Ranger*

Your assignment is to investigate one mask from a culture in India, China, or Japan. (If you find a mask that really intrigues you from another country, you may explore it *pending approval from the instructor*.)   The mask must be associated with a ritual or ceremony. Choose a mask that "has something to say."

The next step is to research your mask.   Discover its origins, its design, its use. Attempt to find out if it is still used by the culture that devised it or if it has evolved into something else. When you have finished your research, write a one to two page paper about the mask.

On the day the assignment is due, bring your paper and a replica of the mask to class. The replica may be your own drawing of the mask or some fascimile.   Please observe copyright rules. You may be asked to discuss your mask in class and to provide us with details about the mask and the ceremony or ritual in which it was used.

This assignment will be evaluated on the following criteria:

1) Quality of the paper—Paper must be typed, punctual, and intelligently written.
2) Use of class time, if any is given.
3) Quality of the presentation, if you are asked to present your work.

Beyond Infinity: Clowning Around

1) Ask the students either through class discussion or in groups to consider how their group functioned. What were the challenges and how did they overcome those challenges?
2) What could the group have done better?
3) What did the group excel at doing?
4) What did students learn about the subject matter (literary work, middle ages, time, interpersonal relations, etc.)?
5) What, if anything, did students learn about themselves, other people, life in general?
6) What questions do they have about themselves, other people, life in general?

Specific to the unit studied:

1) In what ways is non-verbal communication different from verbal communication?
2) On what factors does non-verbal communication depend in order to be effective?
3) Think about some clowns that exist in American culture (Bugs Bunny, Bart Simpson, for example). What values do they represent/satirize? Do they serve a purpose?
4) When we use the term "class clown," what do we actually mean?
5) We use a variety of masks within our society---cars, clothing, tattoos, uniforms, etc. What purposes do masks serve in modern culture?
6) What can you observe about a society through the masks it uses?

Darcy Whodunit

Teacher Notes---The Darcy Whodunit

Let's be honest. For many young male teenagers, appreciating the dramatic tension underlying the social relationships in Pride and Prejudice *does not come easily. I broke the novel up into three chunks, gave the class a week to read the first third, tested the students on how well they read and studied that section (by this time of the year, around February/March, my students know that they will be tested on a close reading of the work!), and discussed the plot, character evolution, and evolving themes. I remember one year, after we had discussed the second third of the novel, a young man came up to me after class, and with a not-so-subtle trace of weariness in his voice, asked, "Mr. Maltese, any chance that some imported Ninja arrive in the third section and wipe out everyone in Netherfield Park?" I had to dash his hopes.*

But all the students, including the males, enjoyed this project. The trial motif for class projects is certainly not new. I used that structure to teach Macbeth, *and adopted a colleague's trial of George from* Of Mice and Men. *We could develop a project using a trial of Creon from* Antigone, *Captain Vere from* Billy Budd, *and Napoleon from* Animal Farm. *Or a teacher could have an actual trial and ask students to reenact it, such as the example in this book involving Galileo. Another option using the trial motif is to place the author on trial. (a number of males wanted Jane Austen in the block!). As Cervantes was "tried" in* Man of La Mancha, *students could accuse John Steinbeck of anti-government sentiment in* The Grapes of Wrath, *or put Ernest Hemingway in the box for writing* The Sun Also Rises *and libeling the real life people through their portrayal via fictional characters in the book.*

The most immediate problem with the trial structure is what to do with the students in the jury. Some students opt to be jurors figuring that they can just sit back, do no research or other work, and wait for the trial. These students would sit around while lawyers and witnesses prepared for the event. I had to change that, and that is why this project has assignments for jurors. This tact worked very well. Students who saw being in the jury as a chance for role playing came to class dressed in the juror's persona.

Ideally, the juror would be members of another class who had yet to read the book, and one year another English teacher volunteered members of her class to serve as the jury. This was fine, but that left me with 12 students with no roles. After that experience, I went back to this format.

There is always at least one student in class who wants to be the judge. I caution that the judge has to do a high degree of research so that the proceedings are in accordance with English law, but, at the same time, I prefer a student judge to a teacher judge. I would advise that you use your discretion in choosing the student for this role. Choose the student who is more likely to benefit from the necessary research and who will listen during the trial rather than the student who gets the rush from power trips. On occasion, especially when the class is overcrowded, it is not a bad idea to have a triumvirate. Three judges whose decision will be based on a majority vote will work well, especially if all three judges will have to explain their individual decisions on a one page paper written after the trial and copied and distributed to the class.

For those teachers who have access to a wiki, this is an ideal project for students to place their individual papers on a wiki---actors, actresses, jurors, and judges. A good closure for this project would be discussion questions and responses on the wiki.

One of the primary goals for any project in language arts (and perhaps other content areas as well) is for the student to go back and revisit the text to find meaning for another purpose. One critic postulated that murder mysteries are ideal subjects for historical inquiry because the author has to research the time period and make certain that the slightest detail is historically accurate. This is also one of the reasons why the trial format often works so well. Students have to go back to the literary work and study it in detail.

I have included a prereading guide for the students to use as they study the novel.

I assigned the novel to be read in sections (volumes) and tested after each volume. Then we discussed, after each volume, questions related to themes. They are included here.

The Darcy Whodunit assignment asks students to reexamine the novel, as all good projects should, and synthesize new conclusions based on the available information. I reiterate, and this bears repeating: **even the males in the classes seemed to enjoy this one.**

Name_____

Date_____

READING GUIDELINE FOR *PRIDE AND PREJUDICE*

This novel is a challenging literary work. The words and phrases are not difficult to read, but there are many characters and subtleties of plot which require concentration and focus. Remember that you are being asked to not only *read* the novel, but to *study* it in preparation for a test as well as future academic projects. The test will be on a *close reading* of the novel, so it is important to pay attention to detail.

Keep in mind that you are also **required** to take notes. Note taking is **NOT** an option. I will check your notes, and, if they are copied or look like they were written the night before or are non-existent, your final marking period evaluation will be adversely affected. I can assure you of that. Good students take notes on their material, and you will be evaluated on how well you adopt the practices of good students. For this novel, especially, it is a good idea to devise a character web and to hypothesize questions as part of your note taking. Review your notes periodically. In an effort to improve your overall performance on the test(s) and projects, I am sharing with you some "tips." Read them carefully.

Tip #1--Give yourself plenty of time to read the book. Sure you can read it the night before, but cramming is a lousy device for studying.

Tip #2--Don't cheat. I believe that there is a strong ethical component to education. Reading the Cliff Notes is cheating, and I will regard those who do use them instead of reading the novel as cheaters. Yeah, yeah, yeah. I know. Your buddy Boris Braindead read the Cliff Notes for *War and Peace* and passed the test. Big deal. There are no Cliff Notes for life, and eventually Boris will have to read something for his college courses or for his job that is not accompanied by short cuts. What does he do then? Most importantly, Boris is using the "end justifies the means" excuse. The last big name in the twentieth century who repeatedly justified his actions by citing the end was a fellow named Adolph Hitler. To say the least, I am not a big fan of his. The *means* are important, especially in something designated as an "honors" course.

Tip #3--At the end of each chapter, hypothesize like crazy. Ask yourself such questions as: "What do I suspect will happen to this or that character?" "Do certain characters seem to be the foils (opposites) of other characters in terms of behavior and attitude?" "What commentary, if any, is Austen trying to make in this chapter?" "Is the action by the characters plausible?" "What people and situations from your own life are similar to the characters and situations in the novel?" "Do supermarkets remove milk that has lasted past its expiration date from the shelves, and, if so, what do they do with that milk?" You get the idea. Good thinkers think as they read.

Tip #4--Slow your reading speed down. I understand. You have two lab reports to file and five chapters of social studies to read, but most of us in education know that students often read too fast and their comprehension suffers--one of the reasons that cramming is a poor strategy. Don't just read words. Read for detail and read for meaning.

Tip #5-- Never bite off the bottom of an ice cream cone on a hot day until the top of the scoops is at cone level.

DISCUSSION TOPICS FOR PRIDE AND PREJUDICE

Discussion following the reading of Volume 1

1) Seinfeld philosophy--a show about nothing

2) What is nothing? Even talking about nothing assumes that nothing is something.

3) Does "nothing" exist?

4) Crouching Tiger--Hidden Dragon--protagonist says, in facing a daunting task, "I am nothing."

5) How many terms do we have using the word, "nothing?"

6) What do we learn about everyday English society?

   Enumerate them on the board or monitor.

7) How can we learn about something if nothing happens? How do we learn those things about English society if nothing happened in the novel?

8) Like Seinfeld, it's in the everyday things that reality really is. Most days we are not hit with Tornadoes, or trapped on a speeding bus with a bomb aboard or attacked by twenty five near sighted ninja.

9) Most people live lives of "quiet desperation."

10) Is Seinfeld really about nothing? Why would we like a show about nothing?

11) Pride and Prejudice is about relationships, and men and women look at them differently.

12) What are modern sitcoms about?

Discussion following the reading of Volume 2

1) How do men and women look at relationships?

2) For example, why does my wife fall asleep during a movie during the most exciting battle scenes, and I fall asleep during the mushy sections?

3) What is the dance routine that men and women perform when they enter a relationship?

4) What do women consider to be a good catch in a man? List them on the board or monitor.

5) What do men consider to be a good catch in a woman. List them on the board or monitor.

6) In the novel, what conclusions can we draw about male/female relationships at that time? How similar are they to our time?

7) What can we tell about the class system in England at that time? On what is their system predicated?

8) Do we have a similar class system? On what is our system predicated?

Discussion following the reading of Volume 3

1) What is Elizabeth's reward for being sensible?

2) What role does reason play in the novel?

Name_____

THE GATHERING AND USE OF INTERNAL EVIDENCE

OR

THE DARCY WHODUNIT

June 27th, 1797. Fitzwilliam Darcy, well-known and well-heeled denizen of Kent County, was found dead in his Pemberley estate last night from unknown causes. Constables are still searching Darcy's home for clues, and further information is forthcoming. Mrs. Robinson, Darcy's housekeeper, noticed that her master had been absent from the fabulous and extravagant ball he was hosting in honor of his newly wed spouse, the former Miss Elizabeth Bennet. When Mrs. Robinson went to her master's bedroom to obtain the key to the wine cellar (the supply of Ripple de Neuf, 1794, needed to be replenished) she found him, apparently unconscious. A physician was immediately summoned, but his medicinal efforts went for naught. After a brief inquiry, local constables suspected foul play and arrested one George Wickham. Wickham is held in police custody, awaiting trial. An autopsy will be conducted.

The purpose of this assignment in multifold, but one of the essential goals is to require you to improve research skills, including the gathering of internal evidence. This assignment will require you to role-play. You may choose to be any one of the following: 1) actor/actress in the role of two or three of the characters from *Pride and Prejudice*

2) a member of a two legal counsel team whose goal is to defend Mr. Wickham

3) a member of a two legal counsel team whose goal is to prosecute Mr. Wickham

4) a member of a newspaper from Kent County reporting on the death of Mr. Darcy and the subsequent trial

5) a jurist that has researched a persona from the novel and written a one and one half page report explaining your occupation, life style, acquaintances, economic status and standing in the novel; you also will be part of a voir dire before the actual trial.

Every student, no matter what role (1 to 5 above) he or she chooses, will be required to 1) conduct research 2) submit at least one small paper 3) maintain historical accuracy in the role both in speech and behavior 4) intellectual effort (which includes use of class time). In essence, these four criteria will be the basis for the your grade on this assignment.

Prosecutors--(Maximum of 2)

I am not asking that you graduate from law school before you complete this assignment, but try to get a sense of courtroom protocol. You may decide *what* to charge Mr. Wickham with--first degree murder, second degree, etc. At some point you must explain these differences to the jury. There will be a voir dire, a chance for you and the defense counsel to question the jurors. In real jury selections, you would have the privilege of rejecting a potential juror. You do not have the option here. The jurists will submit their "profiles" to you and you may question them to unveil any hidden agenda or prejudices. You must submit:

1) to the judge (copies to the defense counsel) a one and one-half page brief explaining what you will try to prove during the trial.

2) a list of witnesses that you wish to call

3) to the judge a one and one-half page summation (if there are two prosecutors, the one who did not write the brief must write the summation)

All written work must meet the criteria outlined at the end of this document.

The trial will begin with an opening statement by you, followed by a statement by the defense. You will then call your witnesses and the defense will then call theirs. After the defense rests, both sides will deliver summations.

You will be evaluated on the depth of your research, the quality of the written material, the maintenance of historical accuracy and the degree of effort exemplified by your behavior.

Defense Counsels--(Maximum of 2)

You task is to provide your client with the best possible defense. You will have to examine the evidence the prosecution presents and decide on a defense strategy. Like the judge and the prosecution, you must do your homework. Research courtroom protocol. You must provide the jury with reasonable doubt. Your task is not to convince the judge or Mr. Maltese, but the *jury*. Consult with your client. Your task is slightly different from most murder trials since everyone in the novel will have had opportunity. One defense might be to demonstrate in court that your client was not the only person with motive. It is necessary that you read the directions for the prosecution detailed above. Your criteria for success is the same as that for the prosecution. **Read these criteria carefully--especially the written work!!**

>>>>>>>>>>One of my best friends is an attorney. He once told me that the best lawyers, during a trial, never ask a question of a witness that they (the lawyers) do not know the answer to. Keep this in mind.<<<<<<<<<<<<

Actors/Actresses

Now is your chance to ham it up. For each character that you choose to be, you must submit beforehand (to the judge) a three paragraph description of who you are and your involvement in the novel. This must be written in the voice of your character. During the trial you may be summoned as a witness, and it is important that you have a good knowledge of your character's role. If you perjure yourself (which means saying something which cannot be substantiated in the novel) you will suffer dire consequences (including a reduced grade!!). You will be graded on the following criteria: the quality of your research, the quality of your written work, the maintenance of historical accuracy (no need to make costumes, but it would be hard for us to swallow that you are Charles Bingley if you take the stand wearing an old Iron Maiden t-shirt!!), and the degree of intellectual effort.

Newspaper people--(Maximum of 3 per paper)--There are two very rival tabloids in Kent County. They will try desperately to outdo each other for the story. Each paper will be required to produce a two to three page newspaper at the end of the trial. The paper may include interviews with trial personalities. The paper must also include some "world" news besides the doings in Kent County, but the big story is the Darcy story. It would be very wise of the reporters at the trial to listen carefully to testimony to spot any witness who may perjure himself/herself by contradicting evidence from the novel. The paper must show evidence of research, maintain historical accuracy in style and content, and demonstrate true intellectual effort.

Jurors-- Jurors, in one way, must do the most work. Mentally they must forget they read the literary work and evaluate the proceedings *based on the evidence presented.* In addition, each jurist will be required to develop a persona. That is, each prospective jurist must research the time period of the novel and construct a person that lived at that time and in that area and plausibly exists within the novel. You cannot simply say I'm Tom Doofus from Meryton, a dope dealer. Find out what people wore, worked at and aspired to. Have your persona be somewhat interwoven with the happenings in the novel. For example, you might be a haberdasher that sold Miss Lydia a hat on one occasion. Study the novel and consult other resources to find out what life was like in that time period. Personae that show no evidence of research will receive no discernible grade of note. This persona must be written up and presented aforehand to the instructor as well as to both legal teams.(minimum of 11/2 pages). The data you use must be drawn from your research. The more accurate and clever this persona, the higher will be the evaluation. During the trial you must listen attentively to the proceedings, and following each day's proceedings, you must complete a jurist's Accountability Sheet. You will be evaluated according to the following criteria: the depth of your research for your persona, the quality of your written work, the maintenance of historical accuracy (again, no tuxedoes necessary, but leave the "I Did Dorney" t-shirt home these days).

Notice to all: talking to reporters may be dangerous. This applies to everyone, but especially the jurists and legal teams. Jurists do not want to seem prejudiced before the verdict and legal teams do not want to spill their strategies to their opponents. At the same time, legal teams and witnesses can use public opinion to their favor. Be judicious.

Criteria

1) Depth of research--your demeanor and your written work should show ample evidence of researching the novel and outside sources. Document any outside sources that you use.

2) Quality of written work--with the exception of the jurist accountability sheets, all work should be typed, punctual, and neatly presented. The voice should be appropriate to the author's role.

3) Maintenance of historical accuracy--claiming that you are a nuclear engineer in 1797 is not a good idea. Dress is up to you, but appropriate deportment is necessary. Think before you speak so that the "Like, yeah, so like I said to Elizabeth, like Beth, what did you ever see, like, in this guy Darcy before?" is eliminated.

4) Intellectual effort--use class time wise, and somewhere in your written or oral performance slip in some originality, some of what is distinctly you.

I stand ready and willing to assist you in this enterprise. Please feel free to call on me. Good luck.

Beyond Infinity: Darcy Whodunit

Generic:

1) Ask the students either through class discussion or in groups to consider how their group functioned. What were the challenges and how did they overcome those challenges?
2) What could the group have done better?
3) What did the group excel at doing?
4) What did students learn about the subject matter (literary work, middle ages, time, interpersonal relations, etc.)?
5) What, if anything, did students learn about themselves, other people, life in general?
6) What questions do they have about themselves, other people, life in general?

The teacher can use the questions below as either closures for the projects or as the inceptions of new projects.

Specific to the unit studied:

1) There are certain conventions between young men and young women in the novel that were expected to be observed. Are any modern conventions observed by today's young men and young women similar to those conventions of Jane Austen's day?
2) There is certainly dramatic tension within the novel *Pride and Prejudice*. What tensions exist between and among characters in the novel?
3) *Pride and Prejudice* is often referred to as a "satire." What do you think Jane Austen is satirizing?
4) Do you believe that the relationships between men and women in western culture are similar to the relationships in Austen's day? If so, why or why not?
5) Many sitcoms on television essentially follow the same patterns in theme and content as in Pride and Prejudice. Consider this statement and agree or disagree.
6) If people three centuries from now studied our contemporary books and television shows, would they possibly react in the same way as you did when you read *Pride and Prejudice*?

The Greek Academy

Teacher Notes: Greek Academy I

A unit on the ancient Greeks was one of the first learning experiences we provided in the humanities course I co-taught with a social studies teacher, an art teacher, and a music teacher. This course was originally designed to teach those creative students who had not succeeded in the conventional classroom which rewarded those students whose primary intelligences were verbal and mathematical. Because the humanities course (entitled Interdisciplinary Studies) tried to address a variety of intelligences and because it was predicated on project based learning and creative problem solving, many other "mainstream" students applied for the course.

The Greek Academy project was a good one for developing collaborative skills in the beginning of the school year (after students received some practice in working together in all the Interdisciplinary subjects through a variety of activities). Every year we changed the "everyday life resources." That is why they are not included here. And the resources we used varied from online research to material found in the library. The following list includes areas of everyday life that seemed to work well:

1) *Diet and eating etiquette*
2) *Holiday celebrations*
3) *Recreation for young people*
4) *Marriage ceremonies*
5) *Personal hygiene*
6) *Transportation*
7) *Entertainment (or what to do on Saturday night)*
8) *School*
9) *Everyday clothing and fashion*
10) *Worship*

Whenever possible, I tried to control the resources students used. Students often tended to choose the online resources that contained the best graphics rather than the most substance. I tried to prepare them for college when much of their reading would not include cartoons.

Name_____

Period_____ Group_____

"I would like to thank the Academy…"

We realize that many of you young and energetic students have traveled many miles by horse and by oxen to apply to the Ancient Academy located at the Oracle at Pendtese. And we, the Masters of the Academy, are anxious to begin the school year. We must begin scheduling classes (young Master Plato's course is filling up quickly), assigning dorm rooms, establishing rules for pledging the Greek system, and lining up concerts. It is hoped that all of you took the time to fill out the personal preferences questionnaire so that we can match you with a roommate who has the same tastes as you, such as an interest in Greco-Greco Wrestling. That is the good news. The bad news is that, once again, we do not have room for everyone who applies to be in our freshman class. As a matter of fact, our hostilities with those nasty Persians have siphoned off some of our facilities and manpower, so that this year we can only accept fifteen new students at the Academy.

Thus, though we know that you have high hopes of enrolling this year, we are afraid that we must limit our acceptances to only fifteen. Therefore we have devised a challenge, a task, a test of your intellectual acumen. Those fifteen who seem to meet the challenge most appropriately will be accepted. Those who do not will be put on the waiting list.

THE CHALLENGE

Your group of applicants will be broken up into trios. Each trio will read and investigate 1) a myth and 2) an aspect of everyday life in contemporary times.

Task 1—The Myth

Your trio will be assigned a myth. Every trio or group will be assigned a different myth. You may find these myths in the library or possibly at home. Each member must read and study the myth. A short quiz will be administered to the trio, and each member will receive an individual score. In addition, each group will receive a composite score composed of its members' scores. This will assist the Admissions Committee in making decisions.

Each group will be asked to make a presentation to the Admissions Committee explaining how this particular myth contributes to our Greek culture. This myth may contribute to our culture by reinforcing our beliefs, explaining phenomenon, or by raising questions. Your group must make intellectual connections between the myth itself and our society. Of course, you may include background material involving the origin and development of the myth and a very brief synopsis of the myth itself.

Task 2—Everyday Life

Your trio will be assigned an aspect of everyday Greek life. It may or may not directly relate to your myth. This is for your group to figure out. Each group will be given resource material on that aspect of Greek life. In addition to the resource material, it is recommended that you search for supplementary material such as illustrations, first hand accounts etc. A short quiz will be administered to the trio, and each member will receive an individual score. In addition, each group will receive a composite score composed of its members' scores. This will assist the Admissions Committee in making decisions.

Each group will be asked to make a presentation to the Admissions Committee explaining describing their particular aspect of Greek social history. You will be asked to analyze how your aspect of everyday life corresponds with the established view of Greek civilization. Explain how the description of everyday life does or does not correspond with your own assumptions about Greek society. To what extent does your knowledge of everyday life in Greek society help you to understand the society you live in today? Your presentation may include illustrations and first hand accounts as supplements.

In order to gain acceptance into the Academy, your group must satisfy the Admissions Committee's **Criteria for Success.** These are detailed below:

CRITERIA FOR SUCCESS

A) *DEGREE OF COLLABORATION*
B) *QUALITY OF COMPOSED MATERIAL*
C) *QUALITY OF PRESENTATION*

DEGREE OF COLLABORATION   40%

1) SHARED LEADERSHIP—Is everyone significantly involved in the activity?
2) USE OF CLASS TIME—Is class time used wisely or wasted?
3) COOPERATIVE SKILLS—Is each group demonstrating good collaborative skills?

QUALITY OF COMPOSED MATERIAL 30%

1) NEATNESS AND PUNCTUALITY—Is the composed material submitted neatly and on time, and in line with acceptable conventions?
2) ABILITY TO ADDRESS AND ANSWER QUESTION—Is the material organized and substantive?
3) DOCUMENTATION—Is the material appropriately documented?

QUALITY OF PRESENTATION   30%

1) EFFECTIVE COMMUNICATION OF CONCEPTS—Is the presentation creative and successful in its communication?
2) PARTICIPATION BY EVERYONE—Is the presentation clear evidence that all members are energetically involved?
3) ENHANCEMENTS—Is the presentation enhanced by audio/visual aids appropriate to the time and setting of the presentation? (using technology available in this time period—charts, oratory style, etc. are appropriate—PowerPoint Presentations are not).

We, the Masters of the Academy, wish to applaud beforehand your diligence and your energy as you embark on these tasks. Please feel free to use us as resources and expect that we will devote our energies into making this a successful enterprise. Alas, those who are incapable of meeting our **Criteria for Success** may still have an opportunity next year to redeem themselves. Until then, they may attempt to find employment in one of our local eateries where they will master the phrase, "Do you want fries with that?" Good luck, and may the trade winds be with you.

Masters of the Ancient Academy located at the Oracle at Pendtese

LIST OF GREEK MYTHS FOR STUDENTS TO INVESTIGATE
FOR *ACADEMY 1* ASSIGNMENT

All students will read Perseus

Perseus

1. Demeter
2. Prometheus and Io
3. Europa
4. Cupid and Psyche
5. Pyramus and Thisbe
6. Orpheus and Eurydice
7. Ceyx and Alcyone
8. Pygmalion and Galatea
9. Pegasus and Bellerophon
10. Phaethon
11. Baucis and Philemon

In addition, students will research aspects of "everyday" lives of the ancient Greeks. What their meals were like, what dinners were like, school, marriage, rituals, shopping, etc.

Beyond Infinity: The Greek Academy

Generic:

1) Ask the students either through class discussion or in groups to consider how their group functioned. What were the challenges and how did they overcome those challenges?
2) What could the group have done better?
3) What did the group excel at doing?
4) What did students learn about the subject matter (literary work, middle ages, time, interpersonal relations, etc.)?
5) What, if anything, did students learn about themselves, other people, life in general?
6) What questions do they have about themselves, other people, life in general?

Specific to the unit studied:

1) From what you learned about everyday Greek life, what essential values do you think the Greeks shared?
2) How do the Greek myths reflect those values?
3) Compare contemporary life in our society with what you learned about in Greek society. What similarities/differences exist?
4) If you were from an alien planet and studied everyday life in American society, what conclusions about our values would you draw?
5) What do the myths that we adhere to say about our values and beliefs?

The Greek Playoff

Teacher Notes—Greek Playoff

As one of the first projects of the school year, this project was effective in developing collaborative skills and understanding the strengths and weaknesses of students in the class. The class had already participated in several small group activities and read several short stories, myths and poems. The class had also read Plato's Apology (which related the trial of Socrates), and, of course, Antigone and Oedipus Rex. I left the entire list out of this project, assuming you would want to use your own works.

Projects which have, at their core, play-acting have a tendency to sort out multiple intelligences and multiple talents. Students volunteer to be actors/set designers/musicians/script writers, etc. But teachers should be careful not to "type-cast" student contributions. The student who enjoys the visual arts must also learn how to compose, and the script writer will benefit from presenting in public, either as an actor or narrator.

In the Greek Playoff, the element of competition is included. Competition, in many forms, plagues education. Class rankings, competing for grades, are not amenable to learning. But competition amongst groups can be helpful to enhance group identity and morale. The focus here should be on a competitive reward that is not high threat. Giving the best grade to the "best" group changes the entire tenure of the assignment, and not for the better. I have seen groups passionately and enthusiastically compete for a candy bar or a title printed up on certificates. **This is one of those areas in which student trust is so important. They have to know that the teacher's goal is true learning, and not the often arbitrary and meaningless letter grade ascribed to performance.** One year, I presented as the ultimate reward for a project well done, an oddly shaped box. Students were allowed to handle the box but not open it. Even though they were acutely aware of the rubric for the evaluation of their projects, the talk in class was about winning "the box." Inside the box was a Pez dispenser. The group that won was thrilled to win, and when the prize was displayed, the whole class laughed and enjoyed the spectacle.

A teacher can maximize the expectations of quality projects from a class but must also, ultimately, minimize the rewarding of grade. The best projects are those in which students participate because of personal pride and enthusiasm for the challenge presented.

A simple spreadsheet like the ones provided earlier is an good example of how to evaluate a project like the Greek Playoff. The major areas of evaluation are Greek Conventions, Greek Themes, and Creativity. You can easily adjust the titles of the columns to accommodate your own rubric. A small spreadsheet is included in this section.

Name_____

Period___ Date_____ Group #ID_____

GREEK

PLAYOFFS

In the fifth century B.C., at the Dionesyian four day festival, there were dramatic competitions. The best playwrights were chosen to present their work; awards were given, honors bestowed, reputations built, feta cheese wantonly consumed. Sophocles was a winner at these events, his Oedipus trilogy propelling him to stardom.

Your group's task is to take one of the literary works we have studied (see the instructor's list) and convert it to a short Greek-style drama. **You will not have a great deal of time to write, stage and rehearse your production**, so in the few days allotted to work on this assignment, every member of the group should be intensely engaged. The following rules must be observed (this is a competition, after all):

1) People off task for any reason will automatically cause points to be detracted from the group's competitive score.

2) The playlet must observe the conventions of Greek drama. Review *Antigone* or examine the editor's notes in the anthology preceding the play *Oedipus Rex*. This means dramatic dialogue, masks, chorus, etc.

3) The playlet should not be a simple reenactment of the literary selection. It should reflect a conventional Greek theme. For example, in Antigone, the myth of Oedipus and the fate of his family is used to demonstrate the conflict of divided loyalties, the consequences of hubris, and the tension between fate and free will. Your playlet likewise must demonstrate those values upheld in Greek society.

4) The playlet should be approximately 8 to 10 minutes long. Your group will be given a total of fifteen minutes to setup and enact the playlet. This means you only have five minutes to set

whatever you need to set up. Therefore your group needs to be organized. (this is a competition, after all)

5) A finished copy of the script, typed, must be presented to the instructor on the day of the presentation.

The Scoreboard

Points will be awarded (and thus grades achieved) according to the following criteria.

1) On task time   40 points. Each person caught off task subtracts three points for each infraction.

2) Greek conventions   20 points.

3) Greek themes   20 points.

4) Greek organization   10 points.

5) Greek script   10 points.

The group which achieves the highest point total wins recognition, awards and, perhaps, a lifetime's supply of feta cheese. Good luck.

Greek Playoff Evaluation Sheet

Greek Playoff

USE WITH SHEET 2, SHEET 3

PERIOD =	2		CRITERIA VALUES						
PROJECT POINTS =	50		100	20	30	30	20		0
GROUP	PROJECT	PERCENT	TOTAL	GROUP	Greek	Greek	Creativity		TEST
#1	POINTS	AGE	POINTS	WORK	Convent	Theme	of group		POINTS
	19	38%	38	18	20	0	0	0	0
Billy the Kid									
Capone, Al									
Tiny Tim									
>>>>>>>>>>>>>>	>>>>>	>>>>>	>>>>>	>>>>>	>>>>>	>>>>>	>>>>>>	>>>>>	>>>>>
GROUP	PROJECT	PERCENT	TOTAL	GROUP	Greek	Greek	Creativity		TEST
#2	POINTS	AGE	POINTS	WORK	QUALITY	QUALITY	of group		POINTS
	10	20%	20	20	0	0	0	0	0
>>>>>>>>>>>>>>	>>>>>	>>>>>	>>>>>	>>>>>	>>>>>	>>>>>	>>>>>>	>>>>>	>>>>>
GROUP	PROJECT	PERCENT	TOTAL	GROUP	Greek	Greek	Creativity		TEST
#3	POINTS	AGE	POINTS	WORK	QUALITY	QUALITY	of group		POINTS
	10	20%	20	20	0	0	0	0	0
>>>>>>>>>>>>>>	>>>>>	>>>>>	>>>>>	>>>>>	>>>>>	>>>>>	>>>>>>	>>>>>	>>>>>
GROUP	PROJECT	PERCENT	TOTAL	GROUP	Greek	Greek	Creativity		TEST
#4	POINTS	AGE	POINTS	WORK	QUALITY	QUALITY	of group		POINTS
	7.2	14%	14.4	14.4	0	0	0	0	0

EVALUATION SHEET FOR GRAMMAR CRITERIA

Greek Playoff

PERIOD = 2

GROUP #	TOT PTS	Greek Convent CIT	PAR A	#	TOT PTS	Greek Theme OR G	CRE A	AL L	TOT PTS	Creativity 10	20 EF F		TOT PTS			TOT PTS		
1	30	10	10	10	30	10	10	10	20	10	10		0			0		
	20	10	10		0				0				0			0		
2	30	10	10	10	30	10	10	10	20	10	10	0	0		0	0		0
	0				0				0				0			0		
3	30	10	10	10	30	10	10	10	20	10	10	0	0		0	0		0
	0				0				0				0			0		
4	30	10	10	10	30	10	10	10	20	10	10	0	0		0	0		0
	0				0				0				0			0		
5	30	10	10	10	30	10	10	10	20	10	10	0	0		0	0		0
	0				0				0				0			0		
6	30	10	10	10	30	10	10	10	20	10	10	0	0		0	0		0
	0				0				0				0			0		

Greek Playoff												
PERIOD =	**2**											
INDIVIDUAL PTS. =	**10**											

GROUP	PROJ PTS.	PER CENT	TOTAL PTS.	# IN GROUP	SESS #1	# IN GROUP	SESS #2	# IN GROUP	SESS #3	# IN GROUP	SESS #4	# IN GROUP
#1			10	4	10	4	0	4	0			
	9	90%	9		9							
Billy the Kid	9	90%	9		9							
Al Capone	9	90%	9		9							
Tiny Tim	9	90%	9		9							
	0	0%	0									
0	0	0%	0									
	36		40	40	36	0	0	0	0	0	0	0
>>>>>>>>>>>>>>>>>	>>>>	>>>>	>>>>	>>>>	>>>>	>>>>	>>>>	>>>>	>>>>	>>>>	>>>>	>>>>

GROUP	PROJ PTS.	PER CENT	TOTAL PTS.	# IN GROUP	SESS #1	# IN GROUP	SESS #2	# IN GROUP	SESS #3	# IN GROUP	SESS #4	# IN GROUP
#2			10	4	10	4	0	4	0			0
	10	100%	10		10							
	10	100%	10		10							
	10	100%	10		10							
	10	100%	10		10							
	0	0%	0									
	0	0%	0									
	40		40	40	40	0	0	0	0	0	0	0
>>>>>>>>>>>>>>>>>	>>>>	>>>>	>>>>	>>>>	>>>>	>>>>	>>>>	>>>>	>>>>	>>>>	>>>>	>>>>

GROUP	PROJ PTS.	PER CENT	TOTAL PTS.	# IN GROUP	SESS #1	# IN GROUP	SESS #2	# IN GROUP	SESS #3	# IN GROUP	SESS #4	# IN GROUP
#3			10	4	10	4	0	4	0			0
	10	100%	10		10							
	10	100%	10		10							
	10	100%	10		10							
	10	100%	10		10							
	0	0%	0									
	0	0%	0									
	40		40	40	40	0	0	0	0	0	0	0
>>>>>>>>>>>>>>>>>	>>>>	>>>>	>>>>	>>>>	>>>>	>>>>	>>>>	>>>>	>>>>	>>>>	>>>>	>>>>

GROUP	PROJ PTS.	PER CENT	TOTAL PTS.	# IN GROUP	SESS #1	# IN GROUP	SESS #2	# IN GROUP	SESS #3	# IN GROUP	SESS #4	# IN GROUP
#4			10	5	10	4	0	4	0			0
	9	90%	9		9							
	0	0%	0		0							
	9	90%	9		9							
	9	90%	9		9							
	9	90%	9		9							
	0	0%	0									

The Greek Playoff

Use this sheet for Individual Test Scores

Period =	2		Use this sheet for entering test data						
Mr. Maltese									
Individual Test Pts.	200		Highest Possible Individual Test Grade =					100	
Group Project Points	0								
GROUP	Percent	Adjusted	Test		# Test	Total Pts.	Total Pts. All	Adjusted	Average
#1	%	Points	Score		Takers	Possible	Takers	Grp. Pts.	Group
	90%	180		90	2	200	340	0	85
Billy the Kid	80%	160		80					
Al Capone	#VALUE!	#VALUE!							
Tiny Tim	#VALUE!	#VALUE!							
	#VALUE!	#VALUE!							
0	#VALUE!	#VALUE!							
>>>>>	>>>>>	>>>>>	>>>>>		>>>>>	>>>>>	>>>>>	>>>>>	>>>>>
GROUP	Percent	Adjusted	Test		# Test	Total Pts.	Total Pts. All	Adjusted	Average
#2	%	Points	Score		Takers	Possible	Takers	Grp. Pts.	Group
	90%	180		90	2	200	340	0	85
	80%	160		80					
	#VALUE!	#VALUE!							
	#VALUE!	#VALUE!							
	#VALUE!	#VALUE!							
	#VALUE!	#VALUE!							
>>>>>	>>>>>	>>>>>	>>>>>		>>>>>	>>>>>	>>>>>	>>>>>	>>>>>
GROUP	Percent	Adjusted	Test		# Test	Total Pts.	Total Pts. All	Adjusted	Average
#3	%	Points	Score		Takers	Possible	Takers	Grp. Pts.	Group
	90%	180		90	2	200	340	0	85
	80%	160		80					
	#VALUE!	#VALUE!							
	#VALUE!	#VALUE!							
	#VALUE!	#VALUE!							
	#VALUE!	#VALUE!							
>>>>>	>>>>>	>>>>>	>>>>>		>>>>>	>>>>>	>>>>>	>>>>>	>>>>>
GROUP	Percent	Adjusted	Test		# Test	Total Pts.	Total Pts. All	Adjusted	Average
#4	%	Points	Score		Takers	Possible	Takers	Grp. Pts.	Group
	90%	180		90	2	200	340	0	85
	80%	160		80					
	#VALUE!	#VALUE!							
	#VALUE!	#VALUE!							
	#VALUE!	#VALUE!							

Beyond Infinity: The Greek Playoff

1. Ask the students either through class discussion or in groups to consider how their group functioned. What were the challenges and how did they overcome those challenges?
2. What could the group have done better?
3. What did the group excel at doing?
4. What did students learn about the subject matter (literary work, middle ages, time, interpersonal relations, etc.)?
5. What, if anything, did students learn about themselves, other people, life in general?
6. What questions do they have about themselves, other people, life in general?

Specific to the unit studied:

1. Having produced, directed, and acted in a play, what distinctions can you make between drama and other forms of literature such as a short story or novel?
2. Would you consider "acting" to be an art form? If so, what are some of the characteristics or skills in the "art" of acting?
3. Why do most, if not all, modern plays NOT have a chorus?
4. The next time you attend a play, either at school, in the community, or on Broadway, what will you focus on in terms of the play itself?

Hard Times, The Musical

Teacher Notes—Hard Times, The Musical

One principle I tried to adhere to with every project involving literature was to have students revisit the text for meaning. The first time a student reads a work, he reads for understanding and some students make connections to other ideas, real world situations, personal experience as they read. Even for these students, revisiting the text to find new/additional meaning is a good strategy. Again, I reiterate the need to test students on a close reading of the book in order to prevent cheating by reading online synopses. A good way to test to see if students read the novel is to require them to read also one or two pieces of literary criticism and then develop test questions that involve both the literary criticism and the literary work. If you do that in the beginning of the year, students who want to achieve will tend to read the assignment. They will hate your "picky" quizzes. I knew other teachers who assigned a reading and did not test. (We are not testing here to see if students can fashion a theme…we are testing to see if they read the book). In talking with the students of those teachers, I learned that, as the year went on, fewer and fewer read the assignment. "Why bother? He's not holding us accountable for it, and we have other homework." English is not like other subjects. There are no Spark Notes for the chapter on "Your Friend the Vector" in the physics textbook.

This project is also high threat, and I was careful to choose those classes in which there was some element of trust to begin with. Singing in public, for most people, is not an easy thing to do. But this project worked out well in a number of ways. First, it bonded students closely. Since they all had to go through the ordeal of singing before the class (some actually enjoyed it), they faced future projects in the school year with greater confidence. They had survive boot camp, with all its rigors, and meeting the enemy in the days ahead could not be as difficult. And they would meet the enemy together. While examining the characters in the novel, in preparation for song lyrics, students seemed to better understand how characterization is developed. They also developed a better understanding of the plot and the novel's themes, and this was good preparation for closure activities.

As part of the project assignment, I issued playbills I created as examples. Of course, students immediately demanded that I sing the songs as they are required to do. Talk about high threat!! As fears slowly subsided in the course of working on the project, students focused on being "the best." Another example of competition among groups being okay as long as the winning stakes, like better grades, were not significant. With a class that you can sense as a group has some good trust and confidence going, try this project in the beginning of the year. Amazing how this will accelerate those collaborative skills for future projects.

Name_____

Prereading Guide

HARD TIMES--WHAT THE DICKENS?

    Hard Times by Charles Dickens is an interesting novel to explore on many levels. As a period piece it provides us with some insight into English society in the nineteenth century. As a philosophical treatise on economics and the class system, it encourages discussion and dispute. As a condemnation of the teaching methodologies of the time, the novel offers us the opportunity to question the structure of our own educational systems. With those themes in mind, here are some guidelines for reading the novel.

1) Read the novel, not the Cliff Notes. I consider Cliff Notes cheating. There won't be Cliff Notes for your college reading material, so you might as well get in the habit of reading and making meaning for yourself.

2) Take notes as you read. You must *study* the text, which essentially means you should interact with it in some way if it is to be a meaningful experience. Writing is a means of doing this. This novel is character intensive, so using a character matrix or character web is advantageous. Focus on relationships between characters and consider what characters may represent, thematically. Dickens gets a great deal of literary mileage out of the names he chooses for his characters. Take the time to examine the names and consider how the names Dickens chooses may provide insight into his characters.

3) Periodically (every chapter if you wish), write a brief plot summary to date. Dickens is fond of subplots, so you might use this strategy in order to develop some coherence in your reading.

4) Most of Dickens work was serialized. That is, he wrote for a periodical and each month or so a chapter of his novel was published. That is why his style seems episodic. The end of chapters causes us to wonder "What will happen next?" When Dickens' novel *The Curiosity Shop*, was being published over several issues, Americans received their copies of the magazine as they were delivered from England. Legend has it that Americans were lined up at the New York dock waiting for the ship with the next installment of the novel, and they were shouting up to the captain, "What happened to Little Nell?" Understanding this structure might help you to better understand the work as a whole.

5) Ask yourself questions. What is Dickens trying to say about the social issues of his day? What connections can you make between other literary works or to scientific or artistic events that may have influenced Dickens?

6) Give yourself plenty of time to do all of the above. You will be tested on a **close** reading of the novel. Read the novel, write about the novel, study the novel, and think about novel. This, if done correctly, needs more time than a few hours the night before the test. Good luck.

Name_____

Period_____ Group ID#_____

HARD TIMES, GOOD TIMES

THE REMAKE

Oh oh!! The Broadway premiere of the musical *Hard Times, Good Times* was not exactly a hit. Reviewers' commentaries were filled with such terms as "a bomb!!," "the worst show since *Beowulf--Part 64--The Geat Retreat*," "major minor," and "El Stinko." The critics focused basically on the musical's inability to capture the "essence and motivations of the characters." Another major area of criticism involved the show's lack of "thematic significance." In other words, none of the major themes of Dickens' novel were present in the Broadway "non-hit."

The producers of the show are now scouring the countryside for a new team of writers to "fix" the show. They want new music and new lyrics. Your group's task is to compete for the right to be this team of writers. Here is what you must do to succeed in this project:

1) Review the characters, plots and themes of *Hard Times*. Decide on five or six characters that you believe you could reveal through song.

2) Choose a **Broadway** show tune (or other tune only after seeking the approval of the instructor) for each character.

3) Write the lyrics to fit the tune. Make certain that the lyrics reveal the character and possesses some thematic implications. Prepare a playbill with an appropriate design and run off enough copies for everyone in class.

4) Prepare a presentation. Do not simply say, "Here's Bounderby's song." Set the stage. Tell the class at what point in the novel this should appear. Set the proper thematic and plot mood or tone.

Ideally your group should sing the songs. However, I do not expect adolescents to jump at this prospect. But think about other ways you can make the presentation besides just throwing the words at us. Perhaps you can make transparencies with the words and provide the musical background via instrument or tape. Karaoke anyone? If you are certain your colleagues in the class know the tune, you may ask them to sing along with you. (This is a good idea, but risky. They may either not know the tune or may not join in, and this would result in a rather lame presentation.) The presentation is your problem. I have enough difficulty dreaming up projects like this one. But seriously consider singing the tunes--no one is expecting a night at the Met.

The purpose of this assignment is multilayered. First I would like you to hone your collaborative skills. Second, I expect that you go back to the text and look further and deeper for meaning. A good knowledge of the text and the dynamics of character and theme should be evident in your presentation. Third I hope to provide a situation for you to demonstrate how deep and how swift flow your creative currents. To those ends I am evaluating this project according to the following criteria:

1) Collaborative efforts--division of labor equitably and use of class time

2) Textual knowledge and composition--extent to which the writing (lyrics) reveals the characters AND thematic implications.

3) Presentation--organization and creativity

Good luck. If the producers decide that your words and your dramatic savoir-faire are the best of the lot, you will be rewarded with fame, fortune, and a pretty good grade. I stand ready and willing to help you in any way possible.

Content for Hard Times Brochure

Page 1

Hard Times,

Good Times

The Musical based

On Dicken's Novel

Maltese Falcon Productions

The Greatest Broadway Hit Since
"Grendel Needs a Hand"

Pick Up Your Tickets

NOW!!

PAGE 2

ORDER NOW!!

People in the loop know that Dickens' marvelous work, *Hard Times,* is being made into a fantastic Broadway musical starring Danny Devito as that lovable Josiah Bounderby, Madonna as the alluring and ever obedient Louisa, Sylvester Stallone as the humble and luckless Tom, Ben Stein as the pedantic McChokaumchild, Fred Savage as the misguided Bitzer and Jenny McCarthy as Mrs. Sparsit. With a cast like this, how can the show miss?

Not only will the acting performances wow you, but the music itself will make you laugh and cry. Gilbert and Sullivan (Bernie Gilbert and Doug Sullivan, both winners of the prestigious 8th grade Creative Writing Awards) were brought in to write the lyrics to some fabulous music!!

Audiences will delight to
Bounderby's Braggadacio!

Sung to the tune of West Side Story's "I Feel Pretty."

I feel self-made,

I feel self made,

I feel self-made, and wealthy and proud.

I   I feel self-made

All Coketown should find me high-browed…

See that rich man in the mirror there…

See that pretty wife that I own.

Such a self-made man, such a wealthy man

Who from nothing I've grown.

PAGE 3

Or who will ever forget McChoakumchild's warm and cuddily address to his students?

Sung to the tune from *The King and I,* "Getting to Know You."

Getting to stuff you,

Getting to stuff you with info.

Getting to fill you,

Getting to fill you with facts.

Haven't you noticed

I'm so pedantic and boring…

Because of all the

Insipid and dull

Things I'm

Putting in your skull

Dayyyy byyyy Dayyyy!!!!

And you will warm to the Bitzer's Ballad of Lament

Sung to the tune of *The Wizard of Oz's* "If I Only Had a Brain."

There ain't no use denying

I've never took to crying

Or giving a loud scream...

A heart is just a pump

And to love's to be a chump,

I will never have a dream.

PAGE 4

With lyrics like that how can you afford to miss the greatest Broadway musical since *Billy Budd Learns to Hang Out.*? So run down to Tic-a-Tron or phone now (555-5559) and get your seats for the show that will take the theatre world by storm!!

HARD TIMES,

GOOD TIMES

Beyond Infinity: Hard Times, the Musical

1. Ask the students either through class discussion or in groups to consider how their group functioned. What were the challenges and how did they overcome those challenges?
2. What could the group have done better?
3. What did the group excel at doing?
4. What did students learn about the subject matter (literary work, middle ages, time, interpersonal relations, etc.)?
5. What, if anything, did students learn about themselves, other people, life in general?
6. What questions do they have about themselves, other people, life in general?

Specific to the unit studied:

1. In *Hard Times*, when Sleary the circus manager, says, "People must have their *fancy,*" he justifies the existence of the circus. Some people say the same thing about art. No matter what the social economic situation, people appreciate whatever art they have available. What do you think of that theory?
2. How does art fit into your lifestyle?
3. Part of the justification of capitalism is that a few make a great deal of money, and the majority make enough to subsist on.....the "trickle down effect." What is your opinion of this concept?
4. There is only so much wealth in the world. Is there any way to distribute that wealth fairly?
5. Someone theorized that everyone exploits everyone else. Your response to this notion?
6. To enjoy a musical, there must be a suspension of disbelief. Isn't this also true of some modern movies? How important is verisimilitude, realism in fiction, in the modern era, especially in cinema?

Holden, We Have a Problem

Teacher Notes: Holden, We Have a Problem

One of my major goals here was for students to develop a deeper understanding of characterization and style. To do this, a teacher often has to place the literary figure in a different context. This is where fantasy analogy (placing a real world person/situation in an other-worldly setting---If Abraham Lincoln were president today, what would he think about the Middle East?). I used this strategy numerous times in assigning term papers, and the amount of plagiarism was significantly curtailed.

I have thought about altering this project in several ways. First, the attached list of literary figures could be changed to authors (or mathematicians, scientists, famous people from history, artists, etc). In a humanities course, this is the direction I would go. Second, I might eliminate the other mission crew members. If Holden or Othello or Huckleberry or Hester Prynne were alone on the spacecraft, the diary/blog might be more interesting.

When I was Pennsylvania's Teacher of the Year, I was fortunate to spend some time at Space Camp in Huntsville, Alabama. We attended classes on space travel, hydroculture, navigation, etc. We also performed missions which emphasized collaboration. The experience was fantastic. The head of NASA education spoke to us about NASA's concerns that not enough young people were becoming engineers or entering the science fields. This, of course, was important to the Space Agency. If you are a teacher and would like to expand your students' interests in these areas, visit their website. http://www.nasa.gov/offices/education/ about/index.html There are resources here, and I am certain that if you contact them, they will respond. You might find materials you could use for this project.

One element that schools should value but usually do not is teacher collaboration. In American public schools, the school schedule is sacrosanct (unless there is standardized testing to be done or an impromptu assembly in the gym to honor the boys' Parcheesi team). Schedules should be modified to accommodate student learning, not the other way around. Optimally a science teacher would work with an English teacher for this project, but, in my case, I had to go it alone. Still, it worked.

Name_____

Group ID_____

"Holden, We Have a Problem"

The National Aeronautics Space Administration (NASA) always has difficulties in raising support for its Apollo program. People have seen astronauts land on the moon several times, and the shine has worn off. In order to rekindle interest, NASA has launched a new program—CAROM (Celebrity Astronauts Report On Moon). Literary figures are on invited to visit the moon. While these characters/writers frolic in weightlessness (actually, technically it is known as micro gravity), and walk on the moon and dine on liquid meatloaf, they file a diary/online blog with the public back on earth.

Your group will be assigned a literary figure. You are to create a diary/blog *from that character's perspective* that includes at least the following events:

1) Space launch
2) Travel time in the spacecraft including eating, dialoguing with crew members and other routine events
3) Walking on the moon
4) Seeing Earth from the moon
5) Return trip to Earth
6) A major malfunction (this malfunction must have be based in a real life possibility. Research on the Apollo missions will be necessary to accurately depict this malfunction.

You may add other events/observations to your diary/blog, but the six above must be included. Your diary/blog may be accompanied by pictures, drawings, video, etc. The group's grade will be determined by the following criteria:

1) Quality of the collaboration---all members must be engaged to more or less the same degree and leadership and responsibility must be shared
2) How the well the character's personality and world view are revealed through the diary/blog
3) Quality of the diary/blog entries. The character's vernacular and style are to be imitated here.
4) Organization of the group. A presentation to the class of your diary/blog should reveal organization and thought.
5) Depth of research, both on the literary figure and the Apollo missions.

Enhancements (pictures, videos, etc.) will contribute to the evaluation of the criteria above.

Divide up the research and the responsibilities and work together as a team. Good luck, and I hope all systems are GO!

"Holden, We Have a Problem"

List of Literary Characters

Your group will be assigned (or you will draw from a pool) one of the following literary characters for this project:

1) Holden Caulfield from *The Catcher in the Rye*
2) Hamlet from *Hamlet*
3) Huckleberry Finn from *The Adventures of Huckleberry Finn*
4) Jim from *The Adventures of Huckleberry Finn*
5) Elizabeth Bennet from *Pride and Prejudice*
6) Captain Ahab from *Moby Dick*
7) Blanche Dubois from *A Streetcar Named Desire*
8) Willy Loman from *Death of a Salesman*
9) Hester Prynne from *The Scarlet Letter*
10) Daisy Buchanan from *The Great Gatsby*
11) Lennie from *Of Mice and Men*
12) Walter Lee Younger from *A Raisin in the Sun*

Beyond Infinity: Holden, We Have a Problem

1. Ask the students either through class discussion or in groups to consider how their group functioned. What were the challenges and how did they overcome those challenges?
2. What could the group have done better?
3. What did the group excel at doing?
4. What did students learn about the subject matter (literary work, middle ages, time, interpersonal relations, etc.)?
5. What, if anything, did students learn about themselves, other people, life in general?
6. What questions do they have about themselves, other people, life in general?

Specific to the unit studied:

1. This project asked you to look at a situation from a certain perspective. How valuable is it in life to look at a problem or situation from other points of view? Can doing this paralyze someone from taking action?
2. Mr. Antolini, the English teacher in *The Catcher in the Rye*, tells Holden that an education "grows one's mind." What does that mean?
3. What does an "education" really mean?
4. Is there ever a time or a situation where you would prefer ignorance over being educated?
5. What, in your opinion, do non-educated people have in common?
6. What, in your opinion, do educated people have in common?
7. Are there things about becoming an adult that frighten you?
8. What things about childhood do you think you will miss when you become an adult?
9. What things about adulthood do you look forward to?
10. What is one major difference between childhood and adulthood?

Jay Gatsby and the Senior Prom

Teacher Notes—The Great Gatsby and the Senior Prom

This is not a project for the beginning of the school year. I choose the groups almost 95% of the time (see my section on collaborative learning). If I allowed students to choose their groups, they would choose to work with their friends, no matter their personal interests. People who advocate appealing to student interests as part of differentiated education seem to ignore this one fundamental concept—students will choose to work with friends over choosing a personal interest most of the time because of peer pressure. One student asked me to put her in a group rather than let her choose. "Mr. Maltese, Desdemona is my best best friend, but in class she wants to gossip instead of work and she pulls my grade down. Please put me in a group and don't tell Desdemona what I just told you." Later I heard the young lady tell Desdemona, "Yeah, I really wanted to be in your group, but Mr. M wouldn't let me. I begged him, but he was pretty mean." I do not mind being the fall guy and taking the pressure off my students in this situation. But if things break right and students develop some very good collaborative skills as well as the courage to choose a project based on interest, I will let them choose.

This project lends itself very nicely to Web 2.0 tools (even though I executed this project during the days of Web 1.0 tools (a chalkboard, chalk, and an overhead projector). Students can construct yearbooks pulling photos from online sources (please demand that they observe copyright laws), as well as making presentations and videos online.

The project "Cooking with Gatsby," in which students present a series of PBS style shows, emanated from an earlier project I conducted involving The Adventures of Huckleberry Finn. That class produced one of the most memorable student productions of my career. PBS had a number of cooking shows, and this was one of the shows the students chose to present (others included a film critic show featuring Huck and Jim, Sesame Street, Mr. Rogers, and Masterpiece Theatre). Cooking with Pap featured a sloppily dressed father of Huck preparing a chicken-in-sherry dish. The seemingly demure and rational Pap became less so as he progressively put more of the sherry into his mouth than into the chicken. Pap ended his show with a harangue against the government and Huck's education. The student pulled it off expertly, and captured the character quite well as well as making us all laugh.

The yearbook project, The West Egg Oracle, expanded exponentially. Students went back to the novel (an action I believe is a prime goal of any project) to find clues as to what to put under a character's picture, "most likely to succeed," clubs the characters belonged to, etc. Students asked if they could include advertisements, and I permitted it as long as they were within historical context.

The other choices appealed to other forms of intelligence, and one colleague liked the musical project so much she extrapolated it to be a major project for all her classes. In fact, one year she reserved the Audion, a small auditorium, and her classes performed the Gatsby musical for all the other English classes.

I met a young woman who had been in my class many years before. We talked about the usual things---her family, work, and the state of the world. She told me in the conversation that she remembers everything about The Great Gatsby because of this project (she chose the yearbook). You just never know where your teaching will take others.

Name_____

Group ID_____

THE GREAT GATSBY

OR

DAISY, TOM, NICK AND DR. T.J. ECKLEBERG ATTEND THE PROM

Your group may choose to complete one (1) of the following projects. Each student will receive two grades. The first grade will be an individual grade based on the input and effort of the student. Each student must produce physical evidence of his/her contribution to the group project. This evidence may take the form of play acting, scriptwriting, musical performance, artwork, etc. **This evidence must demonstrate 1) effort and 2) understanding of the material under study.** Minimal efforts and minimal understanding will be awarded extremely minimal grades.

The second grade will be a group grade based on the following criteria:

1) use of class time and demonstration of group skills--50%

2) understanding of material--themes and characters---20%

3) creativity (clever and not cute)   --10%

4) organization   --10%

5) group involvement (everyone involved equally   --10%

I stand ready and willing to assist you in any way. Good Luck!!

1) Cooking with Gatsby--Create a series of PBS shows that are manned by characters from the novel. Scripts must be written for each show (two or three shows would be fine), and each student must designate what scripts he/she has written. The shows must demonstrate understanding of the motivations and characteristics of the characters as well as the novel's major **themes**.

2) *The West Egg Oracle*--Create a high school yearbook that contains characters from the novel.   Each member of the group should be responsible for certain sections of the yearbook, and this authorship should be identified in the yearbook. The reader should gain insight into the characters and the major themes of the novel by examining the yearbook. What clubs would the owl-eyed man have joined? What captions would appear under Tom Buchanan's senior picture?

3) "MONEY TALKS--AND THERE IS A WHOLE LOT OF SILENCE AROUND HERE"--Conduct a survey on the myths and truths behind the ownership of wealth in the United States. Is it true that ten percent of the population owns ninety per cent of the wealth? Compile research to support your views, and credit authorship of different parts of this paper to different members of the group. This paper should be six (6) to ten (10) pages (typed, double spaced) long. The group will be asked to make a five to seven minute presentation of its findings to the class.

4) "Cole Porter, Eat Your Heart Out!!"--Compose a mini-musical based on the novel. Write the lyrics for songs that reveal either characters or themes of *The Great Gatsby*. You may use melodies from other musicals, but the words must give insight into the characters or major themes.   At least five songs should be composed and demonstrated for the class. When making the presentation, it would be advisable to set the scene for the various numbers. You may make a tape, (video or audio) or enact it live. Members should identify which songs they have contributed.

To the tune of *School Days* when Gatsby is appealing to Daisy to leave her husband.

Daisy, Daisy, give me your answer true,

I'm so crazy, oh for the love of you.

You told me you'd be my honey,

If only I had the money

Well now I am rich

So give Tom the ditch

And I can fulfill my dream with you.

Beyond Infinity: Jay Gatsby and the Senior Prom

1. Ask the students either through class discussion or in groups to consider how their group functioned. What were the challenges and how did they overcome those challenges?
2. What could the group have done better?
3. What did the group excel at doing?
4. What did students learn about the subject matter (literary work, middle ages, time, interpersonal relations, etc.)?
5. What, if anything, did students learn about themselves, other people, life in general?
6. What questions do they have about themselves, other people, life in general?

Specific to the unit studied:

1. In *The Great Gatsby*, Fitzgerald uses the geographical regions of the nation to symbolize past and present, the Midwest the idealized past and the East the corrupt present. Do we still make value judgments about people based on the regions they live in? If so, give examples.
2. To many, as time recedes, we tend to look at the past with "rose colored glasses." Why does that seem to be true?
3. Do you think that in the future you will look upon your childhood as a "golden time?" Why or why not?
4. A great deal of *The Great Gatsby* is devoted to what Fitzgerald considered the excessive materialism of the twenties. Within that regard, how similar do you believe contemporary society is? How different?
5. What value does economic wealth have in your life? Is there more than one way to be "rich?"
6. One theorist argues that an accumulation of things does not lead to happiness, but happy relationships do. What do you think about that theory?

Macbeth and Lord of the Flies
Free Will or Destiny?

Teacher Notes --Macbeth and Lord of the Flies

I created this project for a colleague and very good teacher, Mr. Jonathan Hunt.

Both Macbeth and The Lord of the Flies contain so much material for discussions of themes, that a teacher has to focus on two or three. For example, another project I developed for The Lord of the Flies asked students to consider Freud's id, ego, and superego in relation to the major characters---Jack, Ralph, and Piggy. When we read Macbeth later in the school year, several students opined that Freud's dynamic applied to Macbeth's decision making process— was his id (which tempted him to kill the king) in conflict with his superego (which stressed loyalty and honor)? Another theme that classes discussed in separate units on these literary works involved fate and free will. Does Macbeth really have any choice in his destiny? Likewise, Golding seems to be making the statement that the "beast" in us is stronger than our individual moral perogatives. Following a similar framework that shapes this project, a teacher can tailor his or her themes to fit the goals for the class.

This project is not a beginning-of-the-year project. It requires that students have had some experience in collaborative learning and that they have read the works.

Before starting, please review my notes on collaborative learning. Before attempting any collaborative project, students must learn the skills inherent in successful cooperation.

I Goals:

1) Students will improve the skill of comparison through comparing the characters and themes of Macbeth and The Lord of the Flies.

2) Students will improve the skill of analysis through a textual examination of both works.

3) Students will improve the skill of synthesis by composing and presenting a final produce which expresses their thoughts on certain themes.

4) Students will improve their collaborative skills by working together on a focused problem.

II Necessary Background:

Students should have read and discussed both Macbeth and Lord of the Flies, and the elements of plot, style and characterization should be delineated. I assume that some context for the students has been developed—a description of the Italian Renaissance in terms of its focus on social status and Shakespeare as a product of the later English Renaissance; Golding's war experience and his attempt, as most intellects of his time, to fathom the depth of depravity revealed by the Nazi concentration camps.

III Context:

If we want students to engage in high level thinking skills, we must create problems that force those skills to be exercised and developed. The final two activities in this project attempt to achieve those goals. The first activity is designed as a warm up both in terms of teaching students how to work in groups and to learn to make comparisons between literary works both in terms of theme and purpose.

I think that we notice a decided shift in art during the Renaissance, from a focus on man's relationship to a deity to man's relationship to his fellow man. Now that "Man is the measurement of all things," we cannot hang blame on God when things go wrong. With the central status of man comes enormous responsibility for his actions. The age-old question of whether or not Macbeth has a choice in his fate or if he is simply playing out the role the witches prescribe for him masks an even deeper question about human nature. Does Macbeth fulfill his destiny not because his doom is written in the stars but because human nature is inclined, as in Golding's The Lord of the Flies, to err on the side of self-destruction?

Golding's boyhood generation read Coral Island, a fantasy in which upright British boys are marooned on a desert island and are confronted with starvation, dangerous natural occurrences, and cannibals. Not only do the boys survive and are rescued, but they manage to convert the cannibals on the island to "British ways." Years later, as a navy lieutenant, Golding, upon discovering the magnitude of evil manifested by the Nazis, asked the question, "If British boys were, indeed, stranded on an island, would the scenario play out as it did in "Coral Island?" His answer to his own question is The Lord of the Flies.

IV "Malcolm's Not the Middle" Activity

This and the next activity have several purposes. The first is as a warm up for future collaboration. The second purpose is to make the students revisit the text for deeper meaning. The last reason for this assignment is to begin stretching their minds by asking them to make connections (a high level thinking activity.)

Divide the class into, hopefully six groups with a maximum of five students each. (See my notes on collaborative learning. Assign three groups the characters in Macbeth and the other three groups the characters in Lord of the Flies. The group members may decide which of the following characters each student is responsible for:

Macbeth	Lord of the Flies
Macbeth	Ralph
Lady Macbeth	Jack
Macduff	Piggy

Banquo   Simon

Malcolm   Roger

Distribute the "Malcolm's Not the Middle Individual Assignment" Activity to the students.

Collect the individual worksheets and grade them according to a rubric: 1) Textual Support 2)Degree of Intellectual Thought and Effort 3) On time task. Consult the "Instructions for Using the Group and Grade Assignment Sheet."

V "Maws and Kites" Group Assignment

Distribute the "Maws and Kites" group assignment. I would suggest using the Criteria for Success in this assignment as your rubric for grading the assignment. The focus for this assignment is developing collaborative skills, so I would observe the groups carefully and make certain that off time task by any student adversely affects the group. We are attempting to establish a group mindset, and, especially in the later projects, a "sink or swim together" attitude must be developed.

VI *Survivor—Island of Evil*

This assignment uses, loosely, the Survivor format, but the concept involves students collectively to discuss certain themes and to think.

Using the same groups, ask each group to complete the first activity "Survivor--Island of Evil 1". This is a group of challenges that they would design for a Survivor scenario involving the characters from both literary works. Collect the challenges (4 per group, around 24 challenges total). Choose the best six or seven challenges. Cutting or pasting from the student challenges, combine the challenges on the "Survivor—Island of Evil Deciding a Winner" table.

Assess their challenges based on the Criteria of Success issued to them with the assignment.

VII *Survivor—Island of Evil Deciding a Winner*

Ask each group to predict which team would win each challenge, giving reasons for their choices. Give groups time to complete their answers. How much time is up to you. Walk around the room making certain each team is on task.

Ask them to complete the other questions on that group assignment sheet.

Discuss these predictions and their reasons with the class.

This assignment requires the students to think about open ended questions. The questions guide their thinking, and require analysis and reasoning. Assess based on the quality of collaboration and the quality of their answers, especially the reasons given.

In discussing these answers allude to the similarities of Golding's view of human nature and Shakespeare's view of human nature. Discuss, also, the differences in their perspectives.

VIII *Evil Is As Evil Does*

This is a rather sophisticated project in that it calls upon students to translate their intellectual conclusions into another media. Non-verbal communication can be more precise than verbal communication, so students might find this assignment extremely challenging. Good. You can assess the project using the Criteria for Success outlined in the assignment.

IX *Follow Up*

This project has so many complex themes and implied philosophies that the direction you take after this has many avenues. I would certainly discuss the problems inherent in both non-verbal communication and collaborative learning. Both discussions ask students to be metacognitive about their work.

You can examine the politicizing of the word "evil" in modern venues. Discuss the terms "Evil Empire" and "Axis of Evil" that our political leaders have employed. Using the students' own conclusions about good and evil and human nature, ask them to think about the following: "Are the terrorists evil?" "Are we, the Americans, evil?" (we are constantly referred to as devils by several nations.

You can also explore freedom of choice. If we are basically evil by nature, what is government's responsibility in keeping that evil in check? In fact that question formed the basis in the difference in political mindsets between the former Soviet Union and the United States. The Soviet Union believed that people, left to their own devices, would "do evil," and therefore a demonstrative and omniscient government needed to keep those forces in check. The price the populace paid for secure streets was an oppressive police state. Western culture, especially the United States, seemed to favor the human nature-is-basically-good stance, and even though the crime rate may have risen above that of the Soviet Union, the allowance for good and evil to exist on a somewhat equal footing was preferable than Big Brother. In fact, the Patriot Act and the suspension of some civil liberties in our current political climate is a prime example of the conflict between trust in "good" and the fear of "evil."

Name_____

Macbeth and Lord of the Flies Project

Malcolm's Not the Middle Activity   Group ID#_____ Date:_____

Individual Assignment

"Malcolm's Not the Middle Activity"

Your instructor has assigned your group one literary work. If your group is assigned *Macbeth*, each group member should be assigned one (1) of the following characters: Macbeth, Lady Macbeth, Macduff, Banquo, or Malcolm. If your group is assigned *The Lord of the Flies*, each group member should be assigned one (1) of the following: Ralph, Jack, Piggy, Simon, Roger. No two students in the group should have the same character.

Working *alone* answer the following questions. For each question, you must supply an example from the text to support your choice. Your example may be a quote, a plot development, or a description. No answer will be accepted without support.

1) If your character attended a modern day university, what major would he/she pursue?

Major = _____

Textual Support_____

_____

_____

Page Number_____

2) If your character downloaded music to his/her music player, what music would he/she download (choose 2 pieces)?

Music = _____

Textual Support_____

_____

_____

Page Number_____

3) If your character attended a modern fast food restaurant, what fast food chain would he/she frequent?

Fast Food Franchise = _____

Textual Support_____

_____

_____

Page Number_____

4) If your character attended a modern day high school, what would be his/her primary extracurricular activity?

Extracurricular Activity= _____

Textual Support_____

_____

_____

Page Number_____

Name_____

Macbeth and Lord of the Flies Project

Maws and Kites Activity   Group ID#_____   Date:_____

Group Assignment

Maws and Kites

Group Assignment

Your instructor has assigned you a literary work and, hopefully, each of you has a greater understanding of the literary character you chose for the previous assignment. As a group, (staying in your assigned characters), you have decided to open a restaurant. You are asking your instructor to finance your restaurant, to provide the capital so you can open and maintain your business. Unfortunately, the other groupos I the class will also be asking the instructor for funding. Alas, your poor instructor can only back one group, so you are definitely in competition with the other groups. Working as a group, design your restaurant answering the following questions:

All answers should demonstrate a knowledge of your characters and creativity in applying that knowledge to the questions below.

1) Name of the restaurant   _____

2) You cannot afford a vast menu. Each of the items on the menu must somehow be connected to one of the assigned characters. You must include an appetizer, four entrees, and a dessert.

Type of Dish	Food	Name of Dish	Character Associated with Dish
Appetizer =			
Entrée =			
Entrée =			
Entrée =			
Entrée =			
Dessert =			

3) Provide two illustrations. The first must be of the front of the restaurant, and the second must be of the design of the interior (table arrangement, for example)

4) Provide a sample of non-lyrical music that will be the mood background for the restaurant.

5) Prepare a small presentation to the class, (and particularly to the instructor whose financial support you want!) that explains your restaurant—the name, dishes, illustrations, and music.

Criteria for Success:

Each member of your group will receive the same group grade for this activity. It is, therefore, in everyone's interest that all members are on task at all times and sharing responsibility.

You will be graded according to the following criteria:

1) Quality of the collaboration. Are all members on task at all times?

2) Shared responsibility.   Do all members have equaled workloads?

3) Quality of the textual reference. Do the answers to this assignment demonstrate a good knowledge of the characters and the literary work?

4) Creativity. Do the answers to this assignment demonstrate thought and effort?

5) Quality of the presentation. Is the presentation organized and effective?

I stand ready and willing to help you with this assignment.

Name_____

Macbeth and Lord of the Flies Project

Survivor—Island of Evil 1   Group ID#_____   Date:_____

Survivor—Island of Evil

The producers of a major network have hired your team to develop a series of challenges for the next series, Survivor—Island of Evil. The premise of this show is that two teams of characters from two literary works are on a deserted island in the Pacific engaged in a life and death struggle. The first team is composed of Macbeth, Lady Macbeth, Macduff, Banquo, and Malcolm. The second team is Ralph, Jack, Piggy, Simon and Roger.

Your group's task is to develop four challenges that will engage both teams in struggles that will winnow out the weak from the strong. Each challenge MUST involve both physical and mental components. In other words, the challenge cannot be won by brawn alone. The challenge must require some feat of intellect, including deceit or persuasion. Whichever team loses the challenge must vote one member off the island (and onto the rocks below!) Your group will receive a group grade predicated on the following criteria:

1) Quality of collaboration. Each group member is on task and involved in the assignment.

2) Quality of the challenges. Do the challenges fit the description provided above?

3) Response to assignment. Are the instructions below followed?

Directions:

Provide the instructor with your four challenges in a Microsoft Word file.

1) The word file must have your group number in its title. For example, "challenges group 2."

2) The challenges must be typed in Arial font, font size 9.

3) No automatic numbering

4) Group number and Period number must appear at the top of the document.

Name_____

Macbeth and Lord of the Flies Project

Survivor—Island of Evil Deciding   Group ID#_____ Date:_____

A Winner

Survivor—Island of Evil

Deciding a Winner

"There has to be evil so that good can prove its purity above it." Buddhist quote

As a group, answer the following questions.

1) Which group do you think will win the following challenges and why?

Challenge	Winner	Why

2) Which character on each team do you think will be the first to be eliminated and why?

*Macbeth*_____

Why?_____

*Lord of the Flies--*_____

Why?_____

3) Which character on each team do you think will be the first to betray his/her own team and defect to the other team?

*Macbeth*_____

Why?_____

*Lord of the Flies--*_____

Why?_____

4) What strengths/weaknesses does each team have?

　　　　　Strengths Macbeth　　　　　　　　Weaknesses Macbeth

　　a) _____　　　　a)_____

　　b) _____　　　　b)_____

　　c)_____　　　　c)_____

　　　　　Strengths Lord of the Flies　　　　Weaknesses Lord of the Flies

　　a) _____　　　　a)_____

　　b) _____　　　　b)_____

　　c)_____　　　　c)_____

5) Which team do you think would ultimately win the Survivor—Island of Evil contest?

_____

Why?_____

_____

6) Which character will ultimately win the Survivor—Island of Evil contest?

Why?_____

_____

7) In *Lord of the Flies*, the boys created a chant—"Kill the pig, slit its throat, drink its blood." Develop a chant for *Macbeth*'s team, keeping in mind Renaissance language and style.

Chant_____

_____

8) If your group were on the island, which member would you want to lead you and why?

Member_____

Why?_____

_____

Name_____

Macbeth and Lord of the Flies Project

"Evil is as Evil Does"   Group ID#_____ Date:_____

"Evil Is As Evil Does"

"All that is necessary for evil to succeed is that good men do nothing."

Edmund Burke

Are human beings basically good or are they basically evil? If basically good, then what makes some people "go bad?" If basically evil, then how do some people rise above their nature? If people are neither basically good nor basically evil, then what is responsible for "evil acts.?" These are the questions you are to explore in the following assignment.

Your group's task is to present a pantomime based on a morality play, "The Conflict of Good and Evil." Think about good and evil and human nature. Develop a skit of about five minutes that dramatizes your collective thoughts on the existence of good and evil. For example, you may act out the life of a typical human being, from birth to death, and his/her struggle with the forces of good and evil, the rewards and temptations that all of us experience. This is a very creative assignment, and you have a great deal of latitude, but you must include the following elements:

1) Masks. The easy thing to do is to draw a mask with horns and colored red to represent evil, but that is too simplistic. What is the face of evil in the modern day? What does "good" really look like? How can we recognize either? Give some serious thought to your masks.

2) Mood music. Choose music to accompany the appearance of good and the appearance of evil in your pantomime. The same music may accompany the entire production, or you may have different music for different stages of your playlet. The music *must be non-lyrical. That is, the music must have no words.* We want the mood to be generated not by verbalizing but by the music itself.

3) Pantomime. Body language is very exact. Plan your gestures and movements carefully.

4) Other visual enhancements. You may include backgrounds or posters or any other visual that contributes to the enrichment of your production.

This assignment will be assessed according to the following criteria:

1) Quality of the collaboration. Are all students within a group on task all the time?

2) Quality of the production. Does the production demonstrate depth of thought and creativity?

3) Quality of organization. Does the production seem smooth and well-planned?

3) Quality of the enhancements. Do the masks, visuals, and music contribute greatly to the production?

Brainstorm, plan, organize, divide up the work, and rehearse. I stand ready and willing to assist you in this enterprise.

Beyond Infinity: Macbeth and Lord of the Flies

1) Ask the students either through class discussion or in groups to consider how their group functioned. What were the challenges and how did they overcome those challenges?
2) What could the group have done better?
3) What did the group excel at doing?
4) What did students learn about the subject matter (literary work, middle ages, time, interpersonal relations, etc.)?
5) What, if anything, did students learn about themselves, other people, life in general?
6) What questions do they have about themselves, other people, life in general?

Specific to the unit studied:

1) Did Macbeth really have a choice, or was he simply playing out the role fate created for him?
2) Some researchers who study the cognitive sciences believe that there is no such thing as free will. Our brains, shaped by genetics and environment, dictate our actions. Do you believe you have free will or are you shaped by destiny?
3) Do good and evil exist, or are they figments of our collective imaginations?
4) What separates "being civilized" from "not being civilized?"
5) Is there such a thing as "mob thought," as in Jack's tribe in the novel?
6) When is ambition a good thing? A bad thing?
7) Macbeth thinks that one action (in this case a murder) leads to other actions. The law says that if we plot to commit a crime, such as robbery, and from that crime another occurs, such as a murder, we are equally guilty of that crime. How many times in your life can you recall one action leading to another one that you did not expect?
8) What does the concept of civilization offer? Why would anyone want to be "civilized?"
9) If law did not exist, along with its consequences, would people be mostly barbaric?
10) Do you agree with the romantic notion, that people are basically good, or with the non-romantic notion, that people are fundamentally bad?

Medieval Madness

Teacher Notes-- Medieval Madness

Remember the old adage, "We remember 90% of what we teach?" This project is a perfect example. The difficulty for the teacher here is to maintain the student focus on the intellectualism of the assignment, instead of students falling prey to being cute with the delivery methods. The media, in this case, is decidedly NOT the message. The rubric at the end is deliberately generic so that you can tailor it to your needs.

I begin small group activities at the very beginning of the school year. After assigning and quizzing students on a reading assignment, I ask them to complete a response sheet (some would use the term "worksheet" here, but worksheet implies a busy work activity. My response sheets ask questions that begin with simple feedback information on the content of the reading and end with open ended questions about philosophical issues). I collect the response sheets (individual accountability), break the class into groups and then give the same response sheet for the group to collectively respond to. In this way, students cannot piggy back on the work of others (having turned in their own individual response sheets), and their minds are already setup to discuss the questions with the group.

I evaluate the functioning of the group (see my notes on collaborative learning), and groups choose a members to present their answers to the class at large. These small group activities are sometimes just fanciful ("what cartoon characters do you think best represent the characters in the story" or "what contemporary actors/actresses would you assign to play the part of ....and why?") to more probing questions. The real purpose is to have students develop those necessary collaborative skills for group projects.

Medieval Madness is a small project I used as an introduction to Chaucer and "Sir Gawain and the Green Knight." I found that if I provided reliable resources(and required they use these resources) instead of students choosing the easiest sources for background on the medieval period, I accomplished two things. First, I made certain that they interacted with acceptable academic research, and, second, I eliminated cutting and pasting (see the paragraph referring to the paper).

This is not a high level thinking project. It requires students to collect information and package it in some way without really transforming it. Asking them to develop a small quiz for the class can become a minutiae fest, so some guidance is necessary in helping them develop appropriate questions.

This is one of those projects that can easily become cross disciplinary. A science teacher may require that students examine areas in medieval science—what did the medieval mind know of biology, physics, chemistry? Alchemy? Astronomy? An area of focus could be scientists or mathematicians of the period, from Galen to Kepler. Art teachers may confine research areas to artists and art techniques. Where and how did western artists learn perspective?

Teachers can likewise duplicate the process of this project to accommodate different time periods.

Name_____

Group Id_____ Date Due_____

MEDIEVAL MADNESS

The purpose of this assignment is to help you develop certain skills and to learn specific content involving the period of human history known as the *medieval period* or the *middle ages* or the **dark ages**. The skills that you are expected to develop and refine are collaborative skills, research skills, and synthesizing skills. Please read these instructions carefully because they will provide the criteria for your success on this project.

Were the middle ages really the dark ages, and, if so, what does that mean? What was life like back then? Do we have a stereotypical (and incorrect) view of that time period? What similarities may exist between the medieval period and our own? In what ways is studying the middle ages equivalent to studying an alien culture?

You will be assigned to a group to investigate these and other questions. Each group will have an area of expertise, and within that area members of the group will be assigned the task of becoming experts on subtopics related to that area. After the group has collected and processed the information, each group will teach the class about their respective area. Each group will also submit a paper which documents what they have learned about their specific content area. All areas apply to the time period from approximately 800 A.D. to 1450 A.D. in Europe.

1) The world of **Warfare**--the group assigned to this area should investigate the following:

How was warfare conducted in the Middle Ages? What major wars and battles occurred, and who were the major participants? How did the results of these conflicts change Europe? What weaponry existed? What were the tactics? What happened to the losers? How did kings raise armies? Who treated the wounded? What kind of training did soldiers get? These are just some examples of subtopics you might explore.

2) The world of **Science**--the group assigned to this area should investigate the following:

What role did astrology play in this time period? What was the basis of astrology and what force did it possess in shaping the views of the people? What was the nature of medicine? What kind of training did doctors possess? What were some medical theories? How did people navigate their ships? What were the major means of transportation, and how did these means of travel affect how people viewed the world? What did maps of the world look like? What was the basis of knowledge? How important were facts?

3) The world of **Work**--the group assigned to this area should investigate the following:

What jobs existed, and how did people train for those jobs? What was the educational structure like? What were schools like? How was business transacted? What kind of fees did people charge? In an average village how did most people make their livings, and what was a typical day like?

4) The world of **Justice**--the group assigned to this area should investigate the following: How was the justice system structured in medieval times? What laws existed that we might find strange today? How were trials conducted and juries chosen? What kinds of punishment existed and for what offenses? How was the law made known to the general population? Who were the law enforcers?

5) The world of **Religion**--the group assigned to this area should investigate the following: Religion played a major role in the Middle Ages. What effect, if any, did religion play in the everyday life of an average human being? How religious were most people? What kind of holidays existed that some people still observe today? In what ways are those same holidays similar to and different from our own? Did religion have a more or less separate government from the eccliasiastial government? How did people of the most populous religion treat people who worshipped different religions? What were the Crusades all about?

6) The world of **Art**--the group assigned to this area should investigate the following:

Who built the famous medieval cathedrals and why? What are some of the difficulties faced by the builders? What difference in religious attitude is reflected in the different architectural styles? What was the purpose of painting? What were the usual subjects for painting and why? What music was popular? What crafts were valued by the populace?

7) The world of **Everyday life**--the group assigned to this area should investigate the following: What were the demographics of the day (look up the word demographics). How long did people live? Why did people marry and what was expected of the spouses? How were children viewed by parents? What kind of food did people subsist on and what kind of habitat did they live in? What was the center of the community, spiritually and physically? How important was keeping track of time? What pasttimes did they enjoy, if any? What did these people do for recreation? What were weddings and funerals like?

8) The world of **Women**--the group assigned to this area should investigate the following: What choices did most women have in the medieval period? If unmarried, what did they do? If married, what was life like? What rights did they have, if any?

9) The world of the **Bubonic Plague**--the group assigned to this area should investigate the following: How did the plague start? How did medical people and others try to deal with the plague? What were the results of the plague on the history of Europe, economically, politically and socially? How did the plague die out?

10) The world of **Hundred Years War**--the group assigned to this area should investigate the following: How did the war start? Who were the participants? What were the major battles and who won them? How did this war affect the social fabric of European society?

When each member of your group has finished collecting and processing information, your group is responsible for the completing of three (3) assignments. The three assignments are 1) writing a collaborative paper, 2) preparing a lesson which teaches the rest of your class your area of expertise, and 3) a test on your subject area.

The Paper

Your group should compose a collaborative paper that explains the most important aspects of your research area. Each member is to write a section of the paper (make certain each member identifies the section that he/she wrote). Here are some do's and don'ts. **Do** proofread each other's material. **Do** type the paper (there are facilities in the school for this. **Do** document your resources. **Do** make certain the paper is well-researched, error-free and neat. **Don't** let one person write the paper. No one will receive any credit, including that one person. **Don't** simply copy whole excerpts from resources. You must summarize articles and write the paper in your own words. You will receive no credit for simply cutting and pasting. **Don't** turn in handwritten copy. Your paper will be evaluated based on these criteria.

The Lesson Plan

Your group should prepare a fifteen minute lesson for the class. You may choose any teaching approach you like (lecture, question and answers, Powerpoint presentation, etc.). Do not simply read your information to the class. This is very boring. Your presentation will be evaluated according to the following criteria: The quality of the information presented, the depth of research, the effectiveness of the presentation.

The Area Test

Your group is to prepare a twenty question test for the class on your area of expertise. The test should be "fill-in the blank" format. These questions should come from your presentation. These questions will be evaluated on the following criteria: quality of the questions (questions should be fair but challenging), grammatically correct, and neatly typed. Place the group id on top of the page and prove the instructor with the correct answers.

This assignment is wide and scope and demands organization and cooperation amongst group members. This is a sink or swim project in that all members of a group will succeed or fail together. A member who is uninvolved or who wastes class time will bring down the grade of everyone else in the group. There is enough work here for everyone. If the group claims it is finished then it will be asked to immediately present the assignment to the class. I stand ready and willing to assist everyone on this project. Please do not be afraid to ask.

Group Id_____

EVALUATION SHEET FOR MEDIEVAL PROJECT

GROUP MEMBERS:

1)_____   4)_____

2)_____   5)_____

3)_____   Area of Expertise_____

THE PAPER

CRITERIA	MOST POINTS	POINTS EARNED
DEPTH OF RESEARCH/ DOCUMENTATION	25	_____
HONESTY	25	_____
GRAMMAR/SPELLING	25	_____
NEATNESS	25	_____
TOTAL		_____

THE PRESENTATION

CRITERIA	MOST POINTS	POINTS EARNED
QUALITY OF INFORMATION	50	_____
DEPTH OF RESEARCH	25	_____
EFFECTIVENESS OF PRESENTATION	25	_____
TOTAL		_____

THE TEST

CRITERIA	MOST POINTS	POINTS EARNED
QUALITY OF QUESTIONS	50	_____
GRAMMAR/SPELLING	25	_____
NEATNESS	25	_____
TOTAL		_____

Beyond Infinity: Medieval Madness

1) Ask the students either through class discussion or in groups to consider how their group functioned. What were the challenges and how did they overcome those challenges?
2) What could the group have done better?
3) What did the group excel at doing?
4) What did students learn about the subject matter (literary work, middle ages, time, interpersonal relations, etc.)?
5) What, if anything, did students learn about themselves, other people, life in general?
6) What questions do they have about themselves, other people, life in general?

Specific to the unit studied:

1) What similarities do you see between the Medieval Period and modern times?
2) What major differences do you see between the Medieval Period and modern times?
3) How does a time period or era, like the Medieval Period, get its name? Certainly, the ancient Greeks did not walk around saying, "Hey, we are the ancient Greeks...wish we were modern."
4) Does every time period, including our own, think it is modern? If so, can we ever learn from history?
5) Imagine that you are an historian from the 25th century. What name would you apply to our time period and why?
6) When future archeologists excavate from our time period, what structures do you think they will discover, and what conclusions will they draw from these discoveries?
7) What value, if any, does "newness" have?
8) Is a new work of art superior to an old work of art?

Metaphors: Damarrk at Tanaga

Teacher Notes—Damarrk at Tanaga

I believe that our behavior is dictated by our perceptions (perceptions from the unconscious as well as the conscious), and our perceptions are often shaped by the metaphors we have developed. George Carlin, the comedian, once explained the difference between baseball and football by the terms they used. In football, the more violent sport, we wear a helmet. In baseball, the national "pastime," we wear a cap. In football we play in a stadium (remembrances of the gladiatorial days); in baseball we play in a park. In football we have a "blitz, throw the bomb, play smashmouth ball;" in baseball we strive for a "walk, try to be safe, and run home." Leaders of nations at war spend considerable resources developing metaphors for the enemy, demonizing him, as part of the propaganda machine. In short, the metaphors we use for ourselves and for other people are extremely important. Are teachers assembly line workers, stuffing students with information, or are we creative thinkers who help students create knowledge?

Before beginning this project, I spent time in class helping my students understand the power of metaphors. I drew heavily on the ideas in Metaphors We Live by George Lakoff and Mark Johnson. One lesson involved a discussion of time. In modern American culture, we see time as a commodity. I asked students to come to the board and write down sayings that use time.

"I haven't enough time."

"You are wasting time."

"We are out of time."

"I've invested a great deal of time in that project."

After students write these on the board, I ask them to impose a pattern. They usually come up with the notion that time is a commodity. I then ask them to consider that other cultures do not see time as a commodity....that some other cultures (including some Native American cultures) would not understand the phrase "I was having so much fun I lost track of time." In one class we came to the conclusion that, in 19th century America, land was the overarching commodity, but in the twentieth century, the major currency is time.

There is a wonderful episode of the Star Trek: Next Generation series entitled "Damarrk at Tanaga." In this episode, Captain Picard and an alien are beamed to a planet (ultimately to forge a friendship which they do by combatting a common enemy). Picard is frustrated by his inability to communicate with the alien until he learns that the alien only speaks in metaphors. Picard tells his counterpart the story of Gilgamesh, and this begins the necessary communication. Even though Picard understands the alien's articulation process (only speaking in metaphors), he realizes that without the underlying code, this communication only goes so far. For example, if I met a foreigner and wanted to know if he was trustworthy, asking him with arms outstretched, "Washington and the cherry tree?" would only get a puzzled look in return.

I show this episode to the class before beginning the project, and we discuss how many metaphors we use in everyday life, even though we have no real experience with the metaphor itself. For example, I never saw a "bat out of hell," and do not know if bats fly faster than other animals. However, if I tried to convey speed to a modern audience, saying, "He was as fast as a gerbil out of hell!" would get me those funny looks.

Students found this project to be fun, and, for some of them, they learned from this unit to look at the language we all use somewhat differently.

Name_____

Period_____ Group ID_____

EDMUND HILLARY AND TENZING NORGAY

CLIMBING EVEREST

Human beings in almost all cultures have a penchant for metaphors. Some philosophers might argue that the most important ideas and concepts central to the human condition are best expressed through metaphor (Hello, Shakespeare!). Others like your English teacher will postulate that life without metaphors is appallingly dull. Imagine broadcasting a sporting event without metaphors.

Your group's task is to create a set of metaphors that can represent some fundamental concepts and ideas. These metaphors must be predicated on historical events. Of the ten metaphors you must compose, three may come from the twenty first century, three from the twentieth, three from 1 AD to the end of the nineteenth century, and three from the Hellenistic and/or Roman period.

For example, Crockett at the Alamo has the connotation of self-sacrifice and the commitment to die for a belief as does the Spartans at Thermopylae.

Americans at Pearl Harbor represents surprise and the need to be alert to deceit and chicanery as does 9/11.

Burnside at Fredericksburg may be used to signify a bad decision, particularly a bad military decision.

Charles Lindbergh Crossing the Atlantic represents the human courage and human skill to "push the envelope."

The Challenger Disaster is associated with national tragedy.

The Armistice of 1918 symbolizes relief from war the restoration of world peace, etc.

On a given day you will be given a scenario or situation in which you must converse in only the metaphors provided. Best performance wins academic honors.

Concepts and ideas you might wish to represent:

COURAGE:

METAPHOR:_____

_____

COWARDICE:

METAPHOR:_____

_____

JOY/TRIUMPH:

METAPHOR:_____

_____

DISASTER/DEFEAT:

METAPHOR:_____

_____

SADNESS:

METAPHOR:_____

_____

DEATH:

METAPHOR:_____

_____

IGNORANCE:

METAPHOR:_____

_____

INTELLIGENCE:

METAPHOR:_____

_____

FRIENDSHIP:

METAPHOR:_____

_____

GOOD:

METAPHOR:_____

_____

EVIL:

METAPHOR:_____

_____

SURPRISE:

METAPHOR:_____

_____

Metaphors Damarrk at Tanaga

Scenarios and Situations

When the groups complete their metaphors, give them some time to memorize these metaphors. Then ask each group to stand before the class and engage in a conversation, using only the metaphors they created, within these scenarios and situations.

Your group:

1) is the crew of Apollo 13 when you discover a major mechanical problem with your spacecraft. You are in contact with Command Control in Houston.
2) is broadcasting an exciting football game on Monday Night Football.
3) is opening presents during a holiday event.
4) is on a life raft when a storm appears on the horizon.
5) is on the lunch line in the school cafeteria.
6) is at a car wash for a school fund raising activity.
7) Is confronted by some school bullies
8) Is caught in your backyard when a tornado approaches
9) Is conversing in a cabinet meeting with the President of the United States as he decides what to do about a report that nuclear missiles are heading toward the U.S.
10) finds a mailbag filled with money that has obviously been stolen
11) is a group of passengers on the Titanic waiting for the life boats
12) is on a roller coaster in an amusement park

Beyond Infinity: Metaphors: Damarrk at Tanaga

1) Ask the students either through class discussion or in groups to consider how their group functioned. What were the challenges and how did they overcome those challenges?
2) What could the group have done better?
3) What did the group excel at doing?
4) What did students learn about the subject matter (literary work, middle ages, time, interpersonal relations, etc.)?
5) What, if anything, did students learn about themselves, other people, life in general?
6) What questions do they have about themselves, other people, life in general?

Specific to the unit studied:

1) What would life be like without figures of speech?
2) Do the words and phrases we use shape our reality, or does reality shape the words and phrases we use or both?
3) The philosopher Kant argued that all reality is subjective. Do you agree or disagree with Kant's view?
4) What are the benefits of Kant's view and what are the consequences of believing that all reality is subjective?
5) Suppose there were no such things as metaphors. Would communication be more effective or less effective? Why?
6) Develop your own metaphor for a metaphor.

Metaphors: Atom Smashing

Teacher Notes---Atom Smashing

Please see the Teacher Notes for Damarrk at Tanaga.

John Donne, the poet, was more or less the ringleader of the Metaphysical Poets who seemed to get their thrills by atom smashing. They found metaphors that were not conventional, smashing two apparently dissimilar things together. For example, while many poets compared their lovers to roses or perfumes or celestial bodies, John Donne compares his lover to fish bait. Good metaphors change the way we see both elements of comparison. A college professor once brought in a bucket of frogs to biology class. We stood around the bucket, searching for the appropriate metaphors (although we were not consciously seeking "metaphors") to describe the frogs. "They look like lime jello." "Blob slime." Finally one student said, "Pickles. They look like dark green pickles with bumps." The next day several of us were in a deli, at the cash register, when we noticed a jar of dark green pickles. Of course, we thought of frogs. I cannot look at the moon on a semi-cloudy night without thinking of a galleon because of Alfred Noyes' poem Highwayman. "The moon was a ghostly galleon tossed upon cloudy seas." And when I see a ship on the blue, even though it is not a galleon, I think of the moon. Such is the power of really good metaphors.

In teaching a class of desperate young people, most of whom had been battered by societal misfortunes, I asked them to write metaphors for different things. I was sorry I did so. In reading the metaphors, I received an even truer picture of the lives of these students. The one I remember most vividly is the metaphor one student wrote for a human being: "A human being is like an alkaline battery. Other people use up all the energy and, when they are finished, they throw it away in the garbage." The metaphors we use often reveal who we are and how we see the cosmos, and to communicate that concept, I created this project. It only took two or three days, but the yield was, in my opinion, very high.

This project requires some security issues on the part of the teacher. In my roll book, next to each student's name, I assigned an alphanumeric code. I then asked the students to put this assigned code for each of them in the blank labeled identity. I then drove home the point that they were NOT to share who wrote what. I gave them at least one class period to work on their metaphors. They then turned their metaphors in to me. It is very important that students NOT know that the metaphors they devise will reveal their personality traits, so, as the instructor, you must devise another reason…."we are learning about the power of metaphor, and how to contruct meaningful ones." I usually preface the first handout, Atom Smashing 1, by saying "The best way to complete this assignment is not to find the "right" answer but the "honest" answer. Go with your feelings."

Two days later, I redistributed the lists of metaphors to students in the class making certain that a student did not receive his/her own list. I then distributed Atom Smashing 2. When the class was finished, I collected the lists and gave them and the interpretations (Atom Smashing

2) back to the students who created the lists of metaphors. I gave them some time to look at the interpretations. Every time I issued this project, students were amazed how much of their personal identities was revealed by the metaphors they used.

You can follow this up in a number of ways. My favorite way was to begin a unit on propaganda and the metaphors nations use to wage war. Or we compared metaphors used in everyday life from the past to those we use today, and then drew conclusions about the differences in the two cultures. I included the Metaphor Plan to demonstrate how to begin some discussions about metaphors.

A few scientists (and science teachers) are smug in the belief that science is always predicated on nothing but the facts. The truth is that science is affected by cultural mindsets as well.....and those mindsets are often expressed in metaphor. Aristotle has his "heavenly spheres." Newton described the universe as a mechanical clock, and modern scientists use the metaphor of the "big bang" to express their beliefs in the mechanics of the universe. I think it would be a good idea if all subject areas devoted some time to an examination of the metaphors that are used in their fields. Metaphors express those apparent truths that the facts cannot provide us with.

PLAN FOR A UNIT ON METAPHORS

A great deal of the information in this planning is from *Metaphors We Live By,* by George Lakoff and Mark Johnson.

What I want them to learn:

The power of metaphor and, correspondingly, the power of language.

That our actions are predicated on what we conceive, and what we conceive is based largely on the metaphors we use.

Pre-activities activities—Goal—Get them to think about metaphors, well, metaphorically.

Begin by telling students that metaphors are more than simply figures of speech.

The essence of metaphor is understanding and experiencing one kind of thing in terms of another. Metaphors We Live By

page 8—of Metaphors We Live By—ask students to go to the board and write the many phrases they have heard about time. "We do not have enough time," "How we spend our time." TIME as a commodity, a resource. This is sort of weird when one thinks about it. Other cultures do not see TIME as a commodity, and the statement "We were having so much fun that we did not know where the time went." would have no meaning. Japan, for example, sees space, a limited commodity, as more significant than time.

page 11-same concept applied to language—"He put ideas into his paper." (ideas as carrier or container)—"He carried this idea with him for his entire life."

page 15—Orientational metaphors—Up is good, down is bad.
    I will look you up.
    I will call you up.
    Things are looking up.
    Get up. Wake up.
    The peak of the mountain.
    He's in top shape.
    He rose to the top of his profession
    He fell asleep.
    He's under hypnosis.
    He sank into a coma.
    He came down with the flu.
    He dropped dead.
page 4--ask the students to come up with metaphors for an argument as a war—opposing sides
    Your claims are indefensible.
    He attacked every weak point in my argument.

His criticisms were right on target.
I demolished his argument.
I've ever won an argument with him.
You disagree? Okay, shoot!
If you use that strategy, he'll wipe you out.
He shot down all of my arguments.

SAT's preparation has very little to do with learning anything and everything to do with beating the game. Then, again, taking the SAT's have very little to do with learning anything.

Page 163—Truth is dependent, in large part, on our cultural understanding of a word.

I've invited a sexy blonde to our diner party.
I've invited a renowned cellist to our dinner party.
I've invited a Marxist to our dinner party.
I've invited a lesbian to our dinner party.

Of course, the dinner guest could be all of the above.

Page 165—As opposed to what the objectivists might argue, "there are many celebrated examples to show that sentences, in general, are not true or false dependent of human purposes:

France is hexagonal.
Missouri is a parallelogram.
The earth is a sphere.
Italy is boot-shaped.
An atom is a tiny solar system with the nucleus at the center and electrons whirling around it.
Light consists of particles.
Light consists of waves.

"Each of these sentences is true for certain purposes, in certain respects, and in certain contexts. 'France is a hexagon' and 'Missouri is a parallelogram' can be brue for a schoolboy who has to draw rough maps but not for professional cartographers. 'The earth is a sphere' is true as far as most of us are concerned, but it won't do for precisely plotting the orbit of a satellite. No self-respecting physicist physicist has believed since 1914 that an atom is a tiny solar system, but it is true for most of us relative to our everyday functioning and our general level of sophistication in mathematics and physics. 'Light consists of particles' seems to contradict 'Light consists of waves,' but both are taken as true by physicists relative to which aspects of light are picked out by different experiments."

Activity #1—

Ask students as individuals to make a list of sentences that use the word "time"---these sentences should be common phrases.
Ask students as individuals to make a list of sentences that are used in baseball.
Ask students as individuals to make a list of sentences that are used in football.

Assign these students to groups.

Each group pools the sentences of its members, eliminating duplicates.

A representative from each group goes to the blackboard and writes his/her group's sentences about time.

Do not give these sentences to your students, but many of them will wind up on the board.

You're wasting my time.
This gadget will save you hours.
I don't have the time to give you.
How do you spend your time these days?
That flat tire cost me an hour.
I've invested a lot of time in her.
I don't have enough time to spare for that.
You're running out of time.
You need to budget your time.
Put aside some time for ping pong.
Is that worth your while?
Do you have much time left?
He's living on borrowed time.
You don't use your time profitably.
I lost a lot of time when I got sick.
Thank you for your time.

These sentences and others the students will produce demonstrate that our culture views time as currency.

Divide the groups into two sections. A representative from each group in the first section writes the sentences about baseball on the board. A representative from each group in the second section writes the sentences about football on the board. This is an old comparison that George Carlin made famous. Baseball—wear a cap, run home, try to be safe, play in a park. Football—wear a helmet, the quarterback throws the bomb, defensive players blitz, and it is played in a stadium.

Activity #2

Get a small box and put household items in it.
Ask the class to list ideas or emotions on the board—friendship, love, anger, desire, democracy.

As a class choose one of the ideas or emotions and then pick an item out of the box, say, a glove. Then ask them to create a metaphor. Democracy is a glove which, if ill fitted to a culture, may cut off the circulation to the rest of the body politic, or some such thing.

Activity #3

Study the works of a poet like John Donne and the metaphysical poets—examine the metaphors they use.

Activity #4

Use the handout on developing their (student) metaphors. "A human being is a ...." Etc.

(My thinking…)

How we couch reality in language, and especially metaphors, determines how we act. We demonized Saddam Hussein—the devil, he is Hitler, etc. Suppose in describing students for an IEP we did the same thing? This student is a "devil." He is Hitleresque. We might believe that, but we usually say, "This student is aggressive," "needs to develop social skills," etc.

Metonymy—using one entity to refer to another that is related to it.
Suppose Joe Jones, a handsome, young police officer, walks into a diner, sits at the counter and orders a ham sandwich on rye. The young girl sitting at table 1 with her friends says, "Look at the hunk at the counter." The two mobsters at table 3 say, "Ssh, the fuzz." The waitress identifies him as "The ham sandwich wants ketchup." The young girl wants to meet the hunk, the mobsters want to avoid the fuzz, and the waitress wants a good tip from the ham sandwich.

The Part for the Whole, Produce for Product, Place for the Event, etc.

All hands on deck.
The automobile is clogging our highways.
She's just a pretty face.
I've got a new set of wheels.
He bought a Ford.
The Times hasn't arrived at the press conference yet (reporter from the Times)
The sax has the flu today.
Nixon bombed Hanoi
Exxon has raised its prices again.
The White House isn't saying anything.
Remember the Alamo.
Pearl Harbor still has an effect on our foreign policy.
Watergate changed our politics.

From Metaphors We Live By:

"Thus, like metaphors, metonymic concepts structure not just our language but our thoughts, attitudes, and actions. And, like metaphoric concepts, metonymic concepts are grounded in our experience. In fact, the grounding of metonymic concepts is in general more obvious than is the case with metaphoric concepts, since it usually involves direct physical or causal associations. THE PART FOR THE WHOLE metonymy, for example, emerges from our experiences with the way parts in general are related to wholes, PRODUCER FOR PRODUCT is based on the causal (and typically physical) relationship between a producer and his product, THE PLACE FOR THE EVENT is grounded in our experience with the physical location of events. And so on."

Ask students to come with a list of five metonyms. What associations do we make with these metonyms?

Activity **#5**

Distribute the handout of metaphors. (Inspector Clouseau, Anthropologist)

Students are to circle five of the metaphors on the pages. No name on sheet, but have an identifying id.

Redistribute the papers. Each student is now to complete several activities, (what's in this person's locker, etc.) based on the metaphors.

OR

Better yet. Each student completes a sheet creating his/her own metaphors. Then we exchange them.

From *Metaphors Dictionary* by Elyse Sommer with Dorrie Weiss

Sample Metaphors

#	METAPHOR	AUTHOR	CATEGORY	PAGE #
1.	"Beauty is the melody of features."	Josh Billings	Beauty	36
2.	Beauty alone won't wear well, and there is a great deal of it that won't wash at all and keep its color."	Josh Billings	Beauty	36
3.	Beauty is eternity gazing at itself in the mirror. But you are eternity and you are the mirror."	Kahlil Gibran, The Prophet	Beauty	36
4.	"Beauty is truth, truth beauty."	John Keats	Beauty	36
5.	"Beauty without virtue is a flower without perfume."	Anon. French proverb	Beauty	36
6.	"Beauty's a Flower, despis'd in decay."	John Gay, The Beggar's Opera	Beauty	36
7.	"Beauty is a blind alley…a mountain peak which once reached leads nowhere."	W. Somerset Maugham, *Cakes and Ale*	Beauty	37
8.	"Beauty is a flower which wrinkles will devour."	Thomas Nashe	Beauty	37
9.	"beauty is a witch/Against whose charms faith melteth into blood."	Shakespeare *Much Ado..*	Beauty	37

10.	"Beauty within itself should not be wasted:/fair flowers that are not gather'd in their prime/ Rot and consume themselves in little time."	Shakespeare *Venus and Adonis*	Beauty	38
11.	"She was a phantom of delight/When first she gleamed upon my sight:/ A lovely apparition, sent/To be a moment's ornament."	William Wordsworth, "She was a phantom of Delight?"	Beauty	38
12.	"Death is a fisherman...and we the fishes be."	Anon. English Epitaph	Death	105
13.	"Death...that common revenger of all injuries."	Aphra Behn	Death	105
14.	"Yes, death is the last line of the book."	Giacomo Girolamo Casanova, *Memoirs*	Death	105
15.	"Death is the king of this world: 'tis his park where he breeds life to feed him."	George Eliot	Death	105
16.	"To die is landing on some silent shore."	Samuel Garth	Death	105
17.	"Death is not a period but a comma in the story of life."	Vern McLellan	Death	105
18.	"Death isn't something slimy and catching like life."	A.B. Yehoshua	Death	105
19.	"But he that dares not grasp the thorn/Should never crave the rose."	Anne Bronte	Courage	87
20.	"You're surrounded 24 hours a day. Either you become a herd animal or you dig a cave deep inside your head in which to hide."	John Dulgan	Conformity	80
21.	"For nonconformity the world whips you with its displeasure."	Ralph Waldo Emerson	Conformity	80
22.	"We are grown stiff with the ramrod of convention down our backs."	O. Henry	Conformity	80
23.	"Public men are bees working in a glass hive."	Henry Ward Beecher	Fame	166
24.	"Fame is the thirst of youth."	Lord George Gordon Byron	Fame	166
25.	"Fame is but wind."	Thomas Coryate	Fame	166
26.	"Fame is a food that dead men eat."	Henry Austin Dobson	Fame	166
27.	"Fame is a bugle call/Blown past a crumbling wall."	Lizette Reese	Fame	166
28.	"What is fame? An empty bubble."	Jame Grainger	Fame	166
29.	"Fame is the beauty parlor of the dead."	Benjamin De Casseres	Fame	166
30.	"The state is bodies of armed men."	Nikolai Lenin	Government	194

Atom Smashing 1

Identity_____

Period _____ Date_____

Atom Smashing

Write down metaphors for each of the following. These metaphors should express your beliefs or feelings about the items you write metaphors for.

1) People are _____

_____

_____

2) Friends are (or a friend is)_____

_____

_____

3) Beauty is_____

_____

_____

4) Heaven is_____

_____

_____

5) Life is_____

_____

_____

6) Education/school is_____

_____

_____

7) Family is_____

_____

_____

Identity_____

Atom Smashing 2

Period _____ Date_____

Atom Smashing 2

Inspector Clouseau as Anthropologist

Write the identity of the metaphors you are reading in the space above.

Imagine that you are an anthropologist whose task it is to draw conclusions from a document containing metaphors that a person has written. In the spaces below, write down what you think **based on the metaphors you read.**

1) List the items that the author of this metaphor may have in his/her locker:

_____

_____

_____

2) What career do you think the author wants to someday have? Why do you think so?

_____

_____

3) What family do you think the author does have and will have? Why do you think so?

_____

_____

4) What kind of person would the author want for a spouse? Why do you think so?

_____

_____

5) What do you think the author values most in life? Why do you think so?

_____

_____

6) Describe in as much detail as possible the personality of the author (you may include tastes in music, sports, etc.) You do not have to be right. After all, you do not know the person, but are basing your conclusions *solely and honestly* on the metaphors provided. Use the back of this sheet and then sign your name. You will be evaluated on the logic of your conclusions.

_____

_____

_____

_____

_____

_____

_____

_____

_____

_____

Beyond Infinity: Metaphors: Atom Smashing

1) Ask the students either through class discussion or in groups to consider how their group functioned. What were the challenges and how did they overcome those challenges?
2) What could the group have done better?
3) What did the group excel at doing?
4) What did students learn about the subject matter (literary work, middle ages, time, interpersonal relations, etc.)?
5) What, if anything, did students learn about themselves, other people, life in general?
6) What questions do they have about themselves, other people, life in general?

Specific to the unit studied:

1) Some would argue that the first thing a tribe or nation does to commence war is to demonize the enemy by creating metaphors for the enemy. Cite some examples from history.
2) Our perceptions are shaped by the metaphors we use and by how we name things, and our perceptions shape our behaviors. How does our naming something (or using a metaphor for something or someone) dictate our behavior?
3) Do the lyrics we use in music shape our views toward people?
4) Does the language we use in everyday speech shape our attitudes toward others?
5) Can words hurt, as in the words we use to objectify people, or are words just words?
6) When is a word or a metaphor not acceptable either in speech or in art, including literature and music?
7) What are the consequences for banning any words or metaphors in speech or in art, including literature and music?
8) What would civilization be like if it never had language?

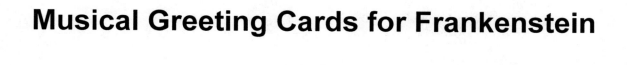

Musical Greeting Cards for Frankenstein

Teacher Notes---'We're in the Money, We're in the Money"

When I was an inexperienced teacher, I asked a class, broken into small groups, to study the themes of a literary work. Having a very rudimentary knowledge of multiple intelligences at the time, I allowed groups to demonstrate their understanding of the characterization of the book's theme and characterization through music, without qualifying the type of music. That was a mistake. The second group that presented to the class played a contemporary song. Every third word of the lyrics began with "F" and ended with "K" and it was not "firetruck." They had played me. When I halted the music and asked how that song, so inappropriate for the setting, could express the theme, they laughed and tried to come up with a lame explanation which even they knew was going to unacceptable. They did not care. They just wanted to play their favorite song (and it was their favorite song) to the class.

Even my slowness has its limitations. From then on I required that all music chosen to accompany a project must be non-lyrical. Or, students can choose the song and write their own lyrics, or they can create their own song and lyrics. This is usually greeted by some students with great chagrin. "Mr. M, why can't we use 'I Hated Her So I Threw Her in the Paper Shredder' by Axel Tulip? It's a great song and really fits the Romantic movement."

Again, in line with my belief that a teacher's goal is to expand, not necessarily indulge, student interest, I sometimes chose the required musical genre----show tunes, classical, jazz. It would not seriously impair their psyches to listen to some Mozart or Bach or Copeland or Berlin or Coltrane. And it did happen that some windows to a different understanding and appreciation of music were opened. I think, on some level, that was definitely my job.

For this particular project I made no such requirement. Choosing the music, the literary work, author, and character, composing the lyrics and illustrating the card were all challenges. I also let students choose the occasion for the same reason.

With the available online software today (Zooburst comes to mind), an online presentation would be acceptable and easily shared with the rest of the class. A cautionary note: copyright laws still apply.

One of the aspects I like about this project is that it is so easily adaptable to other content areas. In science and math the musical cards can represent inventions, equations, scientists and mathematicians, their theories, etc. Social studies could use historical figures, events, policies, eras. Asking students to be clever with the information we give them is a good thing---it helps students develop creative solutions to problems.

As the groups worked on this project, I enjoyed circulating around the groups listening to their conversations and debates. For me, this is where the true learning happens.

Name_____

Group ID_____

"We're in the Money, We're in the Money,"

Or

"Daisy, Daisy, Give Me Your Answer Now"

Tom and Daisy Buchanan

Jay Gatsby

A group of venture capitalists (people who invest in new companies) have decided they wanted to line their pockets with money by investing in an extremely rich source of wealth---people who read literature, like English teachers. They are looking for one company to invest in, and they are looking in the area of musical greeting cards. Your group wants to win the competition, to be that company that gets the bid. To do so, your company (give yourselves a catchy name related to the area) must produce at least three musical cards (hopefully more) that satisfy these requirements:

1) A musical card for an author we have studied in class.
2) A musical card for a literary character
3) A musical card for a literary work

The music for the cards may be from any genre *but the lyrics must be your original lyrics.* You may use famous Broadway musicals for your sources or contemporary tunes, or childhood ditties, *but the lyrics must be your original lyrics.* You may simply record the music and play it when someone opens the card, or you may produce a video highlighting each card.

Each card must also be illustrated as befitting its subject. Nice words inside the card are also things the venture capitalists would like to see. You may use any occasion for your greeting card----holiday, Valentine's Day, sympathy, get well, etc., and the occasion can be different for each card.

On the day this assignment is due, there will be a Musical Card Fair, and the venture capitalists (your instructor) will visit each group and study each card. In fact, all the groups will visit each other's "booth."

Evaluations will be decided on the following criteria:

1) Quality of the collaboration---shared leadership and active involvement by all members.
2) Depth of thought---are the lyrics clever, the music appropriate to the subject, the illustrations likewise subject to the subject
3) Depth of understanding of the subject---are the themes of the literary works expressed, the style and content of the author expressed, the characterization displayed/

So, brainstorm and perform so that those filthy rich bookworms can be exploited!

Beyond Infinity: Musical Greeting Cards

Generic:

1) Ask the students either through class discussion or in groups to consider how their group functioned. What were the challenges and how did they overcome those challenges?
2) What could the group have done better?
3) What did the group excel at doing?
4) What did students learn about the subject matter (literary work, middle ages, time, interpersonal relations, etc.)?
5) What, if anything, did students learn about themselves, other people, life in general?
6) What questions do they have about themselves, other people, life in general?

The teacher can use the questions below as either closures for the projects or as the inceptions of new projects.

Specific to the unit studied:

1) What actually is the ultimate purpose of any greeting card?
2) Was it more difficult to discover the "essence" of the author/character/literary work, or was it more challenging to match that essence with music?
3) What would be an "anti-greeting card?"
4) What will greeting cards say, one hundred years from now, look and sound like?

Myths: Name that Tribe

Teacher Notes—Name Our Tribe

This was a daunting assignment, but a good one. The biggest difficulty students had was thinking of modern heroes from real life. We discussed this. Joseph Campbell bemoaned the loss of a civilization's hero....his argument was that, without looking outward through the eyes of the hero, societies implode. I also had to make the distinction between a celebrity and a hero. Mostly, I wanted the students to realize that we are unique, but no more or no less unique than other cultures. (In 2000, a number of students picked Donald Trump. I asked them what heroic qualities Mr. Trump possessed. "He's rich!" was the reply.). That may or may not tell us something, but you might spend some class time discussing heroism.

The ancient Greeks did not walk around bemoaning the "fact" that they were ancient. "Gee, I wish I was modern like those guys in the 21st century!" I once asked a class to design a National Geographic magazine whose feature article focused on "that mysterious tribe in North America that we called River Dwellers but who called themselves Americans." What tribal rites of passage did they undergo (senior proms)? What odd belief systems did they embrace? (fame for any deed was good). What possessions did they prize? (1957 Chevy).

I was strolling the streets of Tokyo, Japan with some young Americans who were munching on French fries and hamburgers which they had just purchased. I advised them that, in Japan, eating while walking down the street was a social taboo. They all looked at me with both surprise and not a little disdain. "That's stupid. Everyone does that." One of the most difficult challenges in helping students develop an understanding, and sometimes an empathy, for other cultures is to get them to understand that we are a culture as well, with a set of belief systems, ethics, and behavioral patterns that are not written in the heavens.

Name:_____

Group ID_____

Name Our Tribe

This assignment is a quest of sorts. It requires that you go on a journey of exploration, a journey that is both distant and near. You must intellectually step out of the culture that you are in and examine it as an anthropologist from the future would. We are, after all, a culture, a tribe, and some future social scientist will study us. It will be difficult. We are not a static people and we are definitely not all alike. Then again, are the peoples of all the other cultures we have briefly examined more stationary and homogeneous? Are we more complicated than cultures of the past? Who says so? I hope that in attempting to answer these questions, you will 1)improve your critical and creative thinking skills, 2) improve your collaborative skills 3)gain some insight on who we are 4) develop a greater understanding of the nature of culture.

To complete this quest successfully, you and your fellow anthropologists must fulfill the following requirements:

1) Choose five (5) modern heroes of our culture. Make certain that these are "heroes" and not "celebrities." We have discussed heroes as emblems of the cultures that produce them. Each member of the group is to write a one-page paper explaining why one of the heroes fits the description of a cultural hero.
2) Choose one (1) of these heroes collectively. This cultural hero most represents the values and belief systems of our tribe. Create a poster for this hero and write a song celebrating this person. (or online website, video, etc.)
3) Choose five (5) myths that permeate our culture (2 creation myths, 1 value [or belief system]myth, 1 trickster myth, 1 death myth). This is one myth per member of the group. Write a one page paper that explains how the myth reflects the culture.
4) Imagine that anthropologists of the future return from a dig with ten artifacts from our civilization. What artifacts might they be, and how would the anthropologists interpret their significance? Make a list of the artifacts and a brief explanation of the interpretation.
5) Create a presentation that delivers your findings to the class. In essence, you will share the decisions and choices you made in 1 through 4 above. The presentation may include enhancements (audio-visual aids), and should be organized and thought-provoking.

This assignment will be evaluated according to the following criteria:

ACTIVITY	FULL CREDIT CRITERIA	SLIDING CREDIT	NO CREDIT
Group Effort	All members work all the time collectively 200 pts.	>>>>>>>	Members off task, socializing, offering excuses for wasting time.
Each Hero Paper	Each paper is authentic, well-written, typed and documented. No cut and paste 50 Pts. each	>>>>>>>	Non-authentic, cut and paste time, hastily constructed
Each Myth Paper	Same criteria as hero paper	>>>>>>>	Same as above
Hero Poster	Avoids "comic book" style; captures cultural values 25 pts.	>>>>>>>	An advisor room effort
Hero Song	Same as above. Song has original lyrics. 25 pts.	>>>>>>>	Same as above.
Artifact List	Demonstrates thought and intellect. 30 pts.	>>>>>>>	Copied someone else's list. Mental rip off.
Presentation	Organized, clever, good enhancements, all members participate, intelligent thought 100 pts.	>>>>>>>	Poorly organized, few enhancements, some members sitting or reading information. Mentally deficient chipmunks could do as well.

PROCEDURE

1) Spend some time brainstorming. Discuss heroes and myths in general.
2) Agree on the heroes and myths you will use in this assignment. Agree not to waste time and adversely affect each member's grade.
3) Divide up the labor. Set due dates for the group.
4) Develop an artifact list.
5) Plan a presentation.
6) Rehearse the presentation.

This is an ambitious project. It requires that you develop an understanding of the nature of culture and that you become objective in applying that understanding to a study of your own tribe. Good luck, and I stand ready to assist you.

Beyond Infinity: Name Our Tribe

Generic:

1) Ask the students either through class discussion or in groups to consider how their group functioned. What were the challenges and how did they overcome those challenges?
2) What could the group have done better?
3) What did the group excel at doing?
4) What did students learn about the subject matter (literary work, middle ages, time, interpersonal relations, etc.)?
5) What, if anything, did students learn about themselves, other people, life in general?
6) What questions do they have about themselves, other people, life in general?

The teacher can use the questions below as either closures for the projects or as the inceptions of new projects.

Specific to the unit studied:

1) Joseph Campbell, the noted mythologist, worried about the lack of myths, and especially the apparent dearth of heroes in modern culture. Campbell thought that a culture without frontiers or heroes would implode. What does it say about our culture if, indeed, few heroes exist?
2) What is the difference between a hero and a celebrity?
3) Do we, in our society, have a myth of "newness," the belief that not only are we new, but new is genuinely better?
4) Compared to other cultures we have studied or other cultures with which you are very well acquainted, how similar and how different are we?
5) What myths exist in our culture now (remember that myths guide a culture and may be true or untrue)? For example, in contemporary American society, we possess the myth of "from log cabin to White House," the shared belief that anyone can be president of the United States.
6) Examine the myths you listed in #5. If you were an anthropologist from the distant future, what conclusions would you draw about our society based on these myths?

Osiris and Moon Walking

Teacher Notes—Osiris and Moonwalking

In my humanities course, which I collaboratively taught with three other teachers, we developed a small transition unit which attempted to make the connection between the ancient Greeks, which we had just studied, and the Indian cultures which were next up for us. We thought about a small unit on different views of nature. I asked students to read the Osiris and Isis myth, and showed them transparencies of images of Osiris and his rebirth. We also had transparencies of the waxing and waning moons in connection with the Osiris mythology. I decided to focus on the following issues we would discuss in class in preparing for the project:

The connection between the Osiris and Isis myth and other creation myths—myths grow from metaphors grounded in environmental influences—moon, earth, water, sky, are anthropomorphized.

The connection between the Osiris myth and the moon. The moon was important, because every culture could view the moon at night and wonder at its purpose. The most common recognizable shape amongst cultures is the circle, simply because the moon provides that shape. Rather hard to find a triangle in nature.

What are other modern connections between the heavenly bodies and our culture? Movie "stars," horoscope in daily newspaper and online, etc?

Osiris grew out of a metaphorical grounding in what was around them—the moon is seen every night. The crops were important. Nature was not something to be enjoyed. People were part of nature, dependent on nature. In what ways do we see nature today?

I included my ideas at the beginning of this project. A little metacognition is sometimes a good thing.

Ideas for Osiris Unit

What do I want students to learn?

Development of a myth—connection between this myth and other creation myths—myths grow from metaphors grounded in environmental influences—moon, earth, water, sky, are anthromorphized.

Give them Osiris myth to read. What do they find interesting in this myth?

Then show them the connection between Osiris and the moon. Other astronomical connections.

Then what? Ask them to develop a postage stamp or musical score that reflects modern myth. Myth of nature. Nature as we see it.

Today's theme is nature. Illustrate it through a postage stamp, coin, national park service icon, a theme for (play Beethoven's 6th Pastoral Symphony) National Geographic, a nature music for people in hospitals, nature music for people in steel buildings, jingle for radio station.

1) give them a copy of the Osiris myth
2) tell them the connection between the myth of Osiris and the moon and the illustrations.
3) Ask them to come up with connections we still make with the heavens and daily life—stars, horoscope, etc.
4) Discuss nature with them—Osiris grew out of a metaphorical grounding in what was around them—the moon is seen every night. The crops were important. Nature was not something to be enjoyed. People were part of nature, dependent on nature. In what ways do we see nature today?
5) Give them the assignment.

Name_____

Period_____ Group ID_____

"I Got the Sun in the Morning and the Moon at Night..."

Song of the Ancients

My father used to say "you pay for everything in this life." I wonder if cultures pay, as well. For example, I wonder if a person who lives in an air-conditioned, vinyl and plastic home, who takes the plastic and metal commuter train to his office in the city where he works all day in his vinyl and chrome air conditioned office, who then takes the same plastic and metal commuter train to his air conditioned vinyl and plastic home cares anything about the rain forest. What does it mean to him, except for some statistics and dollar signs on a piece of paper? Is a tree a tree, or simply lumber? Is an alligator an animal or a resource for expensive shoes? Is what we call "nature" something apart from humanity, or is humanity a part of "nature?"

The question, to me, is, "Are we paying for being more removed from the natural elements than our ancestors?" The answer may be "no." We get along quite well with Mother Nature—it's simply that we are her rebellious adolescents. Or, maybe the mythology of *Star Wars* ("Luke, the Force is all around us and through us and in us") is closer to the truth, and we are disenfranchising ourselves from the rest of the universe.

In any case, I think you would agree that our view of nature is different from our human predecessors. How you interpret that view is the subject of this next assignment.

Choose one (1) of the following projects:

1) Develop a postage stamp for the United States for the new millenium with "nature" as its subject.
2) Develop a National Park Service Icon (an icon to identify its stationery, signs in national parks, etc.) that has nature as its subject.
3) Create a tape or cd that contains music which conveys our view of nature to severely ill patients in hospitals. The music is intended to soothe and possibly help heal the patients. Music must be non-lyrical, and can be whole works or portion of works combined. You cannot simply bring in a cd of commercially canned "soothing" music. Well, you can, but then I can give you a canned grade.
4) Variation of #3 above, only this tape or cd is designed to help birthing mothers deliver their babies. The belief is that music that reflects a "natural" sound is conducive to the delivery process.
5) Variation of #3 above, only this nature music is designed for people who work in steel office buildings. The intent is to bring them closer to nature.
6) Design a coin (25 cents) for the new millennial with nature as its subject.

It is important to remember that this assignment will be evaluated according to how well you meet the following criteria:

Criteria for Success

1) Time on Task—If class time is apportioned for this project, how well you use that time will be a criterion.
2) Associative Property—how closely does your product reflect **our** culture's view of nature? It is easy to draw a pastoral scene or recreate the sounds of loons drowning in the wild, but does it reflect our stance toward nature?
3) Degree of Effort—this criterion is determined by the obvious thought that you put into the project as well as the aesthetic value.
4) Intangibles—is the product shallow and typical or deep and atypical? Does it move us on a cerebral and passionate level?
5) Is it in harmony with the conjunction of Mars and Venus? (only kidding)

I hope you enjoy this project. I stand ready and willing to assist you in any way possible. Good Luck.

Beyond Infinity: Osiris and Moon Walking

Generic:

1) Ask the students either through class discussion or in groups to consider how their group functioned. What were the challenges and how did they overcome those challenges?
2) What could the group have done better?
3) What did the group excel at doing?
4) What did students learn about the subject matter (literary work, middle ages, time, interpersonal relations, etc.)?
5) What, if anything, did students learn about themselves, other people, life in general?
6) What questions do they have about themselves, other people, life in general?

The teacher can use the questions below as either closures for the projects or as the inceptions of new projects.

Specific to the unit studied:

1) Some modern philosophers and psychologists believe that, in our high tech environment, we are nature-deficient. What do you think that means and how valid is that theory?
2) How does our culture view nature---as something to be exploited, cherished, or negotiated with?
3) What elements of modern living separate us from nature?
4) What advantages/disadvantages exist from being close to nature?
5) Many Native Americans thought it preposterous that one could own a piece of ground. What would you say to those Native Americans about your ownership of property, particularly real estate?
6) As we seemingly become more distant from nature (our ancestors were much better at "reading" nature than the modern common man can), depict humankind's existence on this planet two hundred years from now.

The Pediment Project

Teacher Notes: Pediment Olympics

What fun!!! I originally designed this project, in collaboration with the art teacher, to ensure that students read the assigned myths. The art teacher explained pediments and I assigned the myths (see Pediment Olympic Myths). We were then going to discuss "myths" and "mythology" as Joseph Campbell and Sam Keen described those terms. This project became a terrific lead in to those discussions and projects.

I have a teaching philosophy (described in my book, A Class Act) which says, "Everything must count....even if it really doesn't." Students will not read assigned material unless they know they are going to be held accountable for it, and for many students, even this fact does not convince them to read. The students who worry about their grades will often cheat by reading the Spark notes or online synopses. I knew several teachers who would assign a short story for homework and then not quiz to see if students actually read it. The teacher would argue, "In class discussions I would discover who actually had read it." I doubt that. The smartest students learn to get credit for reading by answering the simplest of questions. Another teacher gave a quick essay question on a novel. The best student writers know how to take a question and pile enough information to make it seem like they read the work. To those students goes the Golden Shovel Award.

My approach to ensure that most students read the assigned work (in other subjects it is easier to make a quiz---there are few Spark notes for chapters in a history or science textbook, but there are many such "resources" for literature), was to give them a detailed quiz, or in the case of the novel, a major test on the content of the reading. Students hated this. And so did some teachers who hated making up quizzes and tests. But even "honor" sometimes evaporates from the persons of honors students who have such an overload of homework that they only focus on the assignments for which they know they will be held accountable.

This particular project was an adjunct to my testing the students on the ten myths. What I did not expect was how much came out of it. Students were incredibly enthusiastic, showed up on the assigned day wearing homemade togas, created props like laurel wreaths, etc. When we completed the project, we had excellent discussions on nonverbal communication, especially how body language is more exact than conventional speech. We also discussed the nature of beauty and the values of Greek culture, as well as kinesthetic intelligence.

You can certainly alter this project to have as its subject Italian Renaissance painting or Medieval architecture or modern sculpture. The students really enjoyed this project and took tons of pictures and shared them around the school.

Group Name(think Ancient Greek)_____

Date Project is Due_____

The Pediment Olympics

You have been assigned ten Greek myths to study. You have also examined a number of ancient pediments which reflected specific styles and arrangements. Your group's task is to prepare for the Pediment Olympics. On a chosen day, the Pediment Impediment Olympic Committee (the IOC) will call up two groups to the stage at a time. The instructors will shout out a Greek myth, and your group will immediately form a pediment based on that myth. The group that forms the best pediment (the myth is accurately captured from the pediment you form and the speed in which you form it) will get points. We will continue in a round robin way so all groups participate in several competitions. This is Round 1.

In Round 2 each group will be given three index cards. On each index card will be one of the ten myths you were assigned to study. Do not share any of the names of these myths with others in the class (failure to obey this caution will result in subtracting points from the group). When called up by the IOC, the group will form the pediment for one of the myths on the index card. Students in other groups will raise their hands (first come, first served), and identify the myth. If correct, both your group and the group that answered correctly will get points. You will do this for two of the three myths on the index cards.

In Round 3 each group presents its best pediment. Points will be awarded on beauty and creativity.

The winner of the Pediment Olympic competition will be showered with rewards....well, maybe not showered. Perhaps just a small stream....or a trickle.....probably just a Greek yogurt for the group. No matter. Your group is doing this for the honor of winning the Pediment Olympics!!! Good luck.

LIST OF MYTHS FOR PEDIMENT OLYMPICS

PERSEUS

DEMETER

PROMOTHEUS AND IO

EUROPA

CUPID AND PSYCHE

PYRAMIS AND THISBE

ORPHEUS AND EURYDICE

PYGMALION AND GALATEA

PEGASUS AND BELLEROPHON

PHAETON

STRUCTURE FOR UNIT ON

GREEK MYTHS AND PEDIMENTS

"SAY CHEESE"

OR

THE PEDIMENT FILE

1. ASSIGN STUDENTS TO GROUPS OF 6.

2. ASSIGN READINGS OF GREEK MYTHS

3. ROUND ONE--EACH GROUP ON THE ASSIGNED DAY WILL RECEIVE THE NAMES OF THREE GREEK MYTHS ON INDEX CARDS.

4. THEY ARE TO POSE (GREEK STYLE) AS A PEDIMENT REENACTING THE MYTH

5. WHEN EVERY GROUP HAS HAD A ROUND, THE COMPETITION BEGINS.

6. ROUND TWO—GROUPS PAIR UP. GROUPS COMPETE, TWO AT A TIME, TO FORM A PEDIMENT ON A GREEK MYTH THAT THE INSTRUCTOR SHOUTS OUT. POINTS ARE AWARDED ON SPEED, ACCURACY, AND CREATIVITY.

7. ROUND THREE—EACH GROUP PRESENTS THEIR BEST PEDIMENT. POINTS ARE AWARDED ON BEAUTY AND CREATIVITY.

Beyond Infinity: The Pediment Olympics

Generic:

1. Ask the students either through class discussion or in groups to consider how their group functioned. What were the challenges and how did they overcome those challenges?
2. What could the group have done better?
3. What did the group excel at doing?
4. What did students learn about the subject matter (literary work, middle ages, time, interpersonal relations, etc.)?
5. What, if anything, did students learn about themselves, other people, life in general?
6. What questions do they have about themselves, other people, life in general?

The teacher can use the questions below as either closures for the projects or as the inceptions of new projects.

Specific to the unit studied:

1. There is an intelligence called "kinesthetic intelligence," the ability for a person to have a good understanding of her body in time and space. Picture Michael Jordan in mid-dunk possessing the intelligence to make a snap decision on what he could do with the ball in mid-air. When forming the pediments, did you experience a heightened sense of kinesthetic intelligence?
2. What are the challenges to modeling?
3. Compared to verbal communication, how exacting is body language?
4. Someone has postulated that it is easier to make a mistake in body language than in verbal language. Do you agree or disagree? Why?
5. When you were actually forming the pediment, what were your feelings?
6. How culturally dependent are our views on aesthetics, on beauty?

Animal Farm—Pinky and the Brain

Teacher Notes—Animal Farm and Pinky and the Brain

There are so many engaging themes to explore in Animal Farm: comparisons of economic systems, kinds of power, the importance of education (if only the animals had written down the history of the revolution and its precepts instead of relying on their faulty memories!), human exploitation, and the nature and use of propaganda, to name a few. Since, as a nation, we were in the midst of a propaganda blitz, I chose that theme and combined it with a typical human fantasy—"What if I ruled the world?"

During the nineties there was a show, popular amongst the brainier students, called Pinky and the Brain. Two laboratory mice, one a genius, the other insane, plot every night to take over the world. http://www.youtube.com/watch?v=iJPFSNu_QNs (for a one minute look at their discussion of the human brain, view http://www.youtube.com/watch?v=Li5nMsXg1Lk) So that became my catcher for the assignment.

I also issued the Washington Post Dispatch Gazette article to rope students in with some humor and to encourage the humor that initiated with Pinky and the Brain. But the student engagement was serious as they focused on buzz words and words that implied certain codes. These discussions in small groups were the meat and potatoes of the actual learning (as they usually are) because students touched on a variety of subjects including politics, human nature, and the meanings of words. More specifically these topics included the proletariat in Animal Farm and the Soviet Union, and the Stalinist regime This was one of those projects in which I had to terminate the discussions and move them on.

I strongly urge that you consider the Criteria of Success that I provided. This project occurred near the end of the year when grades had been pretty much determined and students had developed the collaborative skills I required. Near the end of the school year, a teacher has to develop projects which are appealing to students for factors other than grades, especially seniors. Think about asking students to make online videos or using the internet for propaganda techniques. You might have to adjust Appendix A, the spreadsheet which has the cost list if you make these changes. That should be easy since the spreadsheet is relatively basic.

I have to include a comment here about the closure questions (Discussion Questions for Animal Farm). As I usually did, I issued these questions to each individual student, collected them, and then asked students to convene in their project groups and gave each group the same set of questions. This practice does two things: it allows for individual accountability and it sets up the students' minds for the group discussion of these questions. This closure activity brought the whole notion of propaganda home. We hardly ever imagine that we are bombarded by propaganda on a daily basis. Some of these questions led to rather vociferous conversations. I enjoyed watching minds contemplate something for the first time, the realization that Americans might be played as well as any other culture, and the high cost of ignorance. I did not follow up on these debates. My job was to open the door, but I was careful not to lead anyone through the door. Enjoy.

Name_____

Group ID_____ Date Due_____

"What are we going to do tonight, Brain?"

"Same as we do every night, Pinky…Plan to Take Over the World"

Pinky and the Brain

A nuclear device has been detonated using Washington, D.C. as ground zero. The bomb may have been set off by terrorists, either native or foreign. Or the bomb may have been another nation's revenge for real or imagined atrocities committed by the United States. Or the bomb may have been an accident. No one has yet to claim responsibility, but whoever, if anyone, is accountable, he or she is responsible for evaporating the entire federal government of this nation. There is no President, no Vice-President, no cabinet members, no Supreme Court, no Congress, no Constitution, and no Washington Wizards. Physicists are fond of saying that "Nature doesn't like a vacuum," and currently there is one huge vacuum where once was the seat of American government.

Most people are disturbed by this empty civics hole, but whereas the majority view the recent destruction of American politics as a tragedy, you and your colleagues see the event as opportunity. You can now achieve what you always have wanted to achieve—to take over the most powerful nation in the world, and, thus, for all practical purposes, *to take over the entire world*. However, it has come to your attention that there are several other groups out there who share your vision but not your friendship. You can not simply waltz onto the throne. Some do-gooder group, probably that busybody League of Women Voters has arranged for a national election to choose a party to "rule" the country until a new constitution and a new governmental structure can be created and developed. You will have a short time to concoct a propaganda blitz to sell your group to the American people. Of course, once in power you have no intention of returning the country to that profit-draining moralistic travesty called a "representational democracy." Oh no. Once you and your cronies have mounted Olympus, you will devote most of your energies to staying "King of the Mountain."

Your task, then, has two parts. One, you must develop a series of campaign advertisements, one minute in length, that will convince voters to choose your party. As your opponents campaign, you may change your ads to attack theirs or to defend yourselves from their ads. Before you can develop this campaign, you must discuss within your group a strategy for appealing to the public. What psychological things might work in the current environment?

The second part of your task involves devising your plan to *maintain* power. After all, that, like Napoleon's main objective in the novel, *Animal Farm*, is the prime directive—to achieve and to retain absolute power. How do you keep the people from revolting? What tools should you use? Of course, you can use the Armed Forces to crush rebellion, but that is not the smart way. The smart way is to avoid rebellion altogether. Besides, the Armed Forces will go the way of the American public.

You have money. Lots of it. One hundred million, to be exact. This is not enough to bribe the Armed Forces, but it is enough to purchase commercial time, establish rallies, print posters, compose pamphlets, buy ads. Now for many people, one hundred million would buy quite a few Burrito Supremes at Taco Bell, but pleasure is not your thing—power is. So rather than blow your funds having breakfast with Mickey at Disney World, you will use your economic forces to establish your group as a dictatorship. The trick is to make the American public go along.

Consult Appendix A to find out how much things cost and prepare a budget.

PROCEDURE

This is the sequence of actions that might lead to a successful completion of this assignment:

1) Exhibit good cooperative skills by listening and tuning into fellow group members. Help the brainstorming process. Throw out millions of strategies, but settle on one or two. Keep the plan simple but powerful. In terms of persuasion, what works with the American people? Look at history. Look at the present. Read Appendix A and the excerpt from the newspaper, particularly the article from *The Language of Vision.*

2) Once you have decided on a strategy, divide up the labor. One member can be Minister of Finance (control of budget), Minister of Propaganda, Minister of Education, Minister of Defense, Minister of Silly Walks.... You will have to present your plan to the class, so visual/audio aids will help. Posters, signs, names for the group, symbols, flags, banners, tunes, slogans, etc. may be conceived and produced to enhance your presentation. In my experience, inexperienced students do this first because it is fun. Do not do this first. Do #1 first. Develop a strategy or plan, and then make all the enhancements fit in with this strategy.

3) Each day each group will be permitted one minute to deliver a message live. We are to imagine that this message will go out on major networks to the American people. The content of each message is up to you.

4) Present a one to two page plan of how you are going to accomplish the two tasks listed above—1) the gaining of power and 2) the staying in power. Plan should be neat, signed by all members and submitted on time.

This is what I call an open-ended assignment. It is similar to a game, which has some rules but not many rules. There is plenty of freedom of choice to go around. If I were doing this assignment, I believe that I would find the first part the most difficult—deciding on what strategy, what sort of appeal I can use to get the American people to vote for my group. Other groups will be vying for the same position, so I do not want to be trite. Some politicians today tend to believe that most Americans cannot hold two ideas in their heads simultaneously, hence the sound bites and the simple solutions offered for complex issues. Napoleon (the real one) said that in battle it was necessary to concentrate one's forces at the point of impact. To simplify and drive home the "message" might be the most difficult aspect of this task.

The effort to maintain power is essentially the time to engage in fantasy. Many of us have fantasized, "If I were king…" This is your chance. Here is where the creative freedom of choice comes into play. For the ladies in the various groups, consider this—"Men have been in charge of the political situations in Western Civilization for over two thousand years. Fantasy time though it may be, seize the moment!!"

Your plan can include alliances with other countries, elimination of other countries, development of resources, exploitation of resources, control of the educational system, destruction of the educational system. The only ethic you need follow is the ethic that says, "Whatever keeps you in power is right." Like Napoleon, you are always right.

Criteria for Success

I will evaluate your group's performance on the following criteria:

1) Collaboration within group
2) Class Presentation of Plan
3) Written Plan
4) One minute messages

Incidentally, as a further motivation to succeed in this task, remember that only one group can "win." The losing groups are already scheduled for "execution by gruesome torturing to death." (Rumor has it that this involves strapping each member to chair and forcing him/her to watch 48 straight hours of TeleTubby shows).

Washington Post Dispatch Gazette article

Washington D.C., our nation's capital, evaporated yesterday in a mushroom-shaped cloud. Foul play is suspected. Witnesses say that one minute the city was there, and the next minute, it wasn't. Dennis Gardner, passerby on I-95, said, "One minute I was looking at the Capital, and the next minute it was gone." Amtrak Traveler, Melissa Grey, echoed Gardiner's comment. "We were just on the outskirts of town when suddenly the whole city went up in smoke. The blast rattled the train I was on and caused the Slurpee I was drinking to spill and ruin my pink chiffon dress with gold rhinestones and a lovely lace ruffle around the neck. Now who is going to pay for that cleaning bill?" Grey's lawyer is trying to find someone to sue. Elizabeth Ashlock, famous talk show hostess and her friend, Rachel Hackenberger, known syndicate boss and high stakes gambler, were in Ashlock's Lear jet when the blast occurred. Ashlock noted, "Boy, there was some air turbulence when that baby went off." Hackenberger added, "Hey, I thought that hit was meant for me. But it'll take more than a megaton thermonuclear device to take *me* out." Ashlock and Hackenberger were on their way to a concrete manufacturer's convention when.......

APPENDIX A

You Begin With 100 Million
and Two Cents

With
100,000,000.02

ITEM/AD/EVENT	Cost per Item	# of Items	Total COST	COST	LIST		
Rally in 1 Major U.S. City	5 Million						
1 Minute Commercial Prime Time	300,000						
1 Full Page Ad-top ten magazines	100,000						
1 Million Posters + Distribution	3 Million						
Full Page Ad, New York Times	200,000						
Radio Ad 1 Minute Major Network	100,000						
What you have left =							

Closure Pinky and the Brain

Name_____

Period____ Group ID#_____ Date_____

"Propaganda is to a democracy what a bludgeon is to a totalitarian state."

Noam Chomsky

1) If you were a non-human inhabitant of *Animal Farm*, which animal do you think you would be--the pigs (well-read, relatively educated but corrupt), the sheep, or Boxer, the worker who follows slogans? Give reasons for your choice.

_____

_____

_____

2) Please read and think about the following quotes from Noam Chomsky, "A Brief History of US Corporate & Government Propaganda Operations."

"Lippmann argued that in a properly functioning democracy there are two classes of citizens...the specialized class (distinct minority who runs things) and the big majority of the population...the 'bewildered herd.' The function of the bewildered herd is to be spectators...The bewildered herd are a problem, we've got to prevent their rage and trampling, we've got to distract them, they should be watching the Super Bowl, or sit-coms, or violent movies. Every once in a while you call on them to chant meaningless slogans, like 'support our troops," and you've got to keep them pretty scared because unless they're scared properly and frightened of all kinds of devils that are going to destroy them, they may start to think, which is very dangerous because they're not competent enough to think, and therefore it's important to distract them and marginalize them."

In five lines, react to Chomsky's statement. Is this true, and, if so, will you become one of the educated specialized class or one of the bewildered herd?

_____

_____

_____

_____

_____

3) Let us fantasize for a moment that Lippmann is right and the power of this democracy is in the hands of a few who have wealth and power. Is it in *their* interest to have a well read and educated public? Would they prefer that you not work in school, but prefer to work after school? Is it in their interest to portray an *intellectual* as some kind of nerd who doesn't have the common sense to turn a doorknob? Would they want people to be *educated* voters meaning that people *read and studied* their candidates? Or does the group in power want people who vote for candidates who provided a keg of beer at the company picnic or who gave them slogans that they wanted to hear, or who get most of their information from television and word of mouth?

Does the group in power want an educated population, or is it in their best interest to have essentially an ignorant population? Would they rather have the majority watch Channel 12 or the *Nanny?*

Think about television programs, movies, music, commercials, magazines, etc. Do they seem to support the goals of the minority in power (if such a minority exists), or do they act in the best interest of the majority of the population? In ten lines, address some of these questions. Are your values *your* values or are you playing into the hands of the power brokers?

_____

_____

_____

_____

_____

_____

Beyond Infinity: Pinky and the Brain

1. Ask the students either through class discussion or in groups to consider how their group functioned. What were the challenges and how did they overcome those challenges?
2. What could the group have done better?
3. What did the group excel at doing?
4. What did students learn about the subject matter (literary work, middle ages, time, interpersonal relations, etc.)?
5. What, if anything, did students learn about themselves, other people, life in general?
6. What questions do they have about themselves, other people, life in general?

Specific to the unit studied:

1) As in *Brave New World* people want stability. Change frightens most people. They want certainty. Unfortunately for many, we live in an age of uncertainty. Heisenberg and Neils Bohr changed the vision of science from moving toward the truth to questioning the existence of truth. That's why people who come up with simple solutions to complex problems often get elected. What does civilization promise us? No surprises!!

2) Wrapping oneself in the flag—patriotism—is one way to overcome uncertainty. Everyone wants to belong. Nationalism, ethnicity—all pretty foolish when you think about it. But nobody wants to live as a hermit—humans are social creatures—they need to belong. During a teacher strike opponents of the teachers were marching with the flag—does that make teachers communists? What the hell does that mean—don't argue the issue (teacher salaries); argue the flag. Joe McCarthy threatened to uncover communists in American government. He found none.

3) Another American appeal is freedom of choice—like Burger King. Have your hamburger your way—how much freedom is freedom? Only culture with Bart Simpson mentality—"I do what I want when I want." What is that? What are the consequences of that? Gun Control—opponents wrap themselves in the flag and say it is our freedom to carry weapons. Is that what founding fathers intended? Takes real issue away from fact that a minority of people is making a majority of money off selling death.

Same mindset applies to vouchers. Big problem with vouchers is that how are poor schools supposed to improve? Implies teachers and students are slacking off and just competition Business Style will shape them up. Does competition bring out the best? Biggest issue is that vouchers detract from attempting true school reform. Besides, who said parents will pick "best" schools for their children? Cheapest? Gives most A's?

4) Importance of words—"Genuine Imitation Leather," Food ingredient s "All natural," (arsenic is also "all natural" because it occurs naturally in nature)

So is radioactivity natural.

Renaissance Theme Park

Teacher Notes—Renaissance Theme Park

This project originally was planned as an introduction to Shakespeare. Instead of lecturing for two or three days on Renaissance art, customs, everyday life, etc., I created this project so the students would 1) develop a context for Shakespeare's work and 2) develop research and collaborative skills. As it evolved, the students became more attached to their assigned city, and impromptu discussions of art and architecture broke out amongst the groups. The project itself took on a life of its own, a wish fulfillment that every teacher shares. By the second day, all groups were busily engaged, and I spent my class time circulating among the groups, acting as a resource, putting out fires when necessary and starting a few on my own.

The major difficulty I experienced with this assignment was time. I had not anticipated how their research would lead students into interesting avenues of exploration. "Mr. M., could we include vendors selling food specific to that city or region?" "Can we include a science fair?" "Can we showcase our city leaders in some way?" I had to get to the actual reading and study of Macbeth. Tempted to curtail the Renaissance Theme Park to get on with the curriculum, I listened to my inner teacher voice and let the project play out. I was glad I did. During the study of Shakespeare's plays and poetry, students constantly made connections to what they had learned in this project.

I actually started this assignment with three lectures on successive days. I think lecturing can be a useful methodology if the lectures themselves are engaging. I think I had probably about 8 really good lectures up my sleeve, but I know that I did not have 180. I also learned to construct my lectures in the form of a story. In fact, almost all presentations should be in the form of a story, from the teacher lecturing on the Big Bang to the CEO providing the story of the company. I took a page from the wonderful historian, Barbara Tuchman, and created my stories around people or situations or problems. For example, in developing a context for why people came to northern America, I fashioned my story around Henry VIII. Why not? Henry's story involves temper tantrums, executions, and sex.

The lectures I include here are major concepts and are not meant to be said verbatim. I visited the blackboard/whiteboard frequently and drew diagrams and moats and castles. As technologies emerged, I used the interactive whiteboard to enhance my lectures--- Powerpoints should enrich presentations, not be the heart of the presentations themselves.

I included a handout about Operational Goals. I learned that inexperienced students especially (adolescents as a whole!) have difficulty planning, so I used this template to get them started.

I also included an individual assignment. Working in a group is a privilege for a student. It is NOT a divine right. When, on occasion, a student wasted class time in a group, after a warning or two, I promised the student he would not work in a group until he earned the right.

During the next project, like the one here, I did not assign him to a group, but required that he work alone on this individual assignment during the term of this unit. Of course, he vociferously protested and begged and promised ("I'll be good and work."). I did not relent. To be given an individual assignment he must have really tested my patience and abused his privilege, so my response was that he would have to earn that right back. Grumbling and upset and protesting the unfairness on my part and on the part of the rest of the universe, this student worked alone. The message was not only for him but for the rest of the class. If you do, for the reasons cited above, issue an individual assignment, make certain that the assignment has educational value. Do not relent. The one or two times, early in my career, that I relented, the off task behavior not only intensified but spread to other students. Trust me…hold your ground.

One year I had to, because of time constraints, issue this same assignment to three classes. I simply changed the cities and it worked. Have fun with this one.

Introductory Lecture #1

From Cadavers to Columbus

An Introductory Lecture on the Renaissance

1. Tell a story. The buckaroos love stories rather than the cold imparting of information. Tell them you will use as your central focus of the story, medieval architecture (the cathedrals) and painting to illustrate the change from the medieval period to the Renaissance.

2. Show them an example of Romanesque architecture--the term Romanesque was actually a negative adjective applied to the style that featured big heavy walls, dim light and cubby hole style alcoves. The light was dim because windows weaken a heavy wall, and the walls were heavy because, to be tall, the churches need thick walls. Walking into a Romanesque style church one is inclined to look straight ahead and down--this fitted the medieval temperament just fine. God is omnipotent and, somewhat oppressive. We humble our eyes and ourselves before the Great One. This is a god to be feared. Dark church, dark god. People went to medieval churches to learn their religion through iconography and symbolism. The sculptures and friezes in the church taught them the birth of Christ, the Sermon on the Mount, the Crucifixion, etc. These people could not read. The Romanesque churches (and their descendants) are often called "storybooks in stone."

3. Cathedrals also epitomized man's devotion to God. It would take many years to build a cathedral, and most people who started the building knew they would not live to see its completion. Cathedrals also burned down with unpleasant regularity and a number of cathedrals crumpled and crashed as builders worked in a frenzy to build the tallest structures as a matter of civic pride.

4. Along comes the flying buttress. The support from flying buttresses enabled the walls to be thinner, the windows bigger--hark!! Stained Glass windows!! Now the church is infused with light, colorful light. People now go to church not only for the education but for the entertainment. Medieval and early renaissance life was basically brown--brown earth, brown clothing, brown huts, brown horses, brown dung. But the stained glass windows!! No wonder that churches became centers not only for religious reflection but mercantile foci as well. The high steeples and tall walls force you, when you first walk into a gothic church to look upward. Your eyes naturally go toward the ceiling. Try it!! This is the essence of agape love. You look up to God and God looks down to you. Your heart is uplifted to Him! Quite a change from the Storm and Strife Omnipotent One of the medieval period. This is an example of how art mirrors people's change in their relationships with the universe and how those social changes are reflected in the art. As the Renaissance deepened and expanded, the energies of the populace became increasingly devoted to building not cathedrals (cathedrals were built in church capitals--county seats. Regular old towns had mere churches.) but town halls. City Hall became the center of civic pride reflecting the emphasis on man's relationship not with God but with fellow man. In Salt Lake City, Utah, (this is many moons later) the tallest first building was the church. Later it was City Hall. Now it is a corporate building. What does this mean?

5. Ask them to look at the architecture of the buildings in their area. What conclusions can they draw about the their society based on the buildings? If they were aliens from Alpha Dufusses Star System, what observations would they make about our culture based on the structures that exist? (First there are things called cities where the majority of structures exist--thus centralized populations. Second, stadia and other sport structures along with corporate buildings dominate the skyline. Architecture is basically about the use of space. How do we use space?

Introductory lecture #2

Paintings, Barber Poles and Ptolemy

1) The crusades "liberated" the jewels of the libraries that the Arabs kept intact. They therefore brought back knowledge to Europe--knowledge such as geometry.

2) Meanwhile, barbers were learning a great deal. Doctors prescribed medicines, herbs, but they had no knowledge of what was going on in the human body. It was as if a child were examining an earth worm--the supposition was that there was a lot of gunk inside. (The four humours). But barbers (surgeons) were tending people that were wounded in war--they saw bodies ripped open by shot and shell--"Ooh. Look at that red thing pumping blood. Hey, look at how those muscles are attached to the bones!! Golly, I wonder if this guy really needs this organ?"

3) In the middle ages, art was iconographic and symbolic. The idea of Christ, the idea of the Madonna, the idea of the Crucifixion. All the Christs and all the Madonnas and all the Crucifixions in medieval painting look somewhat the same. Even the Christ child looks like a miniature adult (complete, sometimes with five o'clock shadow!!). Artists often did not sign their works--they were craftsmen, reproducing the ideas for educational purposes. But some painters posed the act of painting as a **problem**. Leonardo and others asked the questions, "What would a grieving mother who watched her son crucified look like?" "If a body is suspended from a cross, what would the musculature look like?" "How would the body hang?" Naturalism, portraying life as accurately as possible, became the fad. Artists like to use the newly discovered "perspective" to trick people into thinking they were seeing the real thing.

What was necessary now was for artists to be good <u>observers</u>. To be *scientists.* They began to accumulate facts. So the barbers (that is why the barber pole is red and white!! symbolizes bandages) provided information on how the blood circulated. Leonardo and others "borrowed" cadavers and placed the bodies in different positions to study musculature. They studied people's faces to see what faces looked like when people cried or laughed or were suspicious.

Artists still worked on commission, and the patron still controlled the process. Blue was expensive and a patron would dictate how much blue he could afford in a painting. And sometimes he demanded from the artist that the artist paint the faces of neighbors in the scenes. So we have the three magi with the faces of Harry's three neighbors!! But now artists had reputations and signed their works. Men and their products became as important as using art to celebrate God's greatest.

Instead of taking the natural world around them for granted, people started to study and catalogue their findings. Linnaeus thought that, within his lifetime, he could catalogue the entire plant world.

4) Meanwhile, back at the ranch of Columbus, good old Christopher was hunched over a map that some crusaders had brought back from some Arab library. It was the work of Ptolemy, the same fellow who centuries earlier had thought that the earth was the center of the universe. People still thought so. But, for Columbus, Ptolemy's measurements of the earth were more important. Ptolemy, using geometry, had calculated the size of the earth.

Now everyone wanted a quick route to get to Spice Land (China), the exotic area that Marco Polo and family had written about. Most people would not sail west because there seemed to be nothing but ocean in that direction, and suppose they ran out of food or water six months out? But Columbus was convinced by Ptolemy's predictions of the earth's size. Columbus believed that the circumference of the earth was small enough that the distance to the China was reachable if he sailed west. He theorized, according to Ptolemy's calculations, that he could reach China in three months. The food and water would held out that long. So off he went. Columbus and Ptolemy were wrong. The circumference of the earth was larger than Ptolemy had theorized. Little did poor Chris know that there was an entire continent, the future home of the strongest nation in the world.

Despite the muff of Columbus, exploration exploded. The result was more and more information shared by more and more people. Getting information became important.

Introductory lecture #3

"Still, the earth moves."
Galileo

1) In China, only the emperor's own astrologers were allowed to practice astrology. This is because the emperor used the astrologer's predictions as the appropriate time to make love with the empress to sire a child. Copernicus was an astrologer. Astrology was the science of the day. The problem was that all models used the earth as the center of the universe. Consequently predicting where the planets would be at a given time became extremely irksome. Therefore astrology was important. Copernicus tried to find a better model for predicting where the planets would be. He was a deeply religious man, and tried to help the church in this enterprise. But every model he tried was wrong, simply because he used the earth as the center of the solar system. One day he, out of frustration, said, "I know this is crazy, but let's try using the sun as the center and the earth going around it." He found that his predictions were much much more accurate. (they weren't perfect because the earth's orbit is not round. It is elliptical. The world had to wait for Johann Kepler to figure that one out.)

So Copernicus wrote a book explaining his heliocentric (as opposed to geocentric) view of the solar system. The Church was not amused, but neither was it threatened. If Copernicus wanted to say elephants had wings, he could go right ahead. If he wanted to say the sun was the center of the solar system instead of the earth, he could go right ahead. He had no proof. As father as Mother Church was concerned, Aristotle, writing centuries before, was still correct. The earth, and mankind, was the center of it all. After all, Aristotle was the smartest man who ever lived, right?!

2) The proof for Copernicus came later. Observation became important. When someone invented the telescope, what was it first used for? It was used for spying in Mrs. Jones' boudoir. More importantly, it was used for war--observing the enemy from afar. Galileo was an astrologer and businessman. He loved inventions. He was messing with the telescope and decided to turn it toward the night sky. Presto!! He discovered that Jupiter had moons, the moon moved, etc. He published a book with his findings, and this time the Church was not only not amused but they felt threatened because Galileo had proof--mathematical proof which the average layman could not understand.

The Church, in no uncertain terms, told Galileo to drop the issue and not refer to his wild, cockamamie ideas again. He did, for a while. But the notion that the solar system was heliocentric and that the earth spun on its axis gnawed at him. He wrote another text (another fine example of scientists getting in trouble through publishing!!) in which a thinly disguised moron becomes an advocate of the geocentric theory and a bright scientist offers the heliocentric view. Galileo's satire was obvious and offensive. Put under house arrest he was eventually tried.

The trial was a real happening.

It is easy to look at the Church elders as Bigger Than Life Deufusses. But people in those days trusted their senses. "You claim the earth spins, Galileo? In other words if I drop a handkerchief when I am on a merry go round, the handkerchief drops to the ground a short distance behind me because the merry go round is spinning. Is that correct?"

"Yes."

"So that if I drop a handkerchief now, because the earth is spinning, as you claim, Galileo, then it should drop a short distance to the side of me? Is that your contention?"

"No. You do not understand. There is this relative thing in which.."

"Galileo, you also postulate that the earth goes around the sun?"

"Yes, my lord, with all due respect it does."

"Are you aware, Galileo, that Aristotle claimed just the opposite?"

"Yes, of course I am aware that he did."

"And the Holy Mother Church as well as all learned men believe that Aristotle was the smartest and wisest man that ever lived. Are you aware of that?"

"Yes, but "

"Are you contending that you are smarter than Aristotle?"

"No, your worship, but"

"Galileo, when I wake up in the morning, the sun is in the East. Is that not true?"

"Yes."

"And as I watch the sun MOVE, it moves toward the middle of the sky and sets in the west. Is that not true?"

"I know it appears that way, your lordship."

"Are you telling me that I am not seeing what I am seeing?"

"But, but, I can explain if you let me explain my calculations."

And so it went. Galileo, under severe threat, recanted his findings. As he left the trial, his assistant said, "Master. What fools they are. Imagine. Thinking that the sun moved around the earth."

Galileo, in a rare moment of intellectual compassion, responded, "I wonder what it would look like if the sun went around the earth?"

In effect, he was saying that they weren't fools. It would look just like it looked.

There are several things to get from the Galileo experience.

1) Galileo's proofs shocked the educated world and later the world at large. The biggest shock came to the collective psyche. If you cannot trust your senses, what could you trust? Now, explaining how the universe "operates," scientists throw layers of calculations and computations on the blackboard which the layman cannot understand.

2) Interesting that today cosmologists would claim that whether the earth goes around the sun or the sun goes around the earth is a moot point. Einsteinian physics says they revolve around each other--the position of the observer is the only relevant factor.

3) The end of the renaissance signals the beginning of the rudiments of the enlightenment. Sensory perception is out, past models are questioned, and the universe becomes a plaything to be observed and measured.

4) Most importantly, people fight change. Metaphors, in this case the geocentric view of the solar system, must be challenged when new information comes into play. Myths are inherently conservative. And when the new information contradicts the myths, we can either be reactionary and hang on to the familiar but incorrect metaphors or invent new metaphors. This is the fundamental reason why school programs do not change!!!!! We teach the way we were taught rather than the ways that research and new models tell us are more effective.

Name_____

Group ID_____

The Renaissance Theme Park
or
forget Mickey and Donald--
We got Michelangelo and Donatello

It is the latter part of the sixteenth century. There is a temporary lull in the hostilities among nations, but the intense rivalries are still there. The leaders of Europe, in an attempt to maintain the relative calm and to unify the peoples of the continent, intend to establish a Renaissance Theme Park in one of the major cities. This theme park must serve several purposes: 1) It must be a testimony to the greatness of the Renaissance 2) It must be an instructive tool for people to learn about the Renaissance and its values so it must be accurate and 3) It must be entertainment for the nobility *and* the masses.

Your group will be assigned a city which would like to host the theme park. This would mean a tremendous economic boon to your city. Even more importantly, it would foster a huge amount of civic pride. As a leading trading company, your group's task is to secure the theme park for your city by presenting your design to the Renaissance Regents (the instructor) who will award one city the prestige of housing the theme park. In effect, you must convince the Regents that your city and your design will provide Europe with a magnificent monument to the Renaissance. In order to accomplish this, your group must research both your city during this time period and the arts, sciences, economics, social life, and politics of the Renaissance. Then you must read the rules!!!

RULES OF THE RENAISSANCE THEME PARK

1) Each city will be awarded the amount of 300,000 Ducats to spend on the design of the theme park. Each structure or amusement costs a specific amount. These amounts can be found on the Cost sheet. No group can exceed this amount.

2) a city can advertise the artwork or technology from another city. For example, London can propose displaying a work by Leonardo da Vinci on the assumption that Leonardo would have wanted his work displayed in such a prestigious place.

3) Each city will submit A model or drawing <u>on time</u>.

4) Each city will submit a written proposal explaining the intent of the design and the attributes of the city.

5) Each city will prepare a presentation to the Regents explaining their design and the attributes of the city. This presentation may be live, accompanied by enhancements or Enhancements include presentations, online and live, music, visuals, etc.

6) Each city will adhere to historical accuracy. An amusement cannot be powered by a nuclear reactor, for example.

7) The Regents look favorably upon specifics. Claiming to display "works by da Vinci" will impress no one. Likewise, stating that there will be "Renaissance music as people enter the gate." will not endear your project to the Regents.

This enterprise demands that your group demonstrate excellent collaborative skills. Other skills that must be employed are research, critical thinking, and creative skills. Division of labor is an extremely relevant strategy here. Divide the research into manageable parts and then discuss everyone's findings *as a group*. Do not simply accept a member's decision that "these are the best paintings of the Renaissance." How do these paintings fit in with the "wholeness" of your theme park? Does everything seem to fit together as a unified whole? Consider not only the arts and sciences of the times, but the social life of the period. How did people amuse themselves? What did they find titillating and intriguing? What were the politics of the time.

This is not a requirement, but your group might consider electing someone as the group's coordinator whose job it will be to, well, coordinate everyone's work. This position is not intended to be a slave driver, but one who tries to keep the group's focus clear and direction steady.

This is a major project. It demands that everyone within a group double and triple up on tasks. If you finish your particular research on one area, help another member with something else. All the requirements--the paper, the design and the presentation--give you the opportunity to be enormously clever and creative. For example, in your theme park, what would satisfy the nostalgia of a visitor? Know your material well, and then let your mind go crazy.

CRITERIA FOR SUCCESS

1. GROUP INVOLVEMENT AND GROUP COHESION--100 POINTS
   a) everyone makes the best use of class time
   b) work is apportioned evenly and fairly
   c) group demonstrates good collaborative skills including communication, trust, leadership and problem solving.
2. THE DESIGN OF THE THEME PARK   --100 POINTS
   a) historical accuracy and attractiveness--25 points
   b) creativity--25 points
   c) captures the essential features and concepts of the renaissance-50 points
3. THE PAPER THAT IS SUBMITTED DETAILING THE DESIGN--100 POINTS
   The paper should
   a) be neat and punctual
   b) explain the group's overall intent and reasons for the design
   c) detail the specific choices that the group has made and the reasons for those choices.

4) THE PRESENTATION OF THE DESIGN TO THE REGENTS--100 POINTS
   The presentation should
   a) be well organized

b) involve everyone in the group
c) utilize enhancements
d) provide a convincing and clever argument for your city

A first step in this project would be to gather information. Find out the names of the people most closely associated with the Renaissance in the fields of art, science, politics and philosophy. Then divide up your group into research teams. Find out what terms most often come up in articles about that time period (humanism, platonism, etc.). Then, *as a group pool,* what each of you has learned and begin to brainstorm about the form and function of your theme park.

This is a demanding and ambitious enterprise that should challenge your critical and creative skills. It will also be a test of your research capabilities. I stand ready to assist in any way possible. Bonne chance!!

CITIES FOR THE RENAISSANCE PROJECT

1) London
2) Florence
3) Venice
4) Amsterdam
5) Milan
6) Paris

EVERYTHING HAS A PRICE!!

Your company has been awarded 300,000 Ducats to design a Renaissance theme park. To include an item in your theme park will cost a specific amount. Below is an explanation of each item:

1) A shop is a retail store that sells a particular group of things. It may be a bakery, a RETAILER OF HORSE AND BUGGY ITEMS OR MUSICAL INSTRUMENTS. a SHOP COSTS 5,000 DUCATS.

2) An EXHIBIT HOUSES A GROUP OF ITEMS THAT HAVE A COMMONALITY. For EXAMPLE, AN EXHIBIT OF PAINTINGS OR INVENTIONS OR ARTIFACTS. Each ITEM IN THE EXHIBIT COSTS 1,000 DUCATS AND MUST BE CATALOGUED IN YOUR PAPER. The EXHIBIT HALL COSTS 10,000 DUCATS, SO IF YOU HAVE AN EXHIBIT OF 10 PAINTINGS THE TOTAL WILL BE 20,000. The PAINTINGS MUST BE NAMED AND THE PAINTER GIVEN CREDIT IN YOUR PAPER.

3) An AMUSEMENT WOULD BE THE EQUIVALENT OF A "RIDE" TODAY. An AMUSEMENT MAY BE A RIDE (WHICH, OF COURSE, CANNOT BE ELECTRICALLY DRIVEN). An AMUSEMENT COSTS 15,000 DUCATS.

4) a THEATRICAL PERFORMANCE REFERS TO ANY OF THE PERFORMING ARTS. It MAY BE A DANCE, A CONCERT, OR A STAGE PLAY OR ANY SIMILAR PERFORMANCE.. Performances COST A ONE TIME FEE OF 15,000.

5) Structures that serve a function, aesthetic or otherwise cost 2,000 ducats. Structures include lost and found stations, restrooms, fountains, ponds, waterfalls, etc. Please specify the nature of each structure in your paper.

Remember that your theme park should be designed to 1) instruct 2) uplift 3)entertain the visitors. You must consider human engineering--how can you make their visit comfortable, enlightening and entertaining?

1. SHOPS	=	5,000 DUCATS
2. EXHIBITS	=	10,000 "
3. ITEMS IN THE EXHIBIT	=	1,000 "
4. AMUSEMENTS	=	15,000 "
5. THEATRICAL PERFORMANCES	=	15,000 "
6) STRUCTURES	=	2,000 " EACH

Group Id#_____ Project_____

Period_____

OPERATIONAL GOALS

Members:1)_____ 2)_____

3)_____ 4)_____

5)_____ 6)_____

What Needs to be Done?	**Whose Responsibility?**	**When Will It be Completed?**
1)_____	1)_____	1)_____
2)_____	2)_____	2)_____
3)_____	3)_____	3)_____
4)_____	4)_____	4)_____
5)_____	5)_____	5)_____
6)_____	6)_____	6)_____
7)_____	7)_____	7)_____
8)_____	8)_____	8)_____
9)_____	9)_____	9)_____
10)_____	10)_____	10)_____
11)_____	11)_____	11)_____
12)_____	12)_____	12)_____

DATES OF SCHEDULED MEETINGS

1)_____

2)_____

3)_____

4)_____

5)_____

6)_____

PURPOSE OF MEETINGS

1)_____

2)_____

3)_____

4)_____

5)_____

6)_____

ACCEPTED ROLES

1) Facilitator/Organizer

2) Script Editor/Reviser

3) On Task Supervisor

4) Audio/Visual/Prop Technician

5) Art/Music Editor/Director

MEMBER

1)_____

2)_____

3)_____

4)_____

5)_____

All students will be writers/composers and researchers. Please follow the descriptions of these roles that follow:

Facilitator/Organizer--Organizes material and helps people in their various tasks. Is sensitive to people's feelings and knows how to get people to work together.

Script Editor/Reviser--Reviews all scripts and revises them for accuracy and language mechanics. Knows how to encourage people and gently criticize the work that comes across his/her desk.

On Task Supervisor--Keeps all members on task and on time. Keeps members on the same track toward the common goals. Frequently reviews assignment to make certain that everyone is "on the same page."

Audio/Visual/Prop Technician--Prepares tapes, both audio and video, edits these materials and helps in their selection. Creates and arranges props.

Art/Music Editor/Director--Chooses musical accompaniment and art displays for presentations and demonstrations. Helps decide artistic choices that are appropriate for the group's goals.

AVENUES OF RESEARCH

The following is a list of people and places and things and ideas you might want to use to begin your research. You certainly do not have to research all of them or even most of them, but in the course of your research I am certain you will come across the overwhelming majority of these items. At least you <u>should</u>.

ART	ARTISTS	PEOPLE	MORE PEOPLE	CONCEPTS
foreshorten	Alberti	Sir Thomas More	Galen	humanism
perspective	Leonardo da Vinci	the Medici	Galileo	platonism
mannerism	Michelangel	Pope Julius II	Copernicus	aristotelianism
fresco	Ralphael	Petrarch	Tycho Brahe	city-state
	Titian	Machiavelli	Johannes Kepler	pragmatism
	Jan van Eyck	Erasmus	Sir Francis Drake	secularism
	Correggio	Henry VIII	Magellan	Thomism
	Botticelli	Elizabeth I	Christopher Columbus	Scholastic theology
	Mantegna	Henry of Portugal	Vasco da Gama	
	Tintoretto			
	Masaccio			
	Donatello			
	Ghiberti			
	Brunelleschi			

Name_____

Individual Assignment #1

1) Write a two to four page essay comparing the cities in terms of
      a) economic resources
      b) artistic resources
      c) cultural advantages and disadvantages

2) Write one page describing which city you would choose to live in during the Renaissance and why.

3) Choose one Renaissance scientist and write a one to two page essay describing his/her contributions to western civilization. If you were to award a Nobel Prize for Science during this time period, who would win it?

4) Choose one artist from the Renaissance and, in a one to two page essay, describe why he was one of the most popular artists of the period. Make certain you refer to specific works by the artist.

All material should be neatly organized, punctual and typed. Evaluation will be made according to the following criteria:

1) Organization
2) Depth and accuracy of research
3) Punctuality
4) Writing Mechanics

Beyond Infinity: Renaissance Theme Park

Generic:

1. Ask the students either through class discussion or in groups to consider how their group functioned. What were the challenges and how did they overcome those challenges?
2. What could the group have done better?
3. What did the group excel at doing?
4. What did students learn about the subject matter (literary work, middle ages, time, interpersonal relations, etc.)?
5. What, if anything, did students learn about themselves, other people, life in general?
6. What questions do they have about themselves, other people, life in general?

The teacher can use the questions below as either closures for the projects or as the inceptions of new projects.

Specific to the unit studied:

1) If you were to apply three adjectives to describe the Renaissance you just studied, what would they be? Explain each choice.
2) Compare and contrast the values/beliefs of the Renaissance and those of contemporary society.
3) Would you prefer to have lived during the Renaissance? Why or why not?
4) Is "Man" truly the measure of all things?
5) Are you a Renaissance person?
6) Does art, especially the visual arts, have as much relevance in the modern era as it did back in the Renaissance? Give reasons for your answer.
7) In the Renaissance, the concept of pragmatism ("if it works it is ethically justified") seemed to be prevalent. In our culture, how prevalent is that concept? Consider the belief that cheating is okay if it gets one into college.
8) Is it possible that, in the near future, some people would initiate a rebirth, a renaissance, and go back to the past to find inspiration?

The Retrial of Galileo

Teacher Notes: The Retrial of Galileo

This is simply a rough outline of a project which is cross disciplinary. If I were actually to employ this project, I would flesh it out, establishing rubrics for each subject and each presentation. All content areas can employ project based learning, and a major argument for pbl is that studies indicate that standardized test scores http://www.bie.org/research/study/meap_outcomes_2004 improve with pbl. This makes sense, because as students engage in a project, they work with the content and often internalize basic principles much better than they would in the conventional classroom. http://www.bie.org/research/study/powerful_learning When working with teachers who use conventional methodologies (teacher talk, student listen), ask them how effective their methodologies are in helping students retain content in long term memory.

This project would appear radical to many high school teachers. The concept of cross disciplinary collaboration is, in truth, more difficult to execute than to conceptualize. Most administrators would appreciate its value, but policy makers and many of these same administrators do little to modify the school schedule so that true collaboration can take place. I know of teachers that have been told, "Meet on your own time---planning periods, lunch, after school." My belief is that, if an institution truly values something, then it demonstrates that value by modifying the system so that that goal is achieved.

I once asked a Latin teacher and later a geometry teacher what value their respective subjects had in the modern world. Ultimately both replied that the logic used in learning Latin and solving math problems was a logic transferable to other disciplines. But research tells us that most students, even the most academic of them, do not automatically make those transfers. So if we want students to see connectivity between both skills and content across disciplines, than we have to do something more than hope students make those connections on their own. That is one of the reasons why cross disciplinary projects are so important.

I experienced one of those rare days when a number of teachers were out sick, and I was called upon to cover their classes. I covered an English class which was studying the novel Animal Farm, then moved to social studies class examining Stalin's Russia, and ended the day in an art class focusing on Nazi art propaganda. As I drove home, I asked myself, "What is wrong with this picture?" What would have happened if all three teachers worked together to develop a unit on propaganda? The only thing stopping us from these enterprises is the human will. We abrogate school schedules for pep rallies and trips to the auditorium for impromptu activities principals deem necessary. Schools have altered school schedules so teachers can collaborate. The people who have overcome these obstacles begin with the principle that the schedule is designed to accommodate student learning and not the other way around.

I originally designed this project with rubrics for evaluation for each participating subject, but I realized that 1) it was a much better idea to give ownership of this project to the participating teachers by having them decide what they wanted to evaluate and 2) hopefully these rubrics would evolve from collaboration amongst the teachers.

Of course, this project, like almost all the others in this book, is a prototype, to be used as a model for projects involving people other than Galileo. Isaac Newton, Charles Darwin, and Albert Einstein are other possibilities. All of them could be the focus of a trial of public opinion.

Name_____

Group ID_____

The Trial of Galileo Galilei

Introduction

Nicholaus Copernicus in the 16th Century, like other astrologers, attempted to find better predictions for the orbits of the heavenly bodies around the earth. In Copernicus' time, astrology was the science of the time, and, in order to make proper forecasts, astrologers needed to have accurate predictions of where the sun, moon, and planets were at a given moment. Unfortunately for the astrologers, the fact that they were basing their predictions on a geocentric model (earth is the center) doomed their predictions to be inaccurate. Copernicus, out of frustration, decided to be radical and rethink the orbits by postulating a heliocentric model (sun as the center). Of course, using the better model, the predictions turned out to be more accurate (although they were still off since they were using cocentric instead of elliptical orbits--Kepler changed that). Copernicus offered his views, but since his work was still fundamentally theoretical, his ideas were not considered a threat to conventional thinking.

Galileo Galilei, using the telescope to examine the night sky, wrote a book detailing his findings back by empirical research. This was a threat. For centuries conventional wisdom held that Aristotle was the smartest man who ever lived, and Aristotle argued for a geocentric view of the solar system. This was congruent with western culture"s belief in a universe that was centered on mankind.

After receiving repeated warnings to repudiate his work, and refusing to do so, Galileo was hauled into court by the Inquisition.

The goal of this project is to defend Galileo in a retrial. To do this, several subprojects must be accomplished in different content areas:

Math students will study the mathematics Galileo used to propose this theory that the earth moved. Galileo's analysis and proofs relied heavily on the Eudoxian theory of proportion. Their subproject will be to understand Galileo's mathematics so that they can be understood by the layman of the 17th Century.

Students will be divided into groups and each group will be given the tasks above. On the assigned day, each group will present its understanding of Galileo's mathematics and a proposal on how to explain this understanding in the early 17th Century.

Science students in groups will address three major questions: First, they will study the science of Galileo's theory. What laws of physics did Galileo rely on? What scientific contribution did Galileo make in terms of the scientific method? Second, students will discuss if and how scientific inquiry and conclusions is culturally biased. That is, how much does the prevailing thinking within a culture affect scientific thought? Third, groups are to prepare a model of what an earth day would look like if the sun did go around the earth.

On the assigned day, each group will present its understanding of Galileo's science and a proposal on how to explain this understanding in the early 17th Century.

Social Studies students will, in small groups, examine the impact Galileo's findings had on the people in his time period. Why was the Inquisition so threatened by Galileo's book? What, if anything, changed sociologically.

On the assigned day, each group will present its understanding of the impact Galileo's theory had on his society, and how the defense counsel can best use this information.

English students will be divided into several groups. One group will be the defense counsel for Galileo in his retrial. Members of this group will study trial proceedings in this time period and prepare a defense after collaboration with math, science, and social studies students. One group will prepare for the trial as the prosecution. This group may either represent either ecclesiastical or civil authorities. This group must also research the trial proceedings of the period. A third group will represent the media of the time, and will issue a newspaper relating the details of the trial to the public. To prepare for this, the group must study the media of the time period with a focus on style. The newspaper may contain advertisements as would be found in the early 17th century. A fourth group will be the jury. Each jurist must research an occupation of the time period, and create a personna based on that occupation and present it to the class. During the trial, each jurist is to keep notes on the trial proceedings which he/she will publish when the trial is over.

Before the actual trial, math, science, social studies, and English students, or representatives of those students, will meet to prepare the defense. The trial will be conducted at a given time and may cover two class periods.

Issues for all classes to consider:

1) What happens when new information, in this case, Galileo's proof that the earth moved and that the earth went around the sun, contradicts established thinking?
2) Is science a march toward the truth, or is science also a product of the thinking of its time?
3) How difficult is it to change what the majority believes to be true? What are some strategies to ask people to question "accepted facts?"
4) What "traditional views," existing in modern society, seem to impede progress?
5) What elements of human nature and human behavior make some humans reluctant to rethink a "truth?"

Beyond Infinity: The Retrial of Galileo

Generic:

1. Ask the students either through class discussion or in groups to consider how their group functioned. What were the challenges and how did they overcome those challenges?
2. What could the group have done better?
3. What did the group excel at doing?
4. What did students learn about the subject matter (literary work, middle ages, time, interpersonal relations, etc.)?
5. What, if anything, did students learn about themselves, other people, life in general?
6. What questions do they have about themselves, other people, life in general?

The teacher can use the questions below as either closures for the projects or as the inceptions of new projects.

Specific to the unit studied:

1. If you were Galileo, do you believe you would have recanted as he did at his trial? What leads you to think this?
2. There is a theory that "no matter how ridiculous an idea is, the more people that believe it, the harder it is to dispel that idea." Do you agree or disagree with that statement? Cite examples to support your opinion.
3. Were Galileo's prosecutors totally ignorant, believing that the sun went around the earth, or were there other factors that made them believe that mistaken idea? If so, what were those factors?
4. Is our view of the universe and its beginning reality or another scientific model of the universe?
5. Is science culturally dependent?   Are scientific theories dependent on what is happening in the rest of the world at the time those theories are formed?
6. We seem to be constantly revising many scientific theories, particularly those in cosmology. Since the human brain is making these decisions, and since the human brain is also part of the universe, can we ever truly be objective in developing our models of the physical universe?
7. When is a mistaken idea dangerous?
8. Is ignorance always "blissful," or can it be dangerous?

Shape Up!

Teacher Notes—Shape Up!

The idea for this project actually arose from a coaching responsibility. I was asked by a young math teacher to observe his class. He did everything a teacher of a conventional classroom would do---he lectured about triangles, drew multiple triangles on the blackboard, and asked students to answer questions about the properties of triangles. But these students were not the most self-motivated. Most were off task, reading other materials, chatting about their weekend exploits, etc. The instructor had to "pull teeth" to get an answer. At the end of the class, we consulted. He was obviously frustrated. I asked him what, ultimately, he wanted his students to learn. Once we got past the delimiting notion of content, "I want them to learn about triangles", we decided on a project that would help develop a context for learning about triangles. This resulted in the following project by enlisting the cooperation of a science teacher who used his students' participation in this project to teach some fundamental principles of science. Before the math teacher embarked on this enterprise, I suggested that he develop a number of small group activities for his classes in order that they develop the necessary collaborative skills for the ensuing project. He did.

When I visited his class as the students worked on the project, I asked the teacher, who was working with a group, to look around and see how many students were fully engaged and on task. He stood up, looked around, and to his surprise, he said, "All of them." He was right.

Group Name_____

Date_____

SHAPE UP!

Your company, Green Mean Machine, is trying to get a contract for a housing contract that will include you as the chief architect. The client, Here Today, Gone Tomorrow Realtors, have some very specific requirements for the houses that they intend to build. The major requirement is that the house be energy efficient. The second requirement is that the house use a minimum of shapes in designing the structure.

Green Mean Machine needs this contract badly, so you will have to do some research about energy conservation and convection currents (and other material information such as Boyle's Law). In order for you to be successful, you must collaborate with students in a physics class to consider how best to heat and cool these future homes. Each house must have the following:

1) Living Room
2) Dining Room
3) Three bedrooms
4) Kitchen
5) Two Bathrooms
6) Garage
7) Utility Room (for washer, dryer, etc.)

You may use any online tools to draw your prototype structure or you may use pencil and paper.

On the assigned day, each group must present its design to the Here Today, Gone Tomorrow Realtors, and explain the rationale behind its blueprints. The realtors will judge the winner of the competition.

Criteria For Success:

1) Quality of the collaboration---how well the group has divided up responsibility, shared the workload, and participated in the presentation. Also, the quality of collaboration with students in the physics class.
2) Rationale for the design—does the design meet/exceed the requirements above?
3) Aesthetics of the design---does this look like a home that someone would want to live in?
4) Quality of the presentation—Are all group members involved and does the presentation demonstrate organization and creativity? Brainstorm, divide up the responsibilities, and conduct the research. Good Luck.

Beyond Infinity: Shape Up!

Generic:

1. Ask the students either through class discussion or in groups to consider how their group functioned. What were the challenges and how did they overcome those challenges?
2. What could the group have done better?
3. What did the group excel at doing?
4. What did students learn about the subject matter (literary work, middle ages, time, interpersonal relations, etc.)?
5. What, if anything, did students learn about themselves, other people, life in general?
6. What questions do they have about themselves, other people, life in general?

The teacher can use the questions below as either closures for the projects or as the inceptions of new projects.

Specific to the unit studied:

1. What shapes seem to be the most common to all peoples? In other words, what shape would most people on the earth readily identify?
2. Examine the rooms in your own home. Do they seem to be designed to serve a function in tune with what the room is for?
3. What connection is there between the materials cultures use to build things and the structures themselves? Consider not just the availability of materials but the philosophy of the culture toward life. (for example, the Egyptians build structures out of stone to last. This implies that the human being, through the entombment in the pyramids, would overcome death.)
4. What value does the study of geometry seem to have on an almost daily basis?

The Show of Shows

Teacher Notes—The Show of Shows

This project, when I first launched it, worked out beyond my expectations. Students were engaged on a daily basis, and their research went beyond my dreams. I think it is important to require that the show be live with video segments. I failed to mention that one year, and one group turned in a 30 minute video that was good but somehow lacking. This group edited and re-edited and edited once again until it was perfect, but what was lost was the improvisation and spontaneity of the live production. So in following years I mandated that the show be performed live with video segments (short video segments).

I also emphasized secrecy. Since the groups were not competing for a higher grade (always a bad tactic), I encouraged group competition through noting that if each group knew what the other was doing, some of their ideas would be snapped up by the opposition and used against them. This worked. I learned early on that competition between or among groups is fine as long as the reward for winning is not a high stakes object....like grades. Students have actively competed, fairly and enthusiastically, for the Grand Imperial Supreme Hershey Bar or the title of Best Actor in the Macademy Awards.

The biggest problems students had with this project included organization skills and timing. Students are big into improvising not because they want to develop improvisational skills but because they are usually not good at preparation, planning, and writing out the details. The more experienced students have complete confidence that they can wing it, especially the boys. In the beginning of the year, I assign a few activities that allows them to not plan just so they can understand how often failure accompanies such a tactic. Even so, with this project I needed to remind them of the importance of planning and rehearsing.

The actual origin of this project was an earlier project I developed on the Medieval Period and the Renaissance(Included in this project, "MMN Poll......")This project was also successful, but I fleshed it out as time went by. With a little imagination the science, art, math teacher can adapt both these projects to accommodate their content areas. Again, in project based learning, the focus is on skill development.

Name_____

Group ID_____

The Show of Shows

In order to study the Enlightenment and the Romantic periods, we are going to create a hypothetical situation. Let us imagine that television, that incredible audio and visual medium, existed in the eighteenth and nineteenth centuries. It is February, and the Nielsen ratings are due to come out. Networks are scrambling to get top ratings by scheduling programs that will capture the viewing public.

One half of the class will represent the EBC, the Enlightenment Broadcasting Company. The EBC's rival represented by the other half of the class, is the RBC, the Romantic Broadcasting Company. On a date in the near future, both companies will have a full class period to present their programming format. Each company will present a schedule of programs for prime time television, and will produce snippets of programs to entice and lure the critics and sponsors who will evaluate the quality of the programming.

The MRC, the Maltese Regulatory Commission (substitute teacher name here), has established certain regulations regarding the content of the programming, and the EBC and RBC will receive guidelines documenting these regulations. Since this project is quite large in scope, it is strongly recommended that the EBC and RBC form subgroups, each with its separate goals and responsibilities. A spokesperson should be selected from each subgroup to participate in a committee which will coordinate all activities for the entire company. Subgroups should be formed as soon as possible. The company might even choose to form subgrops initially in order to develop tighter and more efficient brainstorming sessions. While developing a vision for the overall show is important, it is imperative that operational goals and deadlines be established and adhered to in order for the company to operate efficiently. The company does not want the MRC to revoke its license! Each subgroup should assign members group roles (i.e., coordinator, monitor, timekeeper, liaison and checker) as an initial step.

On the day of the presentation, the company is to present the MRC a detailed scheduling of programming describing the content of the programs and the participants in each of the "snippets." The Criteria for Success are as follows:

1) Quality of the programming. This will be determined by the smoothness of the presentation and the creativity involved in its design and production.
2) Representation of the age (enlightenment/romantic). The intent of this project is to help students understand the values and attitudes of their respective eras. High grades will be awarded to those presentations which accurately (based on research—not what students "think" it may be) depict these values and attitudes.

3) Quality of the detailed scheduling of programming presented to the MRC. This schedule should be typed and signed by each member of the company.
4) Group dynamics. Degree of involvement of *each* member of the company and fulfillment of group roles will be a major source of the evaluation.
5) Quality of the collaborative papers which will be explained in a future handout.

The show must be *LIVE*. The company may use prerecorded videos (even if they are supposedly to take place in real time—"Now to our Man On the Street......" for example.) Notice that, while the class period is 45 minutes long, the show will only be 30 minutes. This means that you have 15 minutes to set up. This is not the time to make major decisions. If you plan well and rehearse, then the 15 minutes should be plenty of time. Remember that Criteria #1 refers to organization. You do not need prerecorded videos. Your "Man on the Street" or other segment can be in another part of the room.

Each company should also remember that it possesses a rival which will try to "scoop" its rival's ideas. A certain degree of secrecy should be maintained by each company to prevent its presentation from being sabotaged. The EBC and the RBC are fighting for the same "information and entertainment" dollar, but each company possesses a definite perspective on the times and must answer to the stockholders who expect their companies to reflect their concerns and views. Do your research well.

Scenery and props are enhancements. They are not necessary, but keep in mind that a "suggestion" with respect to scenery is just as effective as a full blown painted wall.

I will be available to render assistance---I will NOT spy for any group, however! Good luck.

Guidelines—Enlightenment Broadcasting Company

The Enlightenment or Age of Reason did not come into being simply because some men decided to reason things out. One influence was the sheer horror of warfare. Standing armies and cannon fire had converted war from terrifying madness on a small scale to terrifying madness on a large scale. The incredibly horrific Thirty Years War in the early 1600's was still fresh in many memories. Some sort of order had to be imosed on one of mankind's favorite pasttimes. Hence the development of chess style battles and codes of honor---at least for the aristocratic officer class. This did not alleviate the horror of war—it simply made it more "reasonable." There were other reasons for the advent of the Enlightenment, including changes in art, science, and literature.

Perhaps the most beneficial result of the Enlightenment was the belief that man had the power, through reason, to work things out. Our constitution is a direct result of this hope that man could create a rational society if people could learn to use their minds and develop laws which profited all. Certainly the music and art of the time reflected a mathematical precision, a sense of proportion, that appealed the mind's thirst for order. The Enlightenment offered, at least mythically, stability. This may have been an illusion, but, as some religions have been contending for centuries, all life is an illusion. Within this context devise a programming schedule that will include the following:

NEWS Segment—This part of the show should capsulize the major events of the eighteenth and, if desirable, the first fifteen years of the nineteenth century. How would Enlightenment newscasters and commentators have reported and commented on the American and French revolutions? Or the rise of Napoleon? Or Anglo-French relations. Or European events?

SCIENCE Segment—What were the major scientific and technological developments of the age? These can be presented in a Mr. Science Guy format, or NOVA format or any other type of show which focused on the sciences. Scientists that may be included are Carolus Linnaeus, Georges-Louis Leclerc (Comte du Buffon), James Watt.

WEATHER Segment—What would enlightenment forecasts focus on? How would nature be portrayed?

EDITORIAL Segment—An editorial is a commentary on some aspect of contemporary life from a biased perspective, in this case, from the viewpoint of the EBC.

At least two other segments of the company's choice. The following people and their respective contributions to the Enlightenment MUST be highlighted (they can also appear in any of the above segments):

Philosophers: John Locke, Rousseau

Artists: Sir Joshua Reynolds or Sir Thomas Gainsborough, William Hogarth, Jean Antoine Watteau (Rococo style)

Writers: Jonathan Swift, Alexander Pope, Samuel Johnson

Composers: George Frideric Handel, Johann Sebastian Bach, Wolfgang Amadeus Mozart

The formats used to represent the works and ideas of these people is totally up to the judgment of the EBC. Quiz show, interview formats (such as 20/20, Sixty Minutes or Ted Koppel), review formats (such as Movie Critics or At the Movies), or even "kiddie" programming is acceptable. The fundamental goal is to present these intellectual giants in an Enlightenment framework. Ridiculing them is not going to impress the MRC. Communicating their styles and contributions to the age will. This should be foremost in your collective mind as you make your decisions. This does not mean that levity is banished. It *does* mean that the purpose of this project should be evident in your production.

The composers may be represented by theme music or an MTV style format, or they may be a focus of one of your segments. Advertisements for eighteenth century products are also admissible, but must also be within the spirit of the times.

This assignment demands collaboration, a shared workload, organization, and research. The 30 minutes will go fast, and you have a great deal to work in. Be clever, adopt a logo and a slogan for your news show. Who knows? Considering the direction of modern television viewing, you may be able to sell your scheme to the networks!

As always, I am available and willing to help you any way I can.

Guidelines—Romantic Broadcasting Company

Romanticism, rather than a quaint and tidy movement led by homespun clad shepherds, was, in reality, a revolution fueled by a passionate rejection of Enlightenment views and values and a zealous humanitarian spirit. The eighteenth century began with faith in the order of things and ended in two bloody revolutions that shattered the structure of monarchies. From the Romantic viewpoint the scientific discoveries that the Age of Reason pointed to with pride were meaningless because they failed to include the realities of the soul and the spirit. Were human beings only combinations of inexpensive elements that could be separated and reconstructed in the laboratory? Mary Godwin Shelley, wife of the romantic poet Percy Shelley, authored *Frankenstein*. It is interesting to remember that Frankenstein is not he name of the monster but the doctor who "built" him. In attempting to surpass nature, to duplicate the secrets of creation, to obsess with the discreet data rather than the whole, the poor doctor concocted a creature that wreaked havoc on society. He failed to give his creation onot only an adept brain but an ethic (beyond measurement) and a soul. Who is the real monster? It is not strange, then, in our age which points to progress in the scientific and technological sphere, to find the Romantic spirit flourishing. The tumultuous decade of the sixties was largely predicated on the Romantic view, a rejection of conventional values, a "return to nature" motif, and a belief in the dignity and worth of each human being. The RBC, then, is a rebellious network, suspicious of the "advances" of the previous age and inclined to view the historical events of the previous century from a much different perspective than the EBC. Within this context devise a programming schedule which will include the following:

NEWS Segment—This segment should capsulize the major events of the eighteenth and, if desirable, the first fifteen years of the nineteenth century. How would Romantic newscasters and commentators have reported and commented on the American and French revolutions? On the rise of Napoleon? On Anglo-French relations? On European events such as the Greek War of Independence?

NATURE/SCIENCE Segment—The Romantics viewed NATURE rather than the laboratory as the great teacher. How would the Romantics have viewed the discoveries of Carolus Linnaeous and James Watt? Or prepare a nature show—this should not be a simple get acquainted affair introducing Your Friend, the Wily Chipmunk, but an espousal of Nature as the omnipotent and omniscient force in our lives.

At least two other shows of the company's choice. The following people and their respective contributions to the Romanticism MUST be highlighted:

Philosophers—Jean-Jacques Rousseau, Mary Wollstonecraft

Artists—Francisco Goya, Jacques Louis David, John Constable

Writers—William Wordsworth, George Gordon (Lord Byron), Percy Bysshe Shelley, John Keats

Composers—Ludwig Van Beethoven

The formats used to represent the works and ideas of these people is totally up to the judgment of the RBC. Quiz show, interview formats (such as 20/20, Sixty Minutes or Ted Koppel), review formats (such as Movie Critics or At the Movies), or even "kiddie" programming is acceptable. The fundamental goal is to present these intellectual giants in an Romantic framework. Ridiculing them is not going to impress the MRC. Communicating their styles and contributions to the age will. This should be foremost in your collective mind as you make your decisions. This does not mean that levity is banished. It *does* mean that the purpose of this project should be evident in your production.

The composers may be represented by theme music or an MTV style format, or they may be a focus of one of your segments. Advertisements for eighteenth century products are also admissible, but must also be within the spirit of the times.

This assignment demands collaboration, a shared workload, organization, and research. The 30 minutes will go fast, and you have a great deal to work in. Be clever, adopt a logo and a slogan for your news show. Who knows? Considering the direction of modern television viewing, you may be able to sell your scheme to the networks!

As always, I am available and willing to help you any way I can.

Teacher Notes—Traits of Romanticism

To be perfectly honest, I cannot remember the origins of these characteristics of Romanticism. I know I more or less homogenized them from a number of sources. I would not simply copy these and give them to the students. Better they should do the research. But you can use these to guide them in their search.

The Romantic spirit is a state of mind, a way of looking at life for purposes of art. Employing the commonplace, the natural, and the simple as its materials, Romanticism always seeks to find the absolute, the ideal, by transcending the actual. In this context, Romanticism has much in common with Platonism. Listed below are some characteristics of Romanticism. One of the difficulties in teaching the poets is that, since a tenet of Romanticism is individuality, not all the Romantic poets exhibit the same traits. Wordsworth, for example, epitomizes the Romantic dependency on nature, while Byron is better known for his humanitarian spirit. No pigeon-holing here, especially with these gentlemen.

The romantics

1) Liked to indulge in sentimental contemplation, in thinking about things which are seemingly sentimental. Ask students how many indulge in this kind of thinking.
2) Returned to nature as their teacher. They believed that one could learn about the most important questions in life by studying the life process. There is a strong connection here to Taoism, and some students might enjoy studying this religion in connection with Romanticism.
3) Appreciated "natural" nature, that is, nature unspoiled. They enjoyed the wild forest rather than someone's well groomed flower garden.
4) Possessed an emotional sympathy with the humble life and the idealization of it. The simple life was the purest (perhaps because it was the closest to nature—living in a hut is closer to the soil than residing in a palace). Thus the Romantics ere more inclined to write a poem about a shepherd than about someone high up on the social ladder.
5) Were interested in Gothicism and the relics of an idealized past. For the Romantics, knights in shining armor, Greek heroes, damsels in distress all represented ages that celebrated the best of human nature. This was in rebellion to the seemingly endless materialism of the age the Romantics lived in (see Wordsworth's "The World is Too Much With Us" and Thoreau's essays ("we do not ride upon the railroad. The railroad rides upon us.")
6) Were concerned with things of the spirit. They were interested in the possibilities of an afterlife and what happened to the soul at death. Edgar Allan Poe focused more on the emotional spirit than on rationalism.
7) Were interested in symbolism and mysticism. Elements of nature frequently served as symbols in romantic poetry. Mysticism is the belief that direct knowledge of God,

spiritual truth, or ultimate reality can be attained through subjective experience (as intuition or insight).

8) Were intrigued by Orientalism, a fascination with ideas and artifacts from the far east (see #2 above). This should be no surprise. If one considers the above characteristics, it is no wonder that the Orient would be an exotic place for the Romantics.

9) Were dedicated to humanitarianism, a concern for human welfare especially as expressed through philanthropic activities and interest in social reforms.

10) Had a genuine interest in man's inalienable rights.

To the Romantic, the individual, not the structure of society, was the center of art.

If you teach Ralph Waldo Emerson and Henry David Thoreau, you can now understand how Romanticism crossed the Atlantic and found fertile soil, sprouting Transcendentalism. In the United States, there seemed to be unlimited unspoiled nature. Most Americans were farmers, and the bedrock mythology of Americanism was the sanctity of the individual....even in religion. Emerson was noted for saying, "My mind is my own church." Thoreau's self-exile to Walden Pond was for the purpose of the elemental needs of humanity, to "suck out the marrow of life."

Name_____

Group ID_____

SHOWDOWN AT THE MRC CORRAL

The MRC is having a difficult time. IT can only grant one programming license, and it has narrowed its choices down to the EBC and the RBC. The MRC, in its infinite wisdom, has decided to award the license to the network that produces the finest collaborative papers and public defenses of those papers. These public statements will focus on questions that the MRC has designed. Each company should assign its subgroups to answer the questions. The groups will collaborate on the essays and prepare a public presentation of the paper and a possible rebuttal to the paper presented by the opposing company. Each paper must be signed by the authors, typed, and MUST express he viewpoint of the company.

The questions are as follows:

1) The energy crisis in this nation, the United States, is upon us. One of the major solutions is to take land from the National Park Service and use it for strip mining. The coal from this mining venture will fuel quite a few major cities for quite a few years. Would your company publicly support such a venture?

2) The United States is losing the technological war to its foreign competitors. The only viable solution being considered is to fund heavily science and math courses in high school. In order to do so, courses in music and art will have to be eliminated. Would your company be in favor of this proposal?

3) Despite attempts at parental guidance, a large proportion of your viewing audience will be young children under ten years old who will view your programs no matter what time slot they are placed in. Would your company televise programs that are deemed by many to be X-rated material (assuming the X-rating refers to material that may be pornographical and/or violent in tone) regardless of the artistic quality of the programs?

4) The medical community has requested that a show be produced which examines the rights of families whose relatives are connected to life support systems to have legally those connections terminated. What kind of show would your company produce and what angle or slant would it seemingly provide?

Each subgroup of the company should prepare an oral presentation of its paper and a rebuttal to opposing views. *Any member of the subgroup may be interrogated by the MRC as to the content of the paper.* The member's response will critically affect the MRC's evaluation. The MRC *will frown upon a single author responsible* for most of the individual papers. This must truly be a *collaborative paper* demonstrating shared responsibility and shared leadership.

Project Assignment med vs renaissance

Name_____

Period_____   Group ID#_____

"Our MNN Poll of a small village in Burgundy
reveals that 3 people think the plague is nothing to worry about.
The other villagers are dead…"

sometimes we can learn a great deal about realities when we play fanciful games. for example, if we tried to answer the question "What would have happened during Reconstruction if Abraham Lincoln had lived?" we would learn a great deal about both Reconstruction and Lincoln because we would have to research both in depth to make a valid prediction.

The purpose of this assignment is to help you gain an in-depth understanding of two interesting eras, the Medieval Period and the Renaissance. To do this your group must prepare two fifteen minute television news programs(a little fantasy—televisions did not exist). The first news program should be MNN (Medieval News Network—Please change the name of your network and show to reflect your group's character!!). the second news program should be the RNN (Renaissance News Network—again, change the name to suit your fancy.) Your network is in competition with other networks to produce the most **informative, accurate,** and **creative** news program that captures the "spirit" of both time periods and shows the *differences* between the two. To impress the media producers who will hire or fire you, you will prepare this 30 minute program, tape it, and show it for evaluation purposes to the producer(s).

You will be assigned 6 to 8 people in your group. Even though you may decide to separate into two subgroups (a medieval group and a renaissance group) both subgroups will have to communicate and work together to provide a cohesive show that demonstrates the differences (and similarities, perhaps) between the middle ages and the renaissance. There is no doubt that every group member will have to double up on duties, researching, writing scripts, acting, using technology, etc. How well your group demonstrates good collaborative skills will be a major component of your grade.

News program format

1) Approximately fifteen minutes for each show—15 minutes for the medieval period news show, and fifteen minutes for the renaissance news show.
2) Each show must include the following segments:
    a) the announcement of a **NOBLE** (yes, **NOBLE**) **Prize** for the best scientific advancement-- -*predicated on research*
    b) A review of a literary work-- *predicated on research*
    c) The unveiling of a new work of visual art (architecture, painting, sculpture, music-- *predicated on research*
    d) The announcement of a patent granted to the best invention of the period-- *predicated on research*
    e) World news—*predicated on research*
    f) Local news—*predicated on research*
    g) Weather forecast-- *predicated on research*

h) Two commercials-- *predicated on research*

Requirements

1) each segment must be accompanied by a script, typed and proofread.
2) Each segment must have a script of times and arrangements of the segments.
3) Each group must submit a videotape of both shows, edited (within best capabilities).

Criteria for success

1) Collaborative effort—all members of the group should share responsibility equally and demonstrate superb cooperative skills.
2) Organization of the news program
3) Quality of the news program in terms of:

a) creativity—Find stuff about both time periods that one would not usually find in a seventh grade encyclopedia

b) Accuracy (do NOT give information based on what you *think* the middle ages or the renaissance was about.) Accuracy will be evaluated   based on **depth and breadth of research**.

c) Adherence to the format (are all segments included?)

Extra credit: depending on the time available, create the design of a video game program that would be popular in either the medieval period or the renaissance. If the group can actually construct the program then even more points will be awarded. Only attempt this project if all the criteria for success have been satisfied.

Procedure

1) Review this assignment. Make certain you understand the goals (applying good research, for example).
2) Brainstorm ideas.
3) Decide on goals and strategies to achieve those goals. Develop and try to stick to timelines.
4) Assign responsibility. Share leadership.
5) Apportion research assignments. Remember that your group will he held accountable for accuracy and depth of research, so that throwing in a common belief about the middle ages to get laughs will not get your group nearly as many points as revealing unique and interesting insights.
6) Put the show together.
7) Review the **goals** to make certain all requirements are met.
8) Review the **Criteria for success** to make certain that all criteria are met.
9) Rehearse.
10) Proofread scripts.
11) Rehearse.
12) Have a BSD (big something delicious, like a brownie the size of montana).

Final notes: If a member is computer literate, your group may consider a web cam, for example during the weather forecast showing conditions in Siberia or wherever you find a web cam. When you choose the winners of "Best Invention" and "Science Advancement" consider (just consider) some items that are not typically considered advancements. Whether they are good choices depends on how good the research is and the argument the group makes for its selection. For example, the wheelbarrow, the horse collar, etc. Most importantly, get away from previous conceived "assumptions" you may have about those time periods. What will impress the producers are not the trite stereotypes about those time periods, but interesting material, born of research, that makes for interesting and informative presentations.

This project is an ambitious one, dependent on shared leadership, problem-solving, excellent research skills, creativity and trust. Good luck. I stand ready and willing to help you in any way possible.

Beyond Infinity: Show of Shows

Generic:

1. Ask the students either through class discussion or in groups to consider how their group functioned. What were the challenges and how did they overcome those challenges?
2. What could the group have done better?
3. What did the group excel at doing?
4. What did students learn about the subject matter (literary work, middle ages, time, interpersonal relations, etc.)?
5. What, if anything, did students learn about themselves, other people, life in general?
6. What questions do they have about themselves, other people, life in general?

The teacher can use the questions below as either closures for the projects or as the inceptions of new projects.

Specific to the unit studied:

1. If you could choose, would you prefer to have lived during the Enlightenment or during the Romantic periods? Why?
2. Do contemporary times have more in common with the Enlightenment or with the Romantic eras?
3. In the modern period, what Romantic elements do you believe exist?
4. What is our society's view of nature?
5. Edgar Allan Poe, in "The Fall of the House of Usher," explores the relationship between the rational and the emotional aspects of human nature. Are most humans rational or emotional or is there consistent balance?
6. If you were to characterize our contemporary culture, what name would you give to it? In what ways would this name be descriptive of our culture?

Strike Up the Band!

Teacher Notes---Strike Up the Band

During the morning announcements we would ask students to contribute music to be played when announcements were over. That was a disaster. Aside from the language that some students deemed appropriate to be broadcast throughout the school, we forgot how tied into personal identity was the choice of musical genre.

I would be taking attendance or performing some other homeroom responsibility, and a modern piece of music would start over the sound system. No matter what kind of music was played, someone in my homeroom would shout out, "I hate that music....it makes me wanna puke." Or, "What jerks listen to that kind of music?"

To avoid gang wars predicated on musical genre preference, we stopping asking students to contribute music to the morning announcements, and asked the students in charge of the morning program to choose music that was relatively safe from inciting riots. Music from popular movies became a staple.

I tried to think back to my own adolescence to see if there was such loyalty (or, to rephrase, the exclusion of) to one particular type of music. Yes, we were all agog by the Beatles and the Beach Boys, and some of us liked one band better than the others, but this suckling-like attachment to one narrow taste I found in my students of the 80's and 90's was rare, if it existed at all. I, and my college buddies, liked pop, folk, and some music that, to us, was unclassifiable. I remember one classmate who introduced me to jazz via his Herbie Hancock collection. My point is not that we were all so liberal and accepting in those days. I think we simply did not attach so much of our identity to the music we liked.

*In many of my projects I asked students to accompany their presentations with **NON-LYRICAL** music. There were several reasons for this. First, it expanded their repertoire of music; second, I wanted them to focus on the music (in its purest form) and not the words; third, if you taught high school, well, you know the answer. Before I learned to make the non-lyrical stipulation, a group brought in a song where every other word began with the letter "F," and the "theme" concerned stabbing b....es. When I called the group on it, they made a very flimsy connection to their presentation. Basically, they just wanted to hear their music in class.*

I notice a number of novice teachers allowing students to bring in music with lyrics, and, often, they bemoan that decision because there follows a lengthy discussion about student rights, freedom of speech, etc., after some particularly "colorful" piece of music is played during a presentation. The novice teacher, in trying to be democratic (and often trying to be "cool") forgets that democracy applies to all students, including those who are uncomfortable with sexually explicit lyrics or profanity. Forget the argument that students listen "to that stuff anyway on their own." "On their own" does not apply to a classroom setting, no more than playing that music in a place of worship would be appropriate. If we engage in this discussion about "what is appropriate," we must also point out to our students the importance of "context." School is not their basement, or their car, or even the space on the school bus. When the context of the senior prom comes along, they dress up in tuxedos and evening gowns because that what the context tells them to do....exactly.

Novice teachers often had a different take than I did when working with students. For one thing, no matter how much a student may clamor to use his preferred music ("I Loved Her So I Killed Her") in his presentation, I had the fortitude not to cave and said no. Some new teachers find this difficult to do so. Secondly, I defined my teaching responsibilities a little differently than many other colleagues. My job was not to indulge student interest—my goal was to expand student interest, so asking them to listen to classical music or study Greek art or watch a black and white movie classic was simply part of the learning process. You might be surprised to realize how such an approach opened up a new world to some students.

Students really enjoyed this one. I worked with the music teacher on obtaining some "instruments" from around the house/office, and students had to select from these. The inspiration for this came from listening to Leroy Anderson ("Typewriter," and "Sandpaper Ballet"). From the pile of items, the students chose their band's instruments. I sandwiched this unit between some heavy and intense projects. Some of the items were chopsticks, a kitchen timer, spatula, wine glass, etc. As the years went by, I varied this to assign groups to a room---instruments must come from---living room, kitchen, garage, mailroom, library, etc. The presentations were sometimes videoed, which was fine. Amazing how many groups spent time to video their presentations on their own time. This was fun, and it led to some good discussions and insight into the nature of music. Amazing how clever students can be when you build the proper classroom climate and challenge them.

Name_____

Group ID_____

Strike Up the Band!!

This is your chance. Ever since you bought your first album, *The Greatest Hits of the Brady Bunch,* you have wanted to play in your own band. Fate has chosen your fellow band players. Now you have to pool your creative talent and come up with a sound and a style that will pack them in the Carnegie Hall. Actually, since most of you will not have musical instruments and, since you do not have five years to brainstorm and practice, this activity might be a little more difficult than it sounds. *Because you will be asked to produce only* **instrumentals**, you do not have to worry about lyrics. Here are some aspects of this project to consider:

1) Your choice of instruments from the ones supplied by your instructor *[or assigned room of the house/office].* Art is often connected to technology. Think of what Bach could have created with a synthesizer!
2) Brainstorm about what kind of music you want to play....fast, slow, in-between. Mood—relaxing, intense, etc.
3) Consider the purpose of your music—to entertain only or to entertain and to make a statement.
4) What name do you want? This is a fun decision, but also an important one. Names suggest types of music. For example, for a romantic evening, I would not want to take my partner to listen to a band named, *The Human Sacrifice*. Well, maybe some of you would. Consider also the name of the musical piece you create.
5) Rehearsal time in class will be in short supply. Work fast on the preliminaries and the decisions so whatever rehearsal time you have can be used wisely. We prefer a live performance, but will accept a video if no extraneous sounds are used in the editing process.

Each band will have an opportunity to perform and, perhaps, even cut a record, eh, tape, eh, compact disc, eh, cd....Who knows? Maybe those guys from Liverpool started this way.

Beyond Infinity: Strike Up the Band!

Generic:

1. Ask the students either through class discussion or in groups to consider how their group functioned. What were the challenges and how did they overcome those challenges?
2. What could the group have done better?
3. What did the group excel at doing?
4. What did students learn about the subject matter (literary work, middle ages, time, interpersonal relations, etc.)?
5. What, if anything, did students learn about themselves, other people, life in general?
6. What questions do they have about themselves, other people, life in general?

The teacher can use the questions below as either closures for the projects or as the inceptions of new projects.

Specific to the unit studied:

1. How is music, in its pure form (without lyrics), different from the same music with lyrics as an art form?
2. The most abstract form of literature seems to be poetry, and some might argue that the most abstract art form is music. Do you see a connection, in this regard between poetry and music?
3. What observation can you make from the following comment? "Music is usually described in terms borrowed from other art forms: "red hot music," "the blues," "that musical piece was 'velvety," or "tinny," "soft."
4. Apparently, adolescents identify with a particularly musical genre, often to the exclusion of listening to other kinds of music. Later, as adults, people tend to be more accepting of other genres. Do you believe this to be true? Why or why not?
5. If you were living during the early 18th century, what music would you have enjoyed?
6. Are our choices in music dependent on the age and society we live in? How much of our "taste" in music is totally our individual preference and how much is developed by our environment?

Time is Relative

Teacher Notes—Time is Relative

This project certainly knocked off some brain cells. I actually got the idea for this unit from a class discussion about how some Native Americans view time. It is difficult, especially for Westerners, to see time as a human construct. If we are discussing Einstein and relativity, then time seems to have its own relational value to space, but on an everyday basis, we operate according to Newton's laws of time, space and light.

I wanted to jostle students out of this routine and familiar association with time and ask them the larger questions. Originally, I developed this small assignment for a filler between two larger projects. I had hoped that this would be a fanciful refresher for their gray matter. It did not work out that way. Students fussed and argued about this for days, so I included this project in my curriculum and placed it according to dead time in the school year---those times at the end of marking periods or after standardized tests or holidays. Be prepared for a great deal of hand wringing and mental anguish, but students really seemed to enjoy this one.

You can expand on this in so many ways. Ask students to visit websites that discuss time and to research cultural interpretations of time.

Name_____

Group Id#_____

PLAYING WITH TIME

It is the present. In my Warminster basement I perfected the world's first time travel machine. As a long time admirer of Abraham Lincoln, my first journey is to Ford's Theater in Washington, D.C., April, 1865, to stop John Wilkes Booth from assassinating my hero. A flash, a bang and a little presto and I am there to intercept the villain and prevent the deed. Lincoln is not assassinated. Zap—back to the present. The history books make no mention of Booth (except as a minor nineteenth century actor overshadowed by his successful brother, also an actor), and modern texts refer to Lincoln's peaceful death from natural causes in 1887.

The Problem: My dilemma is this: If the event (in this case Lincoln's assassination) did NOT take place, then how could I be aware of it? If I could not be aware of it because it did not take place, then how would I have known about it and gone back to change it? (How can you change something that did not happen?). However, if I did not go back to change it (because the assassination did not take place), then the assassination will take place because I did not go back to change it.
Think about it.

Modern physics tells us that, at least in theory, events can be examined as going forward or going backward in time.

Your group's task is to do the following:
1) Present the problem to yourselves as a group. What actually is the problem? This is called defining the problem.

2) Consider some approaches to solving the problem. This is called planning.

3) Propose a solution. At least try to propose a solution. And try not to spend your time proposing a lynch mob for instructors who give you problems like this one.

On another level, what are some underlying psychological/philosophical/scientific theories involved when we ask, "What time is it?"

Beyond Infinity: Time is Relative

Generic Follow Up Activities:

1. Ask the students either through group discussion or in groups to consider how their group functioned. What were the challenges and how did they overcome those challenges?
2. What could the group have done better?
3. What did the group excel at doing?
4. What did students learn about the subject matter (literary work, middle ages, time, interpersonal relations, etc.)?
5. What, if anything, did students learn about themselves, other people, life in general?
6. What questions do they have about themselves, other people, life in general?

Specific to the unit studied:

1) Stephen Hawking, among others, has suggested that time is curved. Space can also be curved. If space is like the surface of an inflated balloon, we can imagine space as curved, but it is hard to see time as curved. But, if time were curved, that would be a way for time travel—getting quickly from one moment to the other.

> The difficulty with time travel is that the device would have to control everything at that moment in history (say Lincoln's assassination). It would have to freeze the people walking everywhere, the trolley cars, the movement of all the planets and stars to get to that exact moment.

2) Suppose, using a time machine, we went back to assassinate Lincoln. Then (supposing we assassinated him before he had children), none of his children would be born nor would their descendants be born. Then all the events that happened with those descendants would also not have happened (including fender benders!). We wanted to assassinate Lincoln because of the policies he enacted, but, if our assassination through time travel worked, those policies would not have been enacted, so why would we try to go back in time to prevent policies that have not happened? *The Terminator* movie presents the same dilemma.

3) Discuss the Cat in the Box scenario. A person mails you a cat, Fluffy. Before you open the box (a la Christmas Vacation) two realities exist. Either the cat is dead or the cat is alive. Both potential realities exist. In effect, both realities exist. Modern physics considers the possibility of multiverses with multiple realities.

4) History does not exist. Everything is going on simultaneously, including multiple universes. That is why people will claim they looked over their shoulders and momentarily saw a roman legion walk by. Einstein said time exists so everything does not happen at once. Is time simply a human construct?

Time Out!

Teacher Notes—Time Out

I thought I might add this as a "bonus" project. I hope you found some usefulness in these projects.

This project worked out very well following the reading of Stephen Crane's Maggie: A Girl of the Streets. *This is not a beginning-of-the-year project because it really is dependent on efficient student collaboration, so hold off on his one until students have practiced good collaborative skills. Some of these projects are spelled out in great detail. Others, like this one, make certain assumptions about student readiness and comprehension. I tended to tailor the descriptions of my projects to the nature of the class it was assigned to. Even in the very best classes, there are those students who constantly want to "get it right," and who seek affirmation every five minutes from the instructor. That is all right because it is simply part of their individual learning process. Other classes do not like too much direction. Give them a general idea and let them run with it. With the former type of student you have to constantly reassure him that there is no "right" answer but only "good" and "bad" answers. With the more abstract random student, you have to constantly remind her the goals of the assignment, lest she go so far afield that your original objectives are not met. The trick here is to also, somewhere in the messiness of learning, allow her to develop and explore her own objectives along the way.*

If the key word for the naturalist writers was "determinism," then this concept was also reflected in the fields of science and economics. Charles Darwin looks at environmental determinism, while Karl Marx uses Hagel's dialectic opposites to foster the idea that the parameters of one's life are determined by economic factors. Later Sigmund Freud postulates that a human being's personality was determined by the time he/she was five years old, depending on parental influences. You might want to discuss determinism before students embark on this project. Of course, the same basic premise for this task could be applied to any time period. This also allows the students to look at a news magazine (for some of them, for the first time!) This project also makes good use of multiple intelligences. Depending on your school's access to technology, you might change the assignment to an online magazine.

With a little creative thought, teachers in other disciplines can reconstruct this assignment to fit their content area. The concept of naturalism appears in art, science, and politics. Instead of a magazine, teachers can ask students to develop an art gallery, museum, or political campaign with naturalism as the guiding principle.

Name_____

Group ID_____

Time Out

We have studied naturalism and its key accompanying concept, "determinism," the belief that human lives are shaped by forces beyond their control. With this key concept in mind, your group's charge is to reproduce a news magazine (either *Time* or *Newsweek*--no *People*, or *Celebrity Highlights*, or *Martial Arts for the Visually Impaired*)from the middle to late 19th century. The magazine can be online rather than a hard copy, but it must have the following sections representing that time period.

1) National News Section
2) International News Section
3) Literary Review of Books
4) Science Section
5) Art Section
6) Sports Section
7) Letters to the Editor Section

Your magazine can be any date in the time period specified above. You may include advertising, political cartoons, or any other appropriate sections.
Your magazine must reflect in tone and theme the "spirit of the age."

Criteria for Success:

1) Demonstration of excellent collaborative skills.
2) Inclusion of all seven sections of the magazine listed above
3) Depth of research which was used to produce your magazine
4) Magazine reflects the "spirit of the age."
5) Magazine demonstrates thought and intellectual connections. (the reader must learn something from perusing the magazine.)

On a future date, all groups will share their magazines with the rest of the class. Each group will present its product and then share it amongst the other groups for feedback.

Beyond Infinity: Time Out

Generic:

1. Ask the students either through class discussion or in groups to consider how their group functioned. What were the challenges and how did they overcome those challenges?
2. What could the group have done better?
3. What did the group excel at doing?
4. What did students learn about the subject matter (literary work, middle ages, time, interpersonal relations, etc.)?
5. What, if anything, did students learn about themselves, other people, life in general?
6. What questions do they have about themselves, other people, life in general?

The teacher can use the questions below as either closures for the projects or as the inceptions of new projects.

Specific to the unit studied:

1. What naturalistic elements or characteristics seem to exist in modern society?
2. Some neuroscientists believe that our brains are formed by a relatively early age and, therefore, the decisions we make were already made for us. Agree or disagree?
3. Our American culture is predicated on the concept that any citizen can be "whatever he or she wants to be." How valid is this statement?
4. If we believe that no one has freedom of choice, that a person is channeled by fate to make certain decisions, how would our justice system be affected? Could we ethically put anyone in jail for doing what they were destined to do?
5. Are your decisions made through "free will" or are many, if not most, of your decisions beyond your control?
6. What are the consequences of believing that all our decisions are already pre-made?
7. Is "free will" simply an American myth?
8. Does "destiny" really exist?

CPSIA information can be obtained at www.ICGtesting.com
Printed in the USA
LVOW09s0030120614

389702LV00004B/76/P